JOSHUA

The Hodder Bible Commentary

Edited by Lee Gatiss

JOSHUA

GRAHAM BEYNON

HODDER &
STOUGHTON

The Hodder Bible Commentary
Series Editor: Lee Gatiss

First published in Great Britain in 2024 by Hodder & Stoughton
An Hachette UK company

1

The Hodder Bible Commentary: Joshua copyright © Graham Beynon 2024

The right of Graham Beynon to be identified as the Author of the Work has been
asserted by him in accordance with the Copyright, Designs and Patents Act 1988.

Unless otherwise indicated, scripture quotations are taken from
Holy Bible, New International Version® (Anglicised), NIV™
Copyright © 1979, 1984, 2011 by Biblica Inc. Published by Hodder & Stoughton Ltd.
Used with permission. All rights reserved worldwide.
'NIV' is a registered trademark of Biblica Inc.
UK trademark number 1448790.

Scripture quotations marked (ESV) are taken from The ESV® Bible (The Holy Bible,
English Standard Version®), copyright © 2001 by Crossway, a publishing ministry
of Good News Publishers. Used with permission. All rights reserved.

The Last Battle by C.S. Lewis © copyright 1956 CS Lewis Pte Ltd. Extract used with permission.

All rights reserved. No part of this publication may be reproduced, stored in a retrieval system, or
transmitted, in any form or by any means without the prior written permission of the publisher,
nor be otherwise circulated in any form of binding or cover other than that in which it is
published and without a similar condition being imposed on the subsequent purchaser.

A CIP catalogue record for this title is available from the British Library

Hardback ISBN 9781473698512
ebook ISBN 9781473698529

Typeset in Bembo Std and Utopia by Palimpsest Book Production Ltd, Falkirk, Stirlingshire

Printed and bound in Great Britain by Clays Ltd, Elcograf S.p.A.

Hodder & Stoughton policy is to use papers that are natural, renewable and recyclable products
and made from wood grown in sustainable forests. The logging and manufacturing processes
are expected to conform to the environmental regulations of the country of origin.

Hodder & Stoughton Ltd
Carmelite House
50 Victoria Embankment
London EC4Y 0DZ

www.hodderfaith.com
www.hodderbiblecommentary.com

Contents

Dedication ix
Series Preface xi
Consultant Editors xiii
Acknowledgments xv
Maps xvi

Introduction 1
   1. Overview 1
   2. Main themes 8
   3. Biblical theology and application 20
   4. Other issues 28

PART ONE: JOSHUA 1–12

1 The Need for a Leader: Commissioning Joshua (Joshua 1) 35
   1. The instructions to Joshua · Joshua 1:1–9 36
   2. Instructions to the people and their response · Joshua 1:10–18 41

2 Rahab's Faith and God's Encouragement (Joshua 2) 47
   1. The spies and Rahab · Joshua 2:1–7 49
   2. Rahab's example of faith · Joshua 2:8–24 50

3 A Crossing to Remember (Joshua 3–4) 61
   1. The instructions and preparation to cross · Joshua 3:1–13 64
   2. The crossing and its remembrance · Joshua 3:14–4:24 67

4 Identity in the Land (Joshua 5:1–12) 77
   1. Circumcision and reproach · Joshua 5:1–9 78
   2. Passover and the end of the manna · Joshua 5:10–12 82

5	The Coming of the Kingdom (Joshua 5:13–6:27)	87
	1. The commander of the Lord's army · Joshua 5:13–15	89
	2. The circling of the city · Joshua 6:1–14	91
	3. The destruction of the city and the saving of Rahab · Joshua 6:15–25	93
	4. The curse on Jericho · Joshua 6:26–7	94
	Excursus: Devoting to the LORD	101
6	Placing Yourself on the Wrong Side: Achan's Sin (Joshua 7)	103
	1. The defeat at Ai · Joshua 7:1–9	105
	2. God's diagnosis and instructions · Joshua 7:10–15	107
	3. The enactment of God's judgment · Joshua 7:16–26	108
7	Obedience and Success: The Battle Against Ai (Joshua 8:1–29)	117
	1. The plan to attack Ai · Joshua 8:1–9	119
	2. The attack and destruction of Ai · Joshua 8:10–29	120
8	The Shaping of the Relationship (Joshua 8:30–35)	127
	1. The background in Deuteronomy	128
	2. The building of the altar and offering of sacrifices · Joshua 8:30–31	129
	3. The writing and reading of the Law · Joshua 8:32–5	130
9	Salvation by Deception (Joshua 9)	137
	1. The response of the kings of the land · Joshua 9:1–2	139
	2. The response of the Gibeonites · Joshua 9:3–15	140
	3. The revealing of the truth and its consequences · Joshua 9:16–27	141
10	Having God on Your Side (Joshua 10:1–15)	147
	1. The coalition against Gibeon and their call for help · Joshua 10:1–6	148
	2. Israel's victory and God's action · Joshua 10:7–15	149
11	Symbolising and Realising Victory (Joshua 10:16–43)	155
	1. Defeat of the Amorite kings · Joshua 10:16–27	157
	2. Defeat of the southern cities · Joshua 10:28–43	158
12	The Final Victory (Joshua 11)	163
	1. The defeat of Hazor and the northern cities · Joshua 11:1–15	165

	2. *Summary and comment on the conquest · Joshua 11:16–23*	167
13	The Roll Call of Victory (Joshua 12)	173
	1. *Territory and kings east of the Jordan · Joshua 12:1–6*	175
	2. *Territory and kings west of the Jordan · Joshua 12:7–24*	175

PART TWO: JOSHUA 13–21

14	Introduction to Possessing the Land	181
	1. *Conquering and possessing*	181
	2. *The boundaries of the inheritances*	182
15	Inheriting the Land (Joshua 13)	185
	1. *Instructions for possession of the land · Joshua 13:1–7*	187
	2. *Previous division east of the Jordan · Joshua 13:8–33*	189
16	The Model of Inheritance (Joshua 14)	195
	1. *Introduction to division of the land · Joshua 14:1–5*	196
	2. *The commendable example of Caleb · Joshua 14:6–15*	197
17	Judah: Examples and Priority (Joshua 15)	205
	1. *The boundaries of the land · Joshua 15:1–12*	208
	2. *The example of Caleb, Othniel and Aksah · Joshua 15:13–19*	209
	3. *The towns allotted to Judah · Joshua 15:20–63*	210
18	Joseph: Examples and Warnings (Joshua 16–17)	215
	1. *The allotment to Joseph · Joshua 16:1–17:13*	217
	2. *The request from the tribe of Joseph · Joshua 17:14–18*	220
19	Being Slow to Inherit (Joshua 18–19)	227
	1. *Joshua's challenge and the second division · Joshua 18:1–10*	231
	2. *The land allotted to the remaining seven tribes · Joshua 18:11–19:48*	234
	3. *Land allotted to Joshua · Joshua 19:49–51*	236
20	God's Concern for Justice (Joshua 20)	241
	1. *The background to the cities of refuge*	242
	2. *The commands to Joshua · Joshua 20:1–6*	243
	3. *The designation of the towns · Joshua 20:7–9*	244

21 God's Concern for Relationship (Joshua 21)	249
1. The background in Numbers	251
2. The request and allotment in Joshua · Joshua 21:1–42	252
3. The fulfilment of God's promises · Joshua 21:43–5	254

PART THREE: JOSHUA 22–4

22 Unity and Its Preservation (Joshua 22)	263
1. Joshua's speech sending the eastern tribes home · Joshua 22:1–9	266
2. The threat to unity and resolution · Joshua 22:10–34	268
23 Joshua's Call to Loyalty (Joshua 23)	277
1. Introduction: their current position · Joshua 23:1–5	278
2. Joshua's charge and warning · Joshua 23:6–16	280
24 Joshua's Call to Serve the Lord (Joshua 24:1–28)	289
1. A rehearsal of God's goodness to Israel · Joshua 24:1–13	291
2. The call to serve the Lord · Joshua 24:14–28	295
25 The End of an Era (Joshua 24:29–33)	305
1. The death of Joshua · Joshua 24:29–31	306
2. The burial of Joseph · Joshua 24:32	307
3. The death of Eleazar · Joshua 24:33	307
Appendix A: The Tribes of the Promised Land	311
Appendix B: The Borders of the Promised Land	313

To my parents-in-law, Gordon and Helen.
Their example, their encouragement and their
prayers have meant more than they know.

Series Preface

The unfolding of your words gives light.
(Psalm 119:130)

The Hodder Bible Commentary aims to proclaim afresh in our generation the unchanging and unerring word of God, for the glory of God and the good of his people. This fifty-volume commentary on the whole Bible seeks to provide the contemporary church with fresh and readable expositions of Scripture which are doctrinally sensitive and globally aware, accessible for all adult readers but particularly useful to those who preach, teach and lead Bible studies in churches and small groups.

Building on the success of Hodder's NIV Proclamation Bible, we have assembled as contributors a remarkable team of men and women from around the world. Alongside a diverse panel of trusted Consultant Editors, they have a tremendous variety of denominational backgrounds and ministries. Each has great experience in unfolding the gospel of Jesus Christ and all are united in our aim of faithfully expounding the Bible in a way that takes account of the original text, biblical theology, the history of interpretation and the needs of the contemporary global church.

These volumes are serious expositions – not overly technical, scholarly works of reference but not simply sermons either. As well as carefully unpacking what the Bible says, they are sensitive to how it has been used in doctrinal discussions over the centuries and in our own day, though not dominated by such concerns at the expense of the text's own agenda. They also try to speak not only into a white, middle-class, Western context (for example), as some might, but to be aware of ways in which other cultures hear and need to hear what the Spirit is saying to the churches.

As you tuck into his word, with the help of this book, may the glorious Father 'give you the Spirit of wisdom and revelation, so that you may know him better' (Ephesians 1:17).

Lee Gatiss, Series Editor

Consultant Editors

The Series Editor would like to thank the following Consultant Editors for their contributions to the Hodder Bible Commentary:

Shady Anis (*Egypt*)
Kirsten Birkett (*UK*)
Felipe Chamy (*Chile*)
Ben Cooper (*UK*)
Mervyn Eloff (*South Africa*)
Keri Folmar (*Dubai*)
Kerry Gatiss (*UK*)
Kara Hartley (*Australia*)
Julian Hardyman (*Madagascar*)
Stephen Fagbemi (*Nigeria*)
Rosanne Jones (*Japan*)
Henry Jansma (*USA*)
Samuel Lago (*USA*)
Andis Miezitis (*Latvia*)
Adrian Reynolds (*UK*)
Peter Ryan (*Australia*)
Sookgoo Shin (*South Korea*)
Myrto Theocharous (*Greece*)

Acknowledgments

My interest in Joshua began many years ago. I was drawn to wrestle with how to teach an exciting battle narrative to modern believers. I found such wrestling a challenge but also a delight as I saw how Joshua points us to Jesus and has so much to say to the Christian of today. As a result, I was pleased to be asked to write this commentary and to engage in that wrestle again and so to experience that delight more deeply.

There are many people to thank. First, the editor of this series, Lee Gatiss, for his invitation to contribute and then his encouraging editorial guidance on the way through.

Second, my consultant editor Andis Miezitis for his insightful comments.

Third, the staff and readers at Tyndale House, Cambridge. That is where this commentary was written, and a more helpful and pleasant setting could not be imagined. The resources are excellent and the interaction with others stimulating.

Fourth, the leaders and congregation at Grace Church, Cambridge. Having only taught some sections of Joshua previously, I knew I wanted to preach all the way through the book prior to writing. That was done at Grace Church where I received both encouragement and enriching input. It was also a two-month sabbatical period granted by Grace Church that gave me the time to write.

Fifth, the numerous resources from other people I have used, both in preparation of sermons and in writing. I trust I have acknowledged other people's work appropriately in the footnotes that follow, but in teaching a book over a long period of time some insights and understanding become absorbed and it is impossible to trace their origin.

Above all, my heartfelt thanks to our gracious God for all he has given and taught me through this book.

Map 1. The Promised Land at the time of Joshua

Map 2. The division of the land among the tribes

Map 3

The cities of refuge

Map 4

The Levitical cities

Introduction

The book of Joshua is both rich and challenging. It is rich in action and famous events in the history of Israel (such as the battle of Jericho); rich in its portrayal of God and his relationship with his people (such as God's faithfulness to all his promises); and rich in its significance for us today (such as pointing us to Jesus who gains us entry into God's kingdom). It is challenging in much of its content (particularly the killing of the inhabitants of the land); challenging in some of its details (seemingly endless boundary lines and lists of towns); and challenging in its application to us today (it is unlikely we are about to invade a country). This introduction will provide some orientation to the book that will help in how we approach it and understand it for today.

1. Overview

It is vital to see that Joshua is the final stage in a long-running story. The origins of the book start with God's promises to Abraham to make him a great nation, and to give him and his descendants a land to live in (Genesis 12:1–7). Abraham was told that the entry to this land lay more than four hundred years in the future and that his descendants would first be slaves in a foreign land (Genesis 15:12–16). So the nation of Israel grew, and was indeed enslaved in Egypt, but God repeated his promise to Moses:

> Therefore, say to the Israelites: 'I am the LORD, and I will bring you out from under the yoke of the Egyptians. I will free you from being slaves to them, and I will redeem you with an outstretched arm and with mighty acts of judgment. I will take you as my

own people, and I will be your God. Then you will know that I am the LORD your God, who brought you out from under the yoke of the Egyptians. And I will bring you to the land I swore with uplifted hand to give to Abraham, to Isaac and to Jacob. I will give it to you as a possession. I am the LORD. (Exodus 6:6–8)

We see in these verses that the salvation from slavery in Egypt was for the purpose of bringing Israel into the land and giving it to them. The Exodus from Egypt led to the covenant made at Sinai. Then followed forty years in the wilderness because of Israel's failure to enter the land when God had planned (see Numbers 13–14). This abortive entry involved Joshua himself as one of the spies. He, along with Caleb, believed God's promise that they could defeat the inhabitants, but the other spies and God's people at large did not. This event, and the attitudes it exemplified, feature several times in the book of Joshua as they now come again to enter the land.

The disbelieving generation died in the wilderness and God then gave the succeeding generation instructions through Moses about their life as his people. This included lengthy comment on how they needed go about entering the land. This is in the book of Deuteronomy, which forms essential background to much that happens in Joshua. The book of Joshua then sees the nation of Israel poised to enter this long-awaited land a second time. Seeing the book as the continuation and indeed the fulfilment of this deep-rooted story is key in understanding it.

By the end of Joshua, God has fulfilled all his promises to them: the people have entered, have been victorious over the inhabitants and have been given the land. The closing verses, specifying Joseph's bones being buried, reflect Genesis 50:25 and so bring to an end a key chapter in the life of Israel: this is the end of the Exodus movement as a whole. As Mark Biddle expresses it, God's plan was not only 'to deliver *from* bondage, but to deliver *to* rest'.[1] That is what is fulfilled in Joshua, and the foundation is thus laid for Israel's ongoing life in the land seen in the following historical books.

Joshua thus functions as a crucial hinge in the biblical storyline.

---

[1] Mark E. Biddle, 'Literary Structures in the Book of Joshua', *Review & Expositor* 95, no. 2 (1 May 1998): 200, (emphasis original).

INTRODUCTION

This has resulted in it being regarded in two ways. It has been seen as the conclusion to the Pentateuch (the first five books of the Bible), so much so that some include it within a 'Hexateuch'. Alternatively, it is seen as the first of the 'history' books that relay the story of the nation living under the covenant explained in Deuteronomy (and so referred to as the 'Deuteronomic History').[2]

It is, in fact, helpful to see that the book of Joshua looks two ways. As we have commented above, the story of God's promise to Abraham and his descendants is not complete until they have entered and occupied the land that was integral to that promise. Hence, Joshua can be seen as the necessary capstone to the Pentateuch: it is only at the end of the book, with the people sent to their 'inheritance' in the land, that a line can be drawn. At the same time, it is also true that Joshua is the first taste of life under the covenant where Israel experiences the covenant blessings and curses outlined in Deuteronomy, especially in battle. This connects to the calls to live faithfully under the covenant by obeying all that Moses commanded, so that the nation will know success and prosperity under God. Hence, Joshua can also be seen as the first taste of a prolonged history.[3] As John Goldingay puts it:

> The Israelites' arrival in Canaan brings to a happy end the story that began with God's commission and promise to Abraham in Genesis. It also begins the story of the Israelites' life in Canaan that continues until it comes to an unhappy end in 2 Kings.[4]

The man Joshua

We are introduced to Joshua without comment in Exodus 17 when he assists Moses in the battle against the Amalekites (Exodus 17:8–16). He is then referred to as Moses's aide and is at his side during the

---

[2] The term 'Deuteronomic History' often sees the books from Deuteronomy to Kings as having been written by one author to explain the exile. Such a view has been critiqued; however, it is still true that the theology of Deuteronomy is (unsurprisingly) seen through this later history.
[3] For further discussion of how to view Joshua, see David Firth, *Joshua: Evangelical Biblical Theology Commentary* (Bellingham: Lexham Press, 2021), 5–10.
[4] John Goldingay, *Joshua*, Baker Commentary on the Old Testament: Historical Books (Grand Rapids: Baker, 2023), 6.

time at Sinai (Exodus 24:13; 32:17; 33:11). It is later commented that he has been Moses's aide since his youth (Numbers 11:28). Joshua is then one of the twelve spies who go to look over the Promised Land in Numbers 13–14 and is notable, along with Caleb, for his confidence in God that they can enter the land as promised. As a result, he and Caleb are the only spies who survive and are promised they will enter the land (Numbers 14:30).

We are told in Numbers 13 that Moses changed Joshua's name (Numbers 13:16). He was originally called Hoshea, which means 'salvation'. The change to Joshua made it 'the LORD is salvation' or 'the LORD saves'.[5] In Greek his name is 'Jesus', so giving an immediate link with the Lord Jesus, whose name carries the same meaning (see Matthew 1:21).

God later instructs Moses that Joshua is to succeed him (Numbers 27:12–23), and he is commissioned in that role in Deuteronomy 31:1–8:

> Then Moses summoned Joshua and said to him in the presence of all Israel, 'Be strong and courageous, for you must go with this people into the land that the LORD swore to their ancestors to give them, and you must divide it among them as their inheritance. The LORD himself goes before you and will be with you; he will never leave you nor forsake you. Do not be afraid; do not be discouraged.' (Deuteronomy 31:7–8)

These words are echoed in God's encouragement of Joshua in the opening chapter of the book.

There are a remarkable number of parallels between Joshua and Moses: for example, they both send spies, lead a crossing through water and experience a theophany.[6] In some cases, the parallel is spelt out explicitly, such as in Joshua 4:23–4. Other connections form the start and end of key themes, such as the feeding with manna (Exodus 16 and Joshua 5) or the resolution of issues such as the inheritance of

---

[5] Gordon J. Wenham, *Numbers*, Tyndale Old Testament Commentaries (Downers Grove: InterVarsity Press, 1981), 116–17.
[6] See the extensive list of parallels in Biddle, 'Literary Structures', 190–92.

Zelophehad's daughters (Numbers 36 and Joshua 17). All this adds to the picture of Joshua as Moses's successor and the one who finalises the work Moses began in the Exodus from Egypt.

Type of literature

Joshua is written as an account of history. It follows the previous history of God's people in earlier books and leads to that covered later in Judges to Kings. It is also aimed at teaching truth about God, his purposes and being his people. It is therefore a 'theological history'. That is not to downplay the historical elements or the veracity of the account, only to say that it is written in such a way as to teach theological truth as well as to convey history. In fact, the theological truth conveyed is dependent on the historicity of events – as is true throughout Scripture.[7] What this does mean, though, is that the author may use a variety of literary devices to convey the message and so may not abide by modern standards of historical reporting. Accounts of some events may be stylised or include hyperbole; accounts may not be in chronological order or may be framed to highlight certain aspects. This means we should be alert to the composition of the book as a literary document, not simply a historical one.[8]

In addition to this, we must be aware of Joshua being placed in the biblical canon. That means it is to be read in the light of all that comes before it and after it. As we will see, understanding Joshua is very dependent on previous material, especially the promises to Abraham, the Exodus and instructions through Moses. To apply its truths to today, we must also look to see how it is fulfilled in and through the Lord Jesus Christ. We will comment more on this below.

Structure

The book most clearly divides into two halves: chapters 1–12 and 13–24. The first half describes the entry into the land and defeat of the inhabitants, and the second half describes the division of the

---

7 See for example, 1 Corinthians 15:12–19.
8 For more on this topic see J. Gordon McConville and Stephen N. Williams, *Joshua* (Grand Rapids: Eerdmans, 2010), 3–12. Firth, *Joshua*, 14–24.

land among the tribes and final speeches from Joshua. This division of material is reinforced by chapter 12 drawing the first half to a close in its review of Israel's victories and chapter 13 opening in a resumptive fashion, starting a new section.

Within these broad divisions, further comments can be made. Chapters 1 and 2 clearly prepare for the entry into the land; chapters 3–4 describe the crossing of the Jordan. The remainder of the opening half (chapters 5–12) contain a mixture of events internal to Israel and interactions with external groups, primarily in the form of battles.

The second half of the book begins with a summary of land already divided east of the Jordan and then moves to the process of the division of the land west of the Jordan, along with an account of its completion. This divides into two sections itself, with chapters 14–17 relaying the initial phase of division and then a 'second round' of division in chapters 18–19. Chapters 20–21 detail the cities of refuge and towns for the Levites, which finalises the 'setting up' of the nation. This brings the book to its climatic statement: that God has kept all his promises (Joshua 21:43–5, see further below).

The remaining chapters form a conclusion. Chapter 22 relays the eastern tribes returning home; and chapters 23–4 involve two speeches from Joshua, followed by his death and burial. These final chapters form something of an inclusion with chapter 1: the return of the eastern tribes paralleling Joshua's initial commands to them (Joshua 1:12–15); the commands from Joshua to the people paralleling God's commands to Joshua (Joshua 1:7); and the death of Joshua paralleling the death of Moses at the start of the book (Joshua 1:1).[9]

Broadly, we can speak of the first half of the book as focusing on the entry into and conquest of the land, and the second half focusing on the division and possession of the land, with a final charge from Joshua as to how they will go on living in the land. But there is much fine detail within these broad sections. A breakdown of the book therefore is therefore as follows:

---

9 Biddle, 'Literary Structures', 194.

INTRODUCTION

A. Entry and conquest of the land (chapters 1–12)
    a. Entry into the land (chapters 1–5a)
        i. Instruction to Joshua (1:1–18)
        ii. The spies and Rahab (2:1–24)
        iii. Crossing the Jordan (3:1–4:24)
        iv. Circumcision and Passover (5:1–12)
    b. Conquest of the land (chapters 5b–12)
        i. Fall of Jericho (5:12–6:27)
        ii. Achan's sin (7:1–26)
        iii. Defeat of Ai (8:1–29)
        iv. Covenant renewal (8:30–35)
        v. Gibeonite deception (9:1–27)
        vi. Defeat of coalition (10:1–27)
        vii. Defeat of southern cities (10:28–43)
        viii. Defeat of coalition and northern cities (11:1–23)
        ix. Summary of victories (12:1–24)

B. Division and possession of the land (chapters 13–21)
    a. Division of the land (chapters 13–17)
        i. The land yet to be taken (13:1–7)
        ii. Previous division east of the Jordan (13:8–33)
        iii. Caleb and Hebron (14:1–15)
        iv. The inheritance of Judah (15:1–63)
        v. The inheritance of Joseph (16:1–17:18)
    b. Further division of the land (chapters 18–21)
        i. Second division of the land (18:1–19:51)
        ii. Cities of refuge (20:1–9)
        iii. Towns for the Levites (21:1–42)
        iv. Summary (21:43–5)

C. Call to covenant loyalty (chapters 22–4)
    a. Eastern tribes return home (22:1–34)
    b. Joshua's call to leaders (23:1–16)
    c. Covenant renewal for the whole nation (24:1–28)
    d. Conclusion (24:29–33)

2. Main themes

The book is rich in its theological content. Here we will highlight the main themes that run through it.

The Promised Land: inheritance and resting place

The book of Joshua focuses on the Promised Land: entry into it, conquest of it and inheritance within it. We remember that the promise of the land extends back to Abraham in Genesis 12, with specific reference to conquest of the inhabitants in Genesis 15. Hence this is a central and long-standing part of God's plan which has been reiterated many times. The book begins with an assertion that God is 'about to give' them the land (Joshua 1:2), and at the end of the book the climactic statement is that God has given them possession of the land just as he had 'sworn to their ancestors' (Joshua 21:43–5).

The significance of the Promised Land is seen in key words that describe it: it is Israel's *inheritance* and *resting place*. Both these terms are used in chapter 1 (Joshua 1:6, 13, 15). 'Inheritance' is what God has promised to his people: it is his gift to them. 'Rest' is a holistic idea combining peace and harmony. Together they form the capstone of God's salvific promises: his purpose is to rescue his people and place them in the Promised Land so they will have the inheritance promised and will be at rest.

While these terms are used in chapter 1, they do not recur until the conquest for the land is over. The theme of inheritance then dominates the second half of the book, and while rest is only mentioned sparingly, it comes in key sections, especially Joshua 21:43–5. With regard to 'rest', English translations can be misleading as there are references to rest in Joshua 11:23 and 14:15 saying the 'land had rest from war'. However, these use a different word for rest and only mean that war had ceased temporarily, not that the true rest of settlement had started.[10]

---

10 Firth, *Joshua*, 59.

INTRODUCTION

It is helpful to place the theme of land in the wider flow of biblical history. Key components of God's promise to Abraham are to have his people, living in his land, under his blessing and rule.[11] These core elements are what was lost in Eden and then are promised to be regained in the Promised Land. This is why the Promised Land is portrayed as another 'Eden' in references such as Exodus 3:8; Deuteronomy 8:6–9; 11:11–12. After surveying such passages, William Dumbrell says, 'One can hardly escape the impression that what is being depicted through such references is Eden recaptured, paradise restored.'[12] This is of great significance for how we apply promises of the land today, which we will explore below.

God's faithfulness to his promises

Fulfilling the promise to give his people the land leads into the theme of God's faithfulness. The focus of this faithfulness is on the Promised Land, but tied into that are the related promises of being with Joshua and the people and giving them victory over their enemies. The book starts with a reassurance that this is what God will do because this is what God has promised. Many chapters later, we arrive at the high point of the book:

> So the LORD gave Israel all the land he had sworn to give their ancestors, and they took possession of it and settled there. The LORD gave them rest on every side, just as he had sworn to their ancestors. Not one of their enemies withstood them; the LORD gave all their enemies into their hands. Not one of all the LORD's good promises to Israel failed; every one was fulfilled. (Joshua 21:43–5)

---

[11] See, for example, Graeme Goldsworthy, *Gospel and Kingdom: A Christian Interpretation of the Old Testament* (Exeter: Paternoster Press, 1981), chapter 9. Oren R. Martin, *Bound for the Promised Land: The Land Promise In God's Redemptive Plan*, ed. D. A. Carson, New Studies in Biblical Theology (Downers Grove: Apollos, 2015), chapter 2.
[12] William J Dumbrell, *Covenant and Creation: An Old Testament Covenant Theology* (Milton Keynes: Paternoster, 2013), 187. See also Martin, *Bound for the Promised Land*, 87–90.

Joshua later repeats the last sentence, emphasising that God has kept every one of all his promises (Joshua 23:14). Teaching Joshua should encourage us in God's reliability and hence our confidence in his promises made to us.

God's action and the people's response

The relationship between the actions of God and the response of the Israelites is key in Joshua. This is seen in the key area of the land which is constantly seen as a 'gift' from God (e.g., Joshua 1:2, 6, 11). Its nature as 'gift' is repeated verbally but also exemplified and enacted in what happens: God grants victory, he fights for Israel and so he gives them the land (Joshua 10:14, 42). This point is so stressed that the land is already seen as theirs. Hence, David Howard says:

> The land already belongs to Israel; God has already given it to them (i.e. given them the rights or title to it) . . . the giving was yet to be accomplished; it was either imminent or in process. In both perspectives God was the giver and the guarantor of the process.[13]

However, the fact that it is a gift does not mean Joshua and the people are passive in taking it. Rather, they are called to have faith in God's promises and so walk in obedience to his commands. That is what is emphasised to Joshua in chapter 1 (Joshua 1:7) and is then reiterated in various ways through the book, such as the people's faith and obedience in crossing the Jordan or in taking Jericho (Joshua 3–4; 6). We can picture the relationship between these divine and human elements thus:

---

13 David M. Howard, *Joshua, Volume 5 (The New American Commentary): An Exegetical and Theological Exposition of Holy Scripture* (Nashville: Broadman and Holman, 1998), 81.

INTRODUCTION

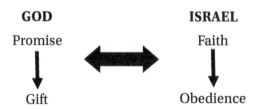

The action of God in promising and so giving means the people are called to respond by believing and so obeying. This dynamic is seen throughout the book.[14]

David Firth uses the analogy of a Christmas present that has our name on it, yet isn't truly ours until we open it. So he says, 'Yahweh is giving the land to Israel, but they have to go forward in faithfulness to him to receive it'.[15] The book begins well in this regard: both Joshua and the people under him trust and obey, and so receive what is promised. Chapter 7 and the sin of Achan is the first black spot on this, but that is dealt with appropriately, and the victories then continue. The overall picture painted in the book, then, is that of faith and obedience, and so success in appropriating God's promises.

Within this overall picture, however, a small but steady drip of failures follow and gradually build, especially in the second half of the book. This is particularly in their failure to drive out some of the inhabitants of the land. Oliver O'Donovan comments, 'The gift fully given was not fully taken'.[16] Hence by the end, when the people promise their ongoing commitment to serve and obey God (Joshua 24:24), one is led to wonder how long this will last.

This also connects to the leadership of Joshua. His faith and obedience are key to Israel's success. This lies behind the commands for

---

14 For more on the theme of gift of the land, see Christopher J. H. Wright, *God's People in God's Land: Family, Land, and Property in the Old Testament* (Grand Rapids: Eerdmans, 1990), chapter 1.
15 David G. Firth, *The Message of Joshua: Promise and People* (Downers Grove: InterVarsity Press, 2015), 33–4.
16 Oliver O'Donovan, 'The Loss of a Sense of Place', *Irish Theological Quarterly* 55, no. 1 (1 March 1989): 51.

him to have strength and to obey in chapter 1 (Joshua 1:7), and it is then emphasised that he obeyed everything God had commanded through Moses (Joshua 11:15). The people then obey Joshua and so the LORD (e.g., Joshua 3:10). But at the end of the book, Joshua's leadership comes to an end. He commands the same strength and obedience he has shown from the next generation of leaders and calls the whole nation to serve the Lord exclusively as he has done (Joshua 23:6; 24:14). This is what is needed for the final taking of the land and for their ongoing possession of it (Joshua 23:6–16). What will happen in Joshua's absence? We are left thinking it is very precarious. We will see this again in discussing the covenant relationship, and this will also lead to some biblical theological reflections.

Covenant relationship

The dynamics between God's gift and the loyalty of his people are an outworking of the covenant. A covenant gives shape to a relationship between two parties. In the Bible, covenants are seen between groups of people (e.g., Israel and the Gibeonites in Joshua 9), but most significantly between God and his people. The covenant with Abraham initiates and then drives the whole story of the Bible (see Genesis 12:1–7; 15:1–21). It contains the promise from God of blessing, a people and a land. Hence the arrival in the land in Joshua is a key part of these covenant promises being fulfilled. The Abrahamic covenant is followed by the covenant made under Moses at Mount Sinai as detailed in Exodus 19–40 and reiterated through Deuteronomy.

There are a number of ways in which the Abrahamic and Mosaic covenants are seen to fit together; the latter is usually seen as a temporary outworking of the former. The Abrahamic covenant is ultimately fulfilled in the gospel of Jesus (Galatians 3:7–9); the Mosaic covenant is the 'old covenant' that is superseded (Hebrews 8:7–13).

A key point for reading Joshua is to know that Israel's relationship with God is being lived out under these covenants. While the word 'covenant' is relatively rarely used in the book, it lies in the background all the time. The Mosaic covenant is very clear in God's blessing of his people's obedience and his cursing in response to their rebellion. For Joshua, that meant they would be successful in their attempts to enter the land and defeat its inhabitants to the extent that they followed the terms of the covenant. The call to Joshua to follow all the Book of the Law and so be successful is a call to live within the covenant (Joshua 1:7–8).

We should make clear, as Terence Fretheim does, that 'success is not to be understood as reward'.[17] Entering the land was claiming an inheritance promised or receiving a gift already given. God had made clear that the Israelites were not being given the land because of anything good in them (Deuteronomy 9:5). Yet they still needed to walk with their God as he fulfilled his promise; not to do so was to spurn it. This outworking of the covenant then gives the background to the dynamic of gift and response outlined above.

Loyalty to the covenant lies behind the approach to war (discussed below) and interaction with the inhabitants of the land (Joshua 6:17–19). It is represented in the setting up of an altar and the reading of the Law on Mount Ebal (Joshua 8:30–35). It comes to a climax in Joshua's final calls for covenant loyalty and warnings against apostasy (chapters 23–4). Covenant has guided their entry into the land and loyalty within it has brought success. Joshua's challenge is then for ongoing life in the land: will they stay within the covenant and know its blessings or stray and experience its curses?

The unity of Israel

While the main activity within Joshua is that of entering and inheriting the land, there is a strong theme of this being done by Israel as a united nation. There is repeated use of the phrase 'all Israel' within the narrative, such that the tribes are portrayed as working together in the common task of entering the land under Joshua.[18] In particular, the unity between the trans-Jordanian tribes and those that will settle west of the Jordan is emphasised. This is seen in the command to the trans-Jordanian tribes to help their fellow Israelites

---

17 Terence E. Fretheim, *Deuteronomic History*, Interpreting Biblical Texts (Nashville: Abingdon Press, 1983), 57.
18 It is used seventeen times.

in chapter 1:12–15. It is highlighted within the subsequent narrative (Joshua 4:12), and then returned to in chapter 22.

Chapter 22 forms an extended reflection on the unity between eastern and western tribes and the link to covenant loyalty to God: it is as each tribe remains loyal to the LORD that they will remain united with each other. Unity between these two groups is also a key theme within the summary section of chapter 12 and the introduction to the inheritance section in chapter 13, as these portray the territories on each side of the Jordan as part of one extended victorious campaign, and as one process of allocation of inheritances. Dale Ralph Davis points out that the unity of Israel in Joshua 'will form a healthy contrast to the increasing fragmentation of Israel in the Book of Judges'.[19]

'Holy war'

Joshua is well known for its battles, especially that of Jericho. The battles involve defeat of the inhabitants of the land but also their death, and this is at the explicit command of God. This is often referred to as a 'holy war'; that is, a battle fought for religious purposes and so sanctioned by God. This is not a biblical term and may not be helpful to use in some contexts because of associations with other religions and even terrorist acts.[20] The background for the battles in Joshua is found in the instructions of Deuteronomy 20. In that passage a clear distinction is drawn between battles in general and those fought when entering the land. For example, in general, an offer of peace was to be made, whereas in the land there was to be no such offer. Hence the battles in the land are of a different nature and purpose.

The command given for the cities in the Promised Land is to 'completely destroy them' (Deuteronomy 20:17). This involves the use of a specific term, often referred to as the 'ban' or 'devoting

---

19 Dale Ralph Davis, *Joshua: No Falling Words* (Fearn, Ross-shire: Christian Focus, 2000), 21.
20 The term 'holy war' has been regularly used in the literature since its use by Gerhard von Rad in 1951. Trent Butler, *Joshua 1–12, Volume 7A* (Nashville: Zondervan, 2014), 353–8.

INTRODUCTION

to the Lord'.[21] The particularity of this term means these are not regular battles; rather, something very specific is happening: God is bringing his sovereign rule over this territory and so exercising his judgment (for more on this understanding see Excursus: Devoting to the LORD).

We should note the two different reasons given for the elimination of the inhabitants.[22] The first reason is the sinfulness of the local population. Genesis 15:16 says that the entry into the land will not happen for four generations because 'the sin of the Amorites has not yet reached its full measure'. In other words, God was waiting until this destruction was deserved. Other passages point to the revolting practices of the inhabitants of the land (such as child sacrifice) as the reason God will drive them out (e.g., Leviticus 18:25; Deuteronomy 9:4–5; 18:12). Hence, the destruction of the inhabitants confronts us with God's right to punish sin, and so points us to the day of final judgment when he will bring such punishment on the whole world. While sobering to contemplate, ultimately the picture we are given of God is reassuring because God will bring justice.

The second reason is the purification of the land. The rationale given in Deuteronomy 20 for the elimination of the Canaanite population is, 'Otherwise, they will teach you to follow all the detestable things they do in worshipping their gods, and you will sin against the LORD your God' (Deuteronomy 20:18). The land is said to have become unclean because of the practices of the inhabitants; now it will be cleansed (Leviticus 18:24). The concern that Israel will be led astray by the practices of the inhabitants of the land is repeated elsewhere (see Deuteronomy 7:2–6; 12:29–31).

These two reasons link to what is happening as Israel enters the Promised Land: this is where God is establishing his kingdom and where he will rule over his people. Meredith Kline has referred to this as 'intrusion ethics'; that is, the intrusion of the eschatological

---

[21] The Hebrew term is *herem*. The term 'the ban' is common in the literature; we will use the term 'devoted' or 'devoted to destruction'.
[22] For an overview of how the inhabitants are viewed, see William Ford, 'The Challenge of the Canaanites', *Tyndale Bulletin* 68, no. 2 (2017): 24.

future into the present.²³ That is why the invasion into the land is not breaking the sixth and eight commandments:

> Only so can the conquest be justified and seen as it was in truth – not murder, but the hosts of the Almighty visiting upon the rebels against his righteous throne their just deserts – not robbery, but the meek inheriting the earth.²⁴

This understanding means we see the Promised Land as the place where a holy God is coming to dwell and rule on earth. This is then incompatible with pagan worship and practices. As Steven Bryan says:

> The conquest is fundamentally a divine action that brings to an end pagan worship and pagan kingship, and the connection of both to the land. God has declared the land holy as preparation for its inhabitants by a holy people and by his own holy presence.²⁵

We should therefore be very careful about the use of the term 'holy war'. Bryan continues, 'It is not war that is holy, but God.'²⁶ What is happening in the conquest of the land is the arrival of God's holy kingdom, and where God rules sin is punished, and the land is cleansed. We must therefore be very clear that the theme of 'holy war' is limited to this establishing of the kingdom in Canaan and so the book of Joshua cannot be used to justify violence against enemies, any kind of military crusade or Christian jihad today.²⁷

We should also note that a connection is sometimes made between the 'God-given' granting of land that belongs to others and colonial

---

23 Meredith G. Kline, *The Structure of Biblical Authority* (Grand Rapids: Eerdmans, 1972), part II, chapter 3.
24 Kline, *Biblical Authority*, 163.
25 Steven M. Bryan, *Cultural Identity and the Purposes of God: A Biblical Theology of Ethnicity, Nationality, and Race* (Wheaton: Crossway, 2022), 116.
26 Bryan, *Cultural Identity*, 119.
27 K. Jesurathnam, 'Joshua', in *South Asia Bible Commentary: A One-Volume Commentary on the Whole Bible*, ed. Brian Wintle (Grand Rapids: Zondervan, 2015), 265.

expansion. One example often cited is that of Puritan settlers in North America, although the connection with the wars in Joshua is contested.[28] It should be clear from the above that Joshua provides no such justification; rather, in Joshua the invasion of the land was for specific, limited reasons within God's plans of salvation history. Broader Christian principles of justice and respect would give us reason to lament much within colonialism. In teaching Joshua in some contexts, it may be helpful to address this issue.

Accusations of 'genocide'

The killing of inhabitants in Joshua has been likened to genocide or ethnic cleansing, and one can see why, as there is indeed the wholescale slaughter of groups of people. In addressing this we should affirm our, and our listeners', instinctive sense of justice. The unjustified invasion of a country and significant elimination of its inhabitants would be appalling. Our moral outrage at contemporary genocides and the like are justified biblically. The issue in Joshua is intensified within the flow of the Bible because we are told of God's intent to use Abraham's descendants to bring blessing to all nations, not destruction (Genesis 12:3).

There are several positions commonly adopted on this issue which we will list and examine briefly.[29]

1. The acts of killing in Joshua are not what they seem
Sometimes this position involves the complete denial of the historicity of Joshua. Such killing simply did not happen and it is written as the creation of a later generation. Other approaches take the language used as metaphorical so that literal killing was never envisaged. These positions simply do not take the text of the Bible seriously.

---

[28] For a view seeing a connection see Pekka Pitkänen, *Joshua: An Introduction and Survey*, Apollos Old Testament Commentary, Volume 6 (Nottingham: Apollos, 2008), 83–9. For denial of this link, see Goldingay, *Joshua*, 15.
[29] For further reading, see Charlie Trimm, *The Destruction of the Canaanites: God, Genocide, and Biblical Interpretation* (Grand Rapids: Eerdmans, 2022). Stanley N. Gundry (ed.), *Show Them No Mercy: Four Views on God and Canaanite Genocide*, Counterpoints (Grand Rapids: Zondervan, 2003).

An alternative is to see the accounts as historical but the language as hyperbolic. There is evidence for this within Joshua itself: for example, in Joshua 10:20 we read that Joshua 'defeated them completely', but the same verse then refers to 'survivors'. David Firth says, 'If intended literally, these statements cannot both be true . . . we need to reckon with the possibility that the text uses an idiom that describes a complete victory, but not one that requires the actual destruction of everyone.'[30] These observations are perfectly valid and may temper our picture of what is happening somewhat, but it does not remove the issue. Even if hyperbolic statements are used, the reality must be close to them or they are inappropriate.[31]

Another approach sees places such as Jericho as 'forts' occupied by military personnel rather than urban environments and so restricts the number and category of people who were killed. This approach does not adequately deal with the biblical text which specifically includes women and children as those killed (Joshua 6:21).

2. The acts of killing in Joshua are what they seem and were wrong
This approach agrees that mass murder is portrayed in Joshua and says it was a moral travesty. The explanations of how it came about vary, broadly blaming either God or the Israelites. Those that blame God take the biblical text at face value and conclude that God is a vindicative murderer. Such has been the accusation of many of the 'new atheists'.[32] Sometimes God is partially excused by saying he accommodated himself to the cultural norms of the day.

Those that blame Israel say that Joshua and the people misunderstood what God was asking for, or that they went much further than commanded.[33] Sometimes Israel is also partially excused by saying they were following the cultural pattern of the day which included such total elimination of enemies. But while Israel and the people's practices were clearly embedded within the cultural setting, they did

---

30 Firth, *Joshua*, 192.
31 Some commentaries so emphasise these points as to say there was no significant killing, for example, Goldingay, *Joshua*, 3–5. This surely runs completely against the text.
32 For example, Richard Dawkins, *The God Delusion* (Boston: Mariner, 2006), 51.
33 As argued by Goldingay, *Joshua*, 51–2, 138–9, 276.

not need to conform to it. Indeed, one of the dominant themes in Deuteronomy is that God's people were not to act as the other nations; why then could they not have been told to act differently in warfare? And God cannot be excused without serious distortion to the text of Deuteronomy and Joshua. God explicitly did require such killing and Israel is commended for their obedience to him.

3. The acts of killing in Joshua are what they seem and were right
As explained above, the rationale for the elimination of the inhabitants was both their sinfulness and the purification of the place of God's kingdom. What was happening with God's people entering the land was therefore unique: God was bringing his rule in time and space in a new way, and as it came, so did his destruction. Canaan was to be a place where every knee bowed before him. It is of great significance that some people in Canaan bowed their knees as God's kingdom came and they were not killed as a result (Rahab in chapter 2 and the Gibeonites in chapter 9 – see commentary). Equally, when an Israelite rebelled against God he received the same punishment as the Canaanites (Achan in chapter 7). Therefore, it is not a matter of ethnicity but of stance towards God. A comment in Hebrews 11 is very illuminating in this regard: 'By faith the prostitute Rahab, because she welcomed the spies, was not killed with those who were disobedient' (Hebrews 11:31). The description of the other inhabitants of Jericho as 'disobedient' (or 'unbelieving') shows that their death was because of their attitude towards God.

As we will see below, the New Testament parallel to this judgment falling on Canaan is the coming judgment of God through the Lord Jesus. What we see in Joshua is an imperfect anticipation of that final judgment and purification of God's world. Ultimately, the question of the killing of the Canaanites is reduced to this: does God have the right to judge and punish people within his creation?[34]

---

[34] Many commentaries have sections dealing with this area. See Howard, *Joshua*, 180–87. Adolph Harstad, *Joshua: Concordia Commentary* (St Louis: Concordia Publishing House, 2004), 256–69.

3. Biblical theology and application

In teaching the book of Joshua today, we need to appreciate both the lessons it teaches within itself and how these are taken up and applied within the rest of the Bible. Some truths are generic and remain as true for us as they were for Joshua's generation, for example God's faithfulness to his promises. However, even then we would want to distinguish between the promises made to Joshua and what he has promised to us.

Other themes require interpreting through the canon of Scripture. For example, the Israelites celebrating the Passover in chapter 5 requires an understanding of how that festival remembering redemption from Egypt is fulfilled in the Lord's Supper remembering redemption from sin. Appropriate connections will be drawn throughout the commentary, but some key 'big picture' moves will be identified here; they will then be drawn on as needed in discussing particular texts.

Old and New Testament appropriation

Some of the groundwork can be laid for this by seeing the way parts of Joshua are appropriated in later biblical texts. It is not that biblical theological moves rely only on passages being quoted later in Scripture, but such quotations do give key guidance. The table below covers this data and makes some brief comments.

Joshua event	Joshua passage	Later reference	Comment
Old Testament			
Crossing the Jordan	Chapters 3–4	Psalm 114:3–6	The blocking of the Jordan by God
Curse on rebuilding Jericho	6:26	1 Kings 16:34	Fulfilled by Hiel showing his disregard for God as part of the apostate house of Ahab
Reference to Joshua; no specific event	No specific passage	Nehemiah 8:17	Celebration at reading of the Law is said to be greatest since days of Joshua

INTRODUCTION

God driving out the nations, defeating kings and giving an inheritance to his people	Multiple passages, see 10:10–11; 11:7–9; 21:43–5; 24:12–13	Psalm 44:1–8	Celebration of entry into the land by God's power
		Psalm 47:1–4	God subduing enemies and giving inheritance
		Psalm 68:12–14	Description of kings fleeing before God
		Psalm 78:54–5	Rehearsal of history of Israel including driving out nations, allotting the land and giving inheritance
		Psalm 105:44–5	Giving the land of other nations, including their cities
		Nehemiah 9:24–5	Taking possession of the land including cities, vineyards, olive trees, etc.
		Amos 2:9	Defeating Amorites
		Micah 6:5	Remembering whole journey from Shittim to Gilgal
Sun and moon standing in battle	10:12–14	Habakkuk 3:11	Included in the recounting of God's great deeds for Israel
Division of the land	Chapters 13–21	Ezekiel 47:13–48:29	A new allotment of land as Israel's inheritance
Not driving out inhabitants of the land	15:63; 16:10; 17:12–13	Psalm 106:34–5	Not destroying the people as commanded
New Testament			
God's promise of presence	1:5	Hebrews 13:5	God promises to be with the believers
Rahab being saved	2:1–24; 6:23	Matthew 1:5	Inclusion in genealogy of Jesus
		Hebrews 11:31	Rahab's faith in welcoming the spies
		James 2:25	Rahab's faith shown in her actions
The Israelites bringing the Tabernacle into the land	Chapters 3–4	Acts 7:45	Tabernacle comes into the land with Joshua until the time of David

Defeat of the tribes in Canaan; giving land as inheritance	E.g., 3:10; 11:23	Acts 13:19	Overthrow of seven nations in Canaan and giving land as inheritance
Walls of Jericho falling	6:20	Hebrews 11:30	The walls of Jericho fell by faith
Gathering of armies to fight	11:4	Revelation 20:8	Gathering of armies for final battle
Being given rest in the land	21:44; 22:4	Hebrews 4:8	The rest given by Joshua does not fulfil what God had promised
Joseph's bones being buried	24:32	Acts 7:16	Recounts Joseph's body being brought up from Egypt and buried at Shechem
		Hebrews 11:22	Joseph's faith shown by his instructions regarding his bones

The Old Testament references demonstrate what a significant moment the entry into the land was. Along with the events of the Exodus, it is celebrated as a key part of salvation history and a prime example of God's momentous acts for his people. It is to be looked back on as a crucial moment of God's goodness, faithfulness and power. Life in the land is to be lived knowing it was given to them by God. There is also reflection on the failure of the people to keep the covenant.[35] Psalm 78 moves from the successful entry into the land to putting God to the test (Psalm 78:56), and Psalm 106 moves from the failure to eliminate all the inhabitants to worshipping their gods and following their customs (Psalm 106:34–9). Within the Old Testament, therefore, Joshua is seen both as a wonderful capstone to God's deliverance from Egypt and a moment where the seeds of failure are already sown.

The reference to the land being allotted again in Ezekiel is very significant for how we understand this theme. In Ezekiel this new inheritance goes alongside a new Temple and a new priesthood. These themes are very clearly picked up in the New Testament as

---

35 Firth, *Joshua*, 12.

INTRODUCTION

referring to the new creation (see Ezekiel 47:1–12 and Revelation 22:1–5). So Oren Martin says of Ezekiel's picture of restoration:

> Thus the promise concerning the renewed Israel's living in the land under a new David is fulfilled in the vision of the temple, recreating Edenic conditions, the boundaries of which are coterminous with the land. From a canonical perspective, then, Revelation presents this worldwide temple as the new heavens and new earth – the new Jerusalem – in the light of the fulfilment of Christ, the true temple.[36]

We will pick this up below, but this indicates we are not to apply the promise of the land as now referring to the land in Canaan; rather, it indicates a new inheritance.

The land, inheritance and rest

Entering the land is a key element in Joshua and, as we saw above, the land is connected with the important themes of God's granting inheritance and rest. The most significant New Testament reference above is from Hebrews 4, which refers to God's promise of rest:

> For if Joshua had given them rest, God would not have spoken later about another day. There remains, then, a Sabbath-rest for the people of God; for anyone who enters God's rest also rests from their works, just as God did from his. Let us, therefore, make every effort to enter that rest, so that no one will perish by following their example of disobedience. (Hebrews 4:8–11)

Here, Joshua is seen as leading the people to rest in the land, but that rest was incomplete and was not the final stage of God's plans. The argument is that Joshua did not give them true rest and that is why God spoke of another day of rest to come. So, David Firth argues:

---

36 Martin, *Bound for the Promised Land*, 112.

The declaration in Psalm 95 about the people not entering God's rest refers in the first instance to the wilderness generation. But in taking up this text and Joshua, the writer to the Hebrews sees a repeated pattern, albeit one tied to God's rest in the Sabbath. Israel's failure to live out the rest God had given under Joshua means there is still a rest to be claimed, and it is this rest that is available to us in Jesus.[37]

We enter the final rest God offers by believing the gospel message of Jesus. In doing so we enter God's promised rest now, but that rest is only finally fulfilled in the new creation. This means that the call in Joshua to believe God's promises and enter the land is now to be applied to believing the gospel and so entering God's rest in Jesus.

This looking forward from a temporary shadow to the eternal reality it anticipates is a frequent theme in Hebrews. Speaking of Abraham, Sarah, Isaac and Jacob, the author says, 'they were longing for a better country – a heavenly one' (Hebrews 11:16). As Palmer Robertson comments, 'They understood, though only dimly, that the land promised them actually had its origins in the heavenly, eternal reality that yet remained before them.'[38] We can therefore see the land as a picture of God's kingdom that we enter now through Jesus and which one day will encompass the whole world.[39]

We see a similar move regarding the theme of inheritance. The land formed the inheritance that God had promised his people in Joshua. That inheritance related to all that would be achieved within the land: it was the place where they would live at peace, with God in their midst. It was, in New Testament terms, a picture of God's kingdom.

Inheritance language is then picked up in numerous places in the New Testament. For example:

---

[37] Firth, *The Message of Joshua*, 348.
[38] O. Palmer Robertson, 'A New-Covenant Perspective on the Land', in *The Land of Promise: Biblical, Theological and Contemporary Perspectives*, ed. Philip S. Johnston and Peter W. L. Walker (Downers Grove: Apollos, 2000), 123.
[39] See also Appendix B: The Borders of the Promised Land.

INTRODUCTION

- We are given an inheritance through the word of God's grace (Acts 20:32).
- The Holy Spirit is a deposit guaranteeing our inheritance (Ephesians 1:14).
- Jesus is the mediator of the new covenant so that we may receive our promised eternal inheritance (Hebrews 9:15).
- We have been we given an inheritance which is kept in heaven for us (1 Peter 1:4).
- Those who are victorious will receive the inheritance of the new creation (Revelation 21:7).

Adolph Harstad summarises:

> The land inheritance is a prelude to the heavenly inheritance awaiting those to whom the Father has been pleased to give the kingdom (Lk 12:32) through the death and resurrection of his Son, the mediator of the new covenant.[40]

We can add to the language of inheritance that of being 'heirs' – those promised an inheritance. We are heirs of the promise to Abraham to inherit the world (Romans 4:13–17); we are Abraham's children and so heirs of his promise (Galatians 3:29); we are heirs of God and co-heirs with Christ (Romans 8:17). Crucially, Jew and Gentile are now joint heirs in Christ (Ephesians 3:6); and men and women are heirs together (1 Peter 3:7). Hence the theme of inheritance connects with those of unity and equality.

Some approaches to the Bible see the promises made to Abraham and then to Israel as independent or semi-independent of this kind of fulfilment in Jesus.[41] There are a number of different schemas as to how this works, but the end result is often that the promise of the land still remains for ethnic Jews today. Some adopting these approaches would therefore see the promises of the land as relating to the modern nation state of Israel. In this commentary we will

---

40 Harstad, *Joshua*, 74.
41 These often go under the broad heading of dispensationalism, but many different versions of this exist.

not follow that line of application; rather, it is our conviction that the promises of the land and inheritance are now received by those who believe in Jesus as outlined above.[42]

The people and the new covenant

We said above that the relationship between God and the people was governed by the covenant – both the background of the Abrahamic covenant and the specifics of the Mosaic covenant. The stipulations of the Mosaic covenant mean we see the potential of God's blessing or curse falling on the nation, depending on their obedience. Teaching Joshua today will therefore require addressing the issue of covenant relationship and that believers today live under the new covenant.

Exactly how this will be addressed will depend on how the teacher sees the old and new covenants relating. With regard to the Abrahamic covenant promises, we can point to their being fulfilled in the blessing we now receive in Jesus (Galatians 3:7–8). With regard to the Mosaic covenant, we can refer to the new covenant which will write the Law on people's hearts such that they will obey (Jeremiah 31:31–4; Hebrews 8:7–13). This will particularly affect the teaching of the covenant renewal passages (Joshua 8:30–35; 24:1–28) but will also pervade the whole book.

Battles and destruction

We stated above that the theme of destruction within the land sees God's sovereign rule being exercised as his kingdom is established. In Canaan that is happening in a limited geographical area. We know that one day God's kingdom will come in all its fullness, which will involve Jesus bringing judgment on those who oppose him (see 2 Thessalonians 1:5–10; Revelation 19:11–21). This means that a main line of application from the battles in Joshua is to the final battle

---

[42] For an examination of this topic, see Munther Isaac, *From Land to Lands, from Eden to the Renewed Earth: A Christ-Centred Biblical Theology of the Promised Land* (Carlisle: Langham Monographs, 2015). O. Palmer Robertson, *The Israel of God, Yesterday, Today, Tomorrow* (Phillipsburg: Presbyterian and Reformed, 2012).

when Jesus returns. The judgment falling on the people of the land is a sobering foretaste of the judgment Jesus will bring.[43]

Within this main line of application, we can also note several other links that are often made. These will not be commonly referred to in the commentary that follows but are included here so that the reader can make their own judgments as to whether to refer to them. Given the theme of battling against evil, some interpreters draw connections to Jesus's battle against demonic forces during his earthly ministry and also through his cross and resurrection (see Matthew 12:22–9; Colossians 2:13–15).[44] Similarly, as the picture in Joshua is of God's kingdom coming, application is made to Jesus bringing God's kingdom through his ministry (see Mark 1:15; 9:1; 14:25).[45] In both these cases the principle is certainly true; what is different in Joshua is the bringing of judgment on those who oppose God's reign. In this commentary we see this as most naturally connecting to the final judgment.

Others have 'spiritualised' these battles and connected them to the Christian's battle against sin today. Certainly, the language of 'putting to death' is used in that regard and one can see a line of application there; Paul tells us that it is because of such things that God's wrath is coming (see Colossians 3:5–6). This also connects to the purification theme explored above and, potentially, to the theme of spiritual warfare (Ephesians 6:10–18).[46] Despite these connections, the focus in Joshua is on the killing of those opposed to God, and hence the main application in the commentary will be to future judgment.

---

43 For a further exploration of this line of thinking, see Daniel L. Gard, 'The Case for Eschatological Continuity', in Gundry (ed.), *Show Them No Mercy*.
44 See comments by Richard Hess, *Joshua: An Introduction and Survey* (Leicester: InterVarsity Press, 1996), 46.
45 For an exploration of this whole area, see Tremper Longman III and Daniel P. Reid, *God Is a Warrior* (Grand Rapids: Zondervan, 1995), chapters 7–9.
46 For an exploration of this theme, see Tremper Longman III, 'The Case for Spiritual Continuity', in Gundry (ed.), *Show Them No Mercy*.

4. Other issues

There are a number of other issues that arise in reading and interpreting Joshua. We can only comment briefly here; further reading is indicated in the footnotes.

Contradictions

We should be aware of the accusation of contradictions within Joshua. This is usually concerning two related issues: (a) the swiftness of the conquest, whether it was quick or prolonged; and (b) the totality of the conquest, whether it was complete or partial. They are related because a slow conquest usually goes hand in hand with a partial one. While the accusation of 'contradiction' is overplayed, we must recognise the truth of what lies behind it.

There are some key background texts to be aware of. Some promise a gradual and prolonged conquest (see Exodus 23:29–30 and Deuteronomy 7:22). These need to put together with the apparent swiftness of conquest recorded in Joshua itself, for example where Joshua is said to have conquered all the southern cities in one campaign (Joshua 10:42). A key issue here is the way Joshua presents 'conquest'. What is described is an overall victory so that the inhabitants can be said to be defeated. However, that is not the same as total elimination. Hence some towns that were 'conquered' were not occupied and needed to be defeated again. Joshua 11:18 specifically says that the wars lasted a long time; and even by the end of the book it is made clear that not all the land had been possessed.

We should therefore see the battles as involving an initial strike in which Israel clearly defeated the inhabitants. Even that took some years, and the actual occupation of each part of the land then followed. The supposed contrast with the picture painted in Judges – of a gradual and slow occupation – is therefore overdrawn.[47]

---

47 See the further discussion in chapter 14, 'Introduction to Possessing the land'.

Date of events and archaeology

There is ongoing debate about the dating of early Old Testament events, especially the Exodus and subsequently the entry into the land. Some Old Testament evidence points to a date as early as the fifteenth century BC.[48] There are some good reasons to accept this, but others argue for a date in the thirteenth century BC.[49] While of significance in other ways, precise dating will not influence our reading of Joshua and so we will not consider it further here.

Relating archaeological discoveries and the biblical narrative to each other is a complex area. While this is a worthwhile pursuit, it is not necessary for our understanding of Joshua. The reader and teacher of Joshua should be confident of approaching the book without any reference to archaeology. It is mentioned here for two reasons. First, it may be encountered in commentaries where it is often used to disagree with or reinforce the biblical text. Second, in some contexts, people may have heard global statements along the lines of archaeology 'disproving' parts of Joshua; for example, that the walls of Jericho did not exist. Such popular reports can easily have an undermining effect and may require an apologetic response. The teacher of Joshua will have to decide what reference to make to this type of concern, if at all.[50]

In considering archaeology in Joshua, there is first the question of what would be expected to be found. We should remember that only a few cities (Jericho, Ai and Hazor) were said to be destroyed and so evidence of an invasion would not even be expected in other locations. Then there are the difficulties of identifying sites, the effects of erosion which would eliminate evidence, the limited areas often involved in excavations, and questions around dating. For example, regarding Jericho, while the site is commonly agreed on, the effects of erosion are significant. There is evidence of significant city walls

---

48 See 1 Kings 6:1 and Judges 11:26. The 1 Kings reference may refer to twelve generations rather than a precise number of years.
49 See the discussion in Harstad, *Joshua*, 15–22. Also, Howard, *Joshua*, 31–35.
50 For a general overview of historicity, see K. A. Kitchen, *On the Reliability of the Old Testament* (Grand Rapids: Eerdmans, 2003), 160–99.

and of destruction by fire, but the dating of such destruction is contested. There are certainly very good reasons to see agreement between the archaeological evidence and the biblical account, but it remains very debated.[51] By comparison, there is significant debate about the site of Ai, and hence the relevance of the data (or lack of it) in the commonly identified location.[52] Within all of this we should remember the well-known maxim that 'absence of evidence is not evidence of absence'.

Dating of writing and audience

The date of writing and intended audience are linked topics. It is common to try to identify the intended audience from themes in the book and so arrive at a date. With Joshua, some have identified a Davidic setting addressing issues associated with his reign.[53] Others see Joshua as being written at a much later date and specifically aimed at the Israelites in exile in Babylon or following the return to the land.[54] However, there is no need to date it that late and there are good reasons to place it much earlier. We should also remember that a biblical author can have broad aims that speak to multiple generations, in which case there is no need to identify a single audience. As John Goldingay says, we can ask 'how the material might function in a context without assuming that it had its origin then'.[55]

An end point to writing is provided by the comment that Jerusalem is occupied by the Jebusites 'to this day' (Joshua 15:63), so placing it before David's conquering of the city in about 1000 BC (2 Samuel

---

51 For an argument in support of the biblical account, see Bryant G. Wood, 'Did the Israelites Conquer Jericho? A New Look at the Archaeological Evidence', *Biblical Archaeology Review* 16, no. 2 (1990): 44–59. This includes evidence of significant grain stores at the time of destruction, indicating that the city fell soon after a harvest and in the absence of a long siege, both of which fit the Joshua account. For an argument that the appropriate evidence is simply lost, see Kitchen, *Reliability*, 187–8.
52 See discussion in Howard, *Joshua*, 177–80.
53 For example, Firth, *Joshua*, 2–5.
54 For example, Jerome F. D. Creach, *Joshua: Interpretation: A Bible Commentary for Teaching and Preaching* (Louisville: John Knox Press, 2003), 9–12.
55 Goldingay, *Joshua*, 11.

INTRODUCTION

5:6–10).[56] We also are told of the Danites losing their inheritance and moving north (Joshua 19:40–48), so placing the writing after these events (Judges 18). The reference to Rahab living among the Israelites 'to this day' (6:25) would place dating within her lifetime – unless a later author was using previously written sources. Other references to situations persisting 'to this day' suggest some indefinite time has passed rather than a contemporaneous account (9:27; 15:63; 16:10), but it may be that Joshua himself wrote sections of the book (see Joshua 24:26). It is assumed here that it was written within a lifetime after the events recorded, but this does not usually affect interpretation of the text.[57]

God's name

The covenant name for God refers to the name God gives himself in Exodus 3. This is represented in most Bible versions by the word 'LORD' (with small capitals to distinguish it from 'Lord'). Some commentaries and books transliterate it as 'Yahweh'. others only using the consonants in the text, 'Yhwh'. In this commentary we will follow the NIV in using 'LORD' when referring to this word. In quoting others, we will retain whatever nomenclature was originally used.

---

56 Howard, *Joshua*, 29–30.
57 See discussion in Harstad, *Joshua*, 8–12.

PART ONE

JOSHUA 1–12

I

The Need for a Leader: Commissioning Joshua

Joshua 1

The book of Joshua picks up where Deuteronomy ends, particularly focusing on the transfer of leadership from Moses to Joshua. The people of Israel are poised on the edge of the Promised Land knowing they are going to enter, which will mean crossing the Jordan River and conquering the native inhabitants (see map 1). They know that this is the plan because the land in front of them was promised to Abraham in Genesis 12, and that promise has been repeated to his descendants over the intervening centuries. This is a long-anticipated entry with deep roots in Israel's history. Before that entry can start, Joshua is commissioned as Moses' replacement and the new leader of Israel. His relationship with God and his trust and obedience will be crucial for this task; in this way he points us forward to the Lord Jesus who gains us entry into God's kingdom.

Joshua installed as leader

1 After the death of Moses the servant of the LORD, the LORD said to Joshua son of Nun, Moses' assistant: 2'Moses my servant is dead. Now then, you and all these people, get ready to cross the River Jordan into the land I am about to give to them – to the Israelites. 3 I will give you every place where you set your foot, as I promised Moses. 4 Your territory will extend from the desert to Lebanon, and from the great river, the Euphrates – all the Hittite country – to the Mediterranean Sea in the west. 5 No one will be able to stand against you all the days of your life. As I was with Moses, so I will be with you; I will never leave you nor forsake you. 6 Be strong and courageous, because you will lead these people to inherit the land I swore to their ancestors to give them.

7 'Be strong and very courageous. Be careful to obey all the law my servant Moses gave you; do not turn from it to the right or to the left, that you may be successful wherever you go. 8 Keep

this Book of the Law always on your lips; meditate on it day and night, so that you may be careful to do everything written in it. Then you will be prosperous and successful. 9 Have I not commanded you? Be strong and courageous. Do not be afraid; do not be discouraged, for the LORD your God will be with you wherever you go.'

10 So Joshua ordered the officers of the people: 11 'Go through the camp and tell the people, "Get your provisions ready. Three days from now you will cross the Jordan here to go in and take possession of the land the LORD your God is giving you for your own."'

12 But to the Reubenites, the Gadites and the half-tribe of Manasseh, Joshua said, 13 'Remember the command that Moses the servant of the LORD gave you after he said, "The LORD your God will give you rest by giving you this land." 14 Your wives, your children and your livestock may stay in the land that Moses gave you east of the Jordan, but all your fighting men, ready for battle, must cross over ahead of your fellow Israelites. You are to help them 15 until the LORD gives them rest, as he has done for you, and until they too have taken possession of the land that the LORD your God is giving them. After that, you may go back and occupy your own land, which Moses the servant of the LORD gave you east of the Jordan towards the sunrise.'

16 Then they answered Joshua, 'Whatever you have commanded us we will do, and wherever you send us we will go. 17 Just as we fully obeyed Moses, so we will obey you. Only may the LORD your God be with you as he was with Moses. 18 Whoever rebels against your word and does not obey it, whatever you may command them, will be put to death. Only be strong and courageous!'

1. The instructions to Joshua • Joshua 1:1–9

The 'death of Moses', recorded in Deuteronomy 34, forms the end of a key period for God's people: Moses led their redemption out of slavery in Egypt and into the covenant at Sinai with the LORD. His designation here as 'the servant of the LORD' would carry these overtones and is emphasised by being mentioned twice (verses 1–2).[1]

---

[1] Moses is repeatedly referred to by this designation throughout Joshua (another four times in the first chapter: verse 2, 7, 13, 15). By the end of the book Joshua is given the same title (Joshua 24:29).

THE NEED FOR A LEADER: COMMISSIONING JOSHUA

Now the baton of leadership is passed to Joshua; Moses's death does not mean God's plans and purposes for his people have died with him. Joshua's leadership has been expected because of God's instructions in Numbers 27. Strictly speaking, his commissioning took place then and is seen later (Deuteronomy 34:9); in this passage, that commissioning comes to fruition. Joshua is described as 'Moses' assistant', which reminds us of his previous appearance in the biblical narrative aiding Moses, most prominently in fighting the Amalekites, being on Mount Sinai and exploring the land.[2]

God's promises (1:2–6)

The opening words to Joshua set the tone for the book as a whole; as Trent Butler says, it is 'a tone dominated by the divine imperative, directing, demanding, and yet encouraging his people into action'.[3] It is in that spirit that Joshua is now called to lead the people to cross the Jordan River and enter the Promised Land (verse 2). The call to 'get ready' is not so much to prepare but to 'arise'; that is, to step up to start to lead the process of entering. In verses 3–6 the overwhelming emphasis is on God's promises and so his reassurance. Virtually all these words spring from the earlier soil of Deuteronomy: the promise to give 'every place where you set your foot' comes from Deuteronomy 11:24; that no one will 'stand against you' from Deuteronomy 7:24 and 11:25; but there is a particular echo of Deuteronomy 31, as seen in the table below.[4]

Deuteronomy 31:6–8	Joshua 1:5–9
Be strong and courageous (x2)	Be strong and (very) courageous (x2)
Do not be afraid; do not be discouraged	Do not be afraid or discouraged
The LORD your God goes with you	I will be with you
He will never leave you nor forsake you	I will never leave you nor forsake you

---

2 See Exodus 17:8–16; 24:13; 32:17; 33:11; Numbers 13–14; 27:12–23. Also see 'The man Joshua' in the Introduction.
3 Butler, *Joshua 1–12*, 7A:230.
4 Goldingay gives a similar list, Goldingay, *Joshua*, 71.

You must go with these people into the land that the LORD swore to their ancestors to give them . . . their inheritance	You will lead these people to inherit the land I swore to their ancestors to give them
The LORD himself goes before you and will be with you	The LORD your God will be with you wherever you go

Such promises and commands are repeated to reinforce them on Joshua. There is also a certainty expressed in God's words: he has already given every place where Joshua will set his foot (verse 3).[5] The significance of this moment should not be lost: this is the time that the land originally promised to Abraham will finally be received (Genesis 12:7). As Dale Ralph Davis says, 'The theological roots of Joshua 1 are sunk deep into the soil of Genesis 12 and following, and that ancient promise is about to receive its contemporary fulfilment.'[6]

The extent of the land is described in verse 4 in south to north (desert to Lebanon) and then east to west terms (Euphrates to Mediterranean), using terminology from Deuteronomy 11:24. This is similar to earlier promises of the land in Genesis 15:18 and Exodus 23:31. We should note the oddity here: if the land extended east to the Euphrates, then where Joshua was standing was already 'in the land'. It is helpful to note that there are two kinds of description of the extent of the land: expansive portrayals of wide borders such as here in verse 4, and more specific delineated boundaries of the land of Canaan west of the Jordan. While the latter is specified as the Promised Land that they are about to enter, the former are indicative of the eventual reign of God across the world (see Appendix B, The Borders of the Promised Land).

Verse 2 refers to giving the land to the people as a whole; in the following verses the people are still in view ('you/r' is still plural in verses 3 and 4), but Joshua takes centre stage. God will be with him (singular) in the same way as he was with Moses (verse 5). If we remember how God was with Moses and what was achieved

---

[5] The NIV has 'I will give' but the tense is perfect and points to the land as already given. See Creach, *Joshua*, 24.
[6] Davis, *Joshua*, 17.

through him, we will realise what a remarkable promise this is. This means Joshua is not simply one in a line of leaders but will play a significant part in advancing God's plans of salvation. God's being with him in this way means no one will be able to withstand him. God's promise to never to leave or forsake him means he will be constantly present to ensure the completion of this task. So, verse 6 summarises, Joshua will lead the people so that they will inherit the land God has promised. Joshua is called to be 'strong and courageous' precisely because of such emphatic reassurance from God. This is not a call to strength and courage in military terms but in grasping God's promises.

Many key themes are raised in these opening verses, which will dominate the following chapters: (a) the giving of the land as fulfilment of previous promises; (b) the experience of entry aided by God such that he 'gifts' them the land; (c) the role of Joshua in leading the people. The land is also spoken of as their 'inheritance', which will be a key theme in the second half of the book.[7]

Strength and courage in practice (1:7–9)

Verse 7 begins with a reiteration of the call to be 'strong and very courageous', which then leads into more precise instructions. These are best seen as an expansion of what such strength and courage will mean in practice, especially as the call to strength and courage are repeated in verse 9, so bracketing this section.

Joshua's strength in God will be shown by his obedience to God's Law. As David Firth says, 'For Joshua, the act of daring is to live wholly by all that Yahweh has revealed in his Torah.'[8] The term 'law' here (Torah) refers to the first five books of the Bible and so is not simply 'law' in the sense of 'command' but rather 'instruction'. Joshua must be careful to live in line with this instruction as given by Moses (verse 7). Such obedience is shown by not turning to the right or to the left; that is, not turning off the prescribed path.

---

[7] For these themes (and others) and their connection with Deuteronomy, see Gordon J. Wenham, 'The Deuteronomic Theology of the Book of Joshua', *Journal of Biblical Literature* 90, no. 2 (1971): 140–48.
[8] Firth, *The Message of Joshua*, 37.

The same phrase in Deuteronomy 28:14 links such deviation with following other gods, meaning that God's word is to be the only source of guidance. Such obedience will be aided by repeating the 'Book of the Law' ('always on your lips') and meditating constantly on it, so that it is obeyed. There is a lovely three-step sequence here of 'saying', 'reflecting' and 'doing': saying the Law as written, consideration of what it means for that situation and then acting in line with it. The implication is that God's commands cannot always simply be followed as a rule book but rather require reflection on how they are to be applied.[9]

We should note here the beginning of a change in God's means of revelation. While special revelation for specific moments would still occur (e.g., Joshua 7:10–15), the Law now existed and was to be studied, applied and obeyed. As David Oginde says, the 'emphasis had started shifting to the written word of God, and Joshua was to be totally committed to this written word'.[10] The Lutheran commentator, Adolph Harstad, sees here the Reformation principle of 'Scripture alone' as the only authority in the Christian's life.[11]

The promised result of such obedience is to be 'prosperous and successful'. Such terms have sometimes been taken to mean success in whatever venture is undertaken, be it a business operation, church ministry or parenting. Similarly, the term 'prosperous' has been utilised by proponents of the prosperity gospel to claim prosperity in financial and other terms. Such readings do not appreciate the context: it is Joshua who is being instructed in entering the land. He is being promised success and prosperity in this task if he sticks to God's commands as to how he undertakes it.[12] There is a more general truth of God blessing our obedience to him, but that cannot be pressed into our definitions of 'success' or 'prosperity' (see further discussion below).

---

9 Firth, *Joshua*, 73.
10 David Oginde, 'Joshua', in *Africa Bible Commentary: A One-Volume Commentary Written by 70 African Scholars*, ed. Adeyemo Tokunboh (Revised edition; Nairobi: Zondervan, 2010), 259–60.
11 Harstad, *Joshua*, 82–3.
12 The word 'prosperous' is unhelpful here with its overtones of financial prosperity; the word rather means 'to bring to success' or 'to succeed in a task'.

THE NEED FOR A LEADER: COMMISSIONING JOSHUA

The section ends with a summary call expressed positively and negatively: be strong and courageous, do not be afraid or discouraged. The reason for such confidence is repeated: God will be with you.

2. Instructions to the people and their response • Joshua 1:10–18

Joshua then gives orders to the people via the 'officers' who go through the camp relaying his instructions.[13] The overall command is to prepare for entering, but within it comes the promise of God because they will prepare to 'take possession' of the land God is giving them. This is the first use of a key word (and so theme) within the book: taking possession or ownership of the land. It is emphasised by being repeated at the end of the verse: God is giving them the land for them 'to possess' (NIV 'for your own').[14]

The Reubenites, Gadites and half-tribe of Manasseh receive specific instructions because they have been granted land as their inheritance on the east side of the Jordan. Numbers 32 relays how these tribes requested, and were granted, this land, but on the condition of aiding the remaining tribes in their conquest of the land. Joshua reminds them of this arrangement and explains that the fighting men must cross over to help their fellow Israelites; indeed, they are to be ahead of the other tribes, as they promised in Numbers 32:17 and which is reported in action in Joshua 4:12. Once the tribes settling west of the Jordan have been given 'rest' in the land, the two and a half tribes can return to their own inheritance.

This section anticipates the end of the book in two ways. First, the return of these two and a half tribes to their land east of the Jordan will come in chapter 22, along with the question of unity between the tribes that their involvement here embodies. Second,

---

[13] The identity of these officials is unclear but fits with previous arrangements such as Exodus 18, and the same word is used in Numbers 11:16–30 and through Deuteronomy. Firth, *Joshua*, 74.

[14] This word (*yarash*) is used frequently in previous books looking forward to entering the land, especially in Deuteronomy. We will discuss it further in chapter 14, 'Introduction to Possessing the Land'.

the theme of rest. This is a significant word in the description of the land, especially in Deuteronomy. It is used infrequently in Joshua but significantly comes here and then again in the closing chapters (see Joshua 21:44; 22;4; 23:1). In entering the land and taking possession of it, the ultimate goal is that of God giving rest.

The response of these tribes (or possibly that of all the people) is given in verses 16–18. This response is significant in showing how Joshua was viewed and in emphasising his role in entering the land. The people pledge an obedience to him paralleled with that towards Moses.[15] As a result, anyone rebelling against Joshua would be subject to death: Joshua's commands relay those of God and so disobedience to him is disobedience to God.

Significantly, the people repeat back to Joshua themes from earlier. They pray that God will be with him just he was with Moses and tell Joshua that he needs to be strong and courageous. This shows us that what is needed for the people to get into the land is a God-empowered, obedient leader. It all turns on God being with Joshua (as he has promised) and for Joshua to trust and obey God (as he is commanded to do); the people will then enter on the basis of what he does, not on their own merits.

KEY THEMES AND APPLICATION

God's working through Joshua
The emphasis in this section is on Joshua being reassured of God's commitment to be with him and so to get the people into the land. What is key is that Joshua is strong and courageous in his trust in God's promises and obedience to his commands; the people are then required to follow him as God's empowered servant.

The promise for God never to leave us or forsake us is true for all believers (see Hebrews 13:5) and so could be applied more generally. However, in this context the focus is on Joshua. Equally it is true that all believers are to be strong in their trust and obedience, but again the focus here is on Joshua. For the people

---

15 While the people's statement seems well meant, Firth suggests there might be some irony given past disobedience to Moses, Firth, *Joshua*, 76.

THE NEED FOR A LEADER: COMMISSIONING JOSHUA

to enter the land, they need this obedient, trusting pioneer. So much so that they repeat the truths of God's presence and the need for strength back to Joshua and pledge allegiance to him: he will get them into the land. Believers today enter the kingdom through the truly faithful servant of the Lord, Jesus Christ. Joshua points us to his namesake, Jesus.[16] The German theologian Johannes Brenz (1499–1570) said:

> Joshua is shown to be a type of Christ, both in name and in deeds. For as Joshua led the Israelites across the Jordan into a land flowing with milk and honey, so Jesus Christ leads believers into an eternal happiness.[17]

Jesus is the one whom God is specially with, who trusts God's promises and who obeys God's commands; so we pledge our allegiance to him. Seen in that vein, the message of Joshua 1 is not that we should 'trust and obey' so that we can be successful, but rather to rejoice that Jesus has trusted and obeyed and has been successful on our behalf, and we can now benefit from his victory.

Past commentators have sometimes taken this theme further in drawing a comparison between Moses and Joshua. Moses is said to represent the Law, which cannot get us into the land, and so we require Joshua, a prototype of Jesus. For example, the early church father Chrysostom (347–407) said:

> [Joshua] brought in the people into the promised land, as Jesus into heaven; not the law; since neither did Moses [enter the promised land] but remained outside. The law has not power to bring, but grace.[18]

---

16 Both names mean 'Yahweh saves'.
17 Johannes Brenz, 'Commentary on Joshua (Preface)', in *Reformation Commentary on Scripture: Joshua, Judges, Ruth*, ed. N. Scott Amos (Downers Grove: IVP Academic, 2020), 5.
18 Chrysostom, 'Homilies on Hebrews 27.6', in *Ancient Christian Commentary on Scripture: Joshua, Judges, Ruth, 1–2 Samuel* ed. John R. Franke, (Downers Grove: InterVarsity Press, 2005), 2–3.

Joshua is indeed a picture of Jesus here, but there is no need to set Joshua against Moses, nor to make him a picture of grace as opposed to law. In fact, we would surely say that Moses was also a type or picture of Christ as he rescued God's people from slavery.[19]

The unity of God's people
We need to appreciate the potential for a split within Israel because of the two and a half tribes residing east of the Jordan. The specific mention of these tribes and their responsibility here is then echoed in the significant events of chapter 22 as they return home and unity is imperilled. The mention of them at the start and end of the book indicates the significance of this theme.

When these tribes first asked for the land east of the Jordan, Moses's great concern was the effect their absence would have on the other tribes entering the land: they would discourage them (Numbers 32:7). He paralleled this with the report of the spies in Numbers 13 that 'discouraged the Israelites from entering the land the LORD had given them' (Numbers 32:9). There is a link, then, between unity and faithfulness; the laxity and separation of some can have a knock-on effect on others. By contrast, there should be a unity that brings encouragement (compare Hebrews 10:24–5).

So here God's people are to operate as one body in the taking of the land; brothers-in-arms (and we can say sisters too) who aid each other in God's purposes. As Trent Butler says of this section:

> Israel is defined as a unified body. The Jordan River does not divide Israel. Threat to Israelite unity lies not in geography but loyalty. The Israelites outside the narrow confines of the land promised by Yahweh must be loyal and support the Israelites within the land. Despite geographical separation, Israel must remain one body dedicated to one land.[20]

---

19 Indeed, Jesus is the new prophet like Moses that God would raise up, Acts 3:22–3.
20 Butler, *Joshua 1–12*, 7A:232.

THE NEED FOR A LEADER: COMMISSIONING JOSHUA

The prosperity gospel
The message of this passage is not that we can claim God's power and presence for our purposes now, nor that this gives us the steps to success and prosperity in life. Unfortunately, such a 'soft' prosperity gospel is found in some sermons and commentaries on this passage.[21] Such teaching can harm people by saying that if they do not know such success it must be because they are untrusting or disobeying in some way.[22] God does indeed promise to be with us, and we should all look to obey his word – there is the possibility of that general application – but that is not the focus here, and certainly not the dynamic at play for the people at large. They, and so we, look to God's anointed servant who wins entry into his land for us.

Christian living within God's unfolding plan
This chapter exemplifies how we live relating to the past, present and future.[23] Joshua and the people are instructed how to live now in the present, based on what God has promised and done in the past, and on what he says he will do now and in the future. That is true of many passages in the Bible, but particularly so here. This illustrates a key dynamic in the life of God's people: we are to be looking backwards to God's past actions, forward to the fulfilment of his promises and around at his work in and through us now. We live within the unfolding story of his plan of redemption. We should then be orientated to that story and seeking to live well within it; it is what gives shape and purpose to our lives. We might warn people of the danger of creating our own life story aside from God's grand narrative.

Within this is the specific link between God's promises and our living: we always live in the light of what God has promised. Plus, we see God's faithfulness to his plan of salvation: he promised to get his people into the land, and he is advancing that plan here and

---

21 For example, John A. Huffman, *The Communicator's Commentary: Joshua* (Waco: Word Books, 1673), 30–38.
22 For an overview of this area from Old Testament texts, see Walter C. Kaiser, 'The Old Testament Promise Of Material Blessings and the Contemporary Believer', *Trinity Journal* 9, no. 2 (1988): 151–70.
23 Firth, *Joshua*, 77–8.

will continue it in the future; his people are called to rely on his faithfulness. All this can be reapplied to Christian believers looking back to God's work in Jesus, around at the growth of the church now and forward to his second coming.

Appointing leaders
This chapter is often referred to when appointing leaders. The points made vary but often include the need for timely succession in leaders, the challenge of a change in leadership and the importance of God's choice of leader. These points may be true but are not the primary aim of this passage. We must see that Joshua is in a different category from church leaders today: he operates as God's chosen leader to achieve the next phase of salvation history.

Having said that, we can certainly ask what we should look for in leaders. What we see in Joshua is not a great strategist or commander but great trust and obedience. We should want and pray for leaders who repeat God's Law, meditate on it and are careful to do everything written in it. We may also anticipate Joshua passing on similar commands to later leaders of God's people (see Joshua 23:6–7). This leads then to the character qualifications for leaders seen in the New Testament (1 Timothy 3:1–7; Titus 1:5–9). Each culture will face its challenges in what is looked for in church leaders or what leaders are inclined to in themselves. In most places, accruing power or influence rather than obedience is a constant temptation.[24]

---

24 Ovidiu Creangă, 'Joshua', in *Central and Eastern European Bible Commentary*, ed. Corneliu Constantineanu (Carlisle: Langham Global Library, 2022), 220.

2

Rahab's Faith and God's Encouragement

Joshua 2

Joshua has been appointed as leader of God's people and called to trust and obedience in leading Israel into the Promised Land. Now, before the main event of the entry into the land, he sends spies to reconnoitre the territory. This leads to the well-known story of Rahab, who hides the spies from the king of Jericho and so sides with the Israelites. In doing so, she exemplifies faith and enters the 'hall of fame' of faith in Hebrews 11. At the same time within the flow of the narrative the spies return, not with military knowledge, but with a specific encouragement to Joshua.

Rahab and the spies

2 Then Joshua son of Nun secretly sent two spies from Shittim. 'Go, look over the land,' he said, 'especially Jericho.' So they went and entered the house of a prostitute named Rahab and stayed there.

2 The king of Jericho was told, 'Look, some of the Israelites have come here tonight to spy out the land.' **3** So the king of Jericho sent this message to Rahab: 'Bring out the men who came to you and entered your house, because they have come to spy out the whole land.'

4 But the woman had taken the two men and hidden them. She said, 'Yes, the men came to me, but I did not know where they had come from. **5** At dusk, when it was time to close the city gate, they left. I don't know which way they went. Go after them quickly. You may catch up with them.' **6** (But she had taken them up to the roof and hidden them under the stalks of flax she had laid out on the roof.) **7** So the men set out in pursuit of the spies on the road that leads to the fords of the Jordan, and as soon as the pursuers had gone out, the gate was shut.

8 Before the spies lay down for the night, she went up on the roof **9** and said to them, 'I know that the LORD has given this land to you and that a great fear of you has fallen on us, so that all who live in this country are melting in fear because of you. **10** We have heard how the LORD dried up the water of the Red Sea[a] for you when you came out of Egypt, and what you did to Sihon and Og, the two kings of the Amorites east of the Jordan, whom you completely destroyed.[b] **11** When we heard of it, our hearts sank[c] and everyone's courage failed because of you, for the LORD your God is God in heaven above and on the earth below.

12 'Now then, please swear to me by the LORD that you will show kindness to my family, because I have shown kindness to you. Give me a sure sign **13** that you will spare the lives of my father and mother, my brothers and sisters, and all who belong to them – and that you will save us from death.'

14 'Our lives for your lives!' the men assured her. 'If you don't tell what we are doing, we will treat you kindly and faithfully when the LORD gives us the land.'

15 So she let them down by a rope through the window, for the house she lived in was part of the city wall. **16** She said to them, 'Go to the hills so that the pursuers will not find you. Hide yourselves there for three days until they return, and then go on your way.'

17 Now the men had said to her, 'This oath you made us swear will not be binding on us **18** unless, when we enter the land, you have tied this scarlet cord in the window through which you let us down, and unless you have brought your father and mother, your brothers and all your family into your house. **19** If any of them go outside your house into the street, their blood will be on their own heads; we will not be responsible. As for those who are in the house with you, their blood will be on our head if a hand is laid on them. **20** But if you tell what we are doing, we will be released from the oath you made us swear.'

21 'Agreed,' she replied. 'Let it be as you say.'

So she sent them away, and they departed. And she tied the scarlet cord in the window.

22 When they left, they went into the hills and stayed there three days, until the pursuers had searched all along the road and returned without finding them. **23** Then the two men started back. They went down out of the hills, forded the river and came to Joshua son of Nun and told him everything that had happened to them. **24** They said to Joshua, 'The LORD has surely given the whole land into our hands; all the people are melting in fear because of us.'

---

[a] 10 Or *the Sea of Reeds*
[b] 10 The Hebrew term refers to the irrevocable giving over of things or persons to the LORD, often by totally destroying them.
[c] 11 Hebrew *melted in fear*.

RAHAB'S FAITH AND GOD'S ENCOURAGEMENT

1. The spies and Rahab • Joshua 2:1–7

Joshua's sending these two spies is one of the many parallels between him and Moses who sent spies in Numbers 13. Under Moses, however, they are not called 'spies' and it is not done 'secretly' (verse 1). The secrecy here is most probably from the rest of Israelites; at the conclusion of the chapter the men report back to Joshua specifically. It is hard to know Joshua's motivation given the assurances he has just been given, and some commentators question his actions. However, God's assurances and prudent action are not in opposition to each other, and no negative comment is made in the biblical text. As it turns out, Joshua gains no strategic information but does receive significant encouragement.

Jericho is the specific object of Joshua's concern because it would be the first city in their path (see map 1). Why they stayed at the home of Rahab is not stated; it is most likely that she offered lodging as well as her sexual services, and the language of entering 'the house of . . . Rahab' aids that interpretation.[1] We should note that at this stage there would be negative resonances for an Israelite reader: a pagan prostitute is exactly the sort of person who represents a danger to God's people and a test of their faithfulness to God. The background of sexual immorality and turning away from God in Numbers 25:1–5 could be in mind, especially with the mention of 'Shittim', which is where this took place. Such presumptions are about to be overturned! Firth summaries this point: 'Rather than playing the harlot, Israel was saved by one.'[2]

There is no explanation of how the spies' presence and whereabouts are made known, but they are reported to the king who immediately sends a message that Rahab should turn the men over.[3] They have come to 'spy out the whole land' and so are enemies, and aiding them will aid those planning to invade. It appears that Rahab has previously decided where her loyalties lie because she has already

---

[1] That she was indeed a prostitute is clear by the word used and the comments in the New Testament (Hebrews 11:31; James 2:25).
[2] Firth, *Joshua*, 81.
[3] The word 'king' probably means more of a local ruler, as Jericho was not large.

hidden the men (verse 4) and she then spins a tale that sends the messengers off in a false pursuit. The comment on the closing of the city gate behind them (verse 7) now means the spies are trapped and will have to find an alternative way out of the city. We must not miss the drama of these opening verses, as Adolph Harstad says:

> The drama in Josh 2:1–7 is intense. The facts make it so: spies, a prostitute, a king in panic, cover blown, a cover-up, the dark cover of night, the men covered by flax on a roof, a misguided wild chase, and a quick closing gate that squeaks of Canaanite fears.[4]

2. Rahab's example of faith • Joshua 2:8–24

Rahab's knowledge and response (2:8–11)

The importance of Rahab's words to the spies is shown by the significant space given over to them in verses 9–13; they form the heart of the passage as the dramatic narrative now pauses until verse 15 (but only really resumes in verse 21). Rahab speaks of what she now *knows* because of what she has *heard*.[5] What she knows is that the LORD has already given the land to the Israelites, and that everyone is 'melting in fear' because of them (verse 9). What she has heard is how God has acted on behalf of his people, specifically in the drying up of the Red Sea and in the defeat of two significant kings, Sihon and Og.[6] In speaking of these kings, Rahab uses a particular term which denotes the giving over things to the LORD by destroying them.[7] Hence she sees these victories as more than revealing military ability; rather they are the sovereign judgment of God.

---

[4] Harstad, *Joshua*, 119.
[5] The chiastic structure of Rahab's speech is helpfully laid out by Hess, *Joshua*, 89–90.
[6] For the Red Sea see Exodus 14; for the defeat of Sihon and Og see Numbers 21:21–35.
[7] This is the word *herem*. See 'Holy war' in the Introduction and Excursus: Devoting to the LORD.

RAHAB'S FAITH AND GOD'S ENCOURAGEMENT

The result of this news is repeated in verse 11: everyone's hearts 'melted in fear'.[8] This emphasises the response of all the inhabitants and will be the key component of the spies' report in verse 24. Such a response was foretold following the victory at the Red Sea: the song of Moses looked ahead to the victories to come and said, 'the people of Canaan will melt away; terror and dread will fall on them' (Exodus 15:15–16). Rahab is echoing these very words back to God's people.

Rahab's conclusion in verse 11 is that the LORD is God in heaven and earth. This is very different from the view that different gods have authority over different regions, or that there are numerous gods who might be in competition with each other. Such views would have been common in Canaan and are found today in some parts of the world.[9] Rahab has moved to see there is only one true God, and so, by implication, the gods of her people, such as Baal, are false.[10] God's status means he can do as he pleases, wherever he pleases, including in the land of Canaan. This is the basis of Rahab's statement at the start: that the LORD has given them the land.

We should note that all the people have heard the same news reported, all have melted in fear as a result, but Rahab has gone an additional step in what she now believes about Israel's God. That is what has motivated her to hide the spies and leads to her plea in the next verses. In her response to the spies, Adolph Harstad sees an example of Jesus's representative principle: 'he who receives you receives me' (Matthew 10:40).[11] The reception of God's people reveals one's reception of God himself. This 'receiving' of the spies is what is highlighted in both Hebrews 11 and James 2 – see below.[12]

---

8 NIV footnote. This is a different verb from verse 9 but with a similar meaning.
9 Jesurathnam, 'Joshua', 269.
10 Howard, *Joshua*, 103.
11 Harstad, *Joshua*, 132.
12 Although note that the NIV translation of both these passages means the word 'received' is somewhat obscured.

Rahab's call for kindness (2:12–16)

Rahab implores the spies to promise safety for her and her family. She uses significant terms in doing so. They are to swear 'by the LORD', using the covenant name for God. They are asked to 'show kindness' to her just as she has 'shown kindness' to them. This word is commonly used of God's steadfast love or loyalty, but also that shown by his people to each other.[13] Rahab knows what is coming and so she changes loyalties and sides with the Israelites.

The spies respond positively to her request. She has already hidden them; they only ask that she continues in this vein by remaining silent. If so, they will treat her 'kindly and faithfully', repeating the theme of loyalty and adding that of reliability. While these are all on a horizontal plane – between Rahab and the spies – the words used are resonant of God and so suggest the vertical plane of God's kindness and faithfulness expressed through his people. The spies escape by a rope from her house and Rahab shows her concern for their safe return by advising them to hide while the hunt for them is still active rather than trying to cross the Jordan immediately.

The scarlet cord (2:17–21)

The narrative jumps back to a condition that the men had given for Rahab's protection, and that of her family.[14] A scarlet cord must be tied in the window of her house and her family must be with her in the house. If anyone were to leave the protection of that place, then the spies would not be responsible for their safety. The 'scarlet cord' is referred to as 'this cord' but it is unlikely to be the 'rope' by which they were let down (different words are used of each). Rahab readily agrees and quickly complies.

---

13 The word is *hesed*.
14 This is related as if the conversation happened after the men were let down. The NIV places it in the past tense to smooth the sequence.

RAHAB'S FAITH AND GOD'S ENCOURAGEMENT

The spies report (2:22–4)

The spies hide in the hills as Rahab proposed, keeping them from those searching for them on the travel routes. After three days the men make their way back and report to Joshua everything that has happened to them, as opposed to what they have achieved.[15] We are given a summary of that report which focuses on their conclusion: that the LORD has surely given them the land. The reason for their certainly comes in the following phrase: that the people are melting in fear because of the Israelites. The spies may draw their conclusion purely because their enemy is so frightened, or they may be thinking of the prediction of Exodus 15:15 and so see God's promise being fulfilled. For the later reader of the text, though, the echo of Exodus 15 is clear.

By the end of the chapter, it is interesting to ask what has been achieved by this ploy of spying out the land. Joshua doesn't appear to have gained any significant military or strategic knowledge. But he has received a report that confirms God's promises and predictions and so encourages him in his task. There is also a significant contrast with the original spying mission that Joshua himself was part of (Numbers 13–14). That resulted in the Israelites themselves trembling with fear, whereas now they return with a report of the inhabitants doing the same.[16]

KEY THEMES AND APPLICATION

God's encouragement of Joshua
Within the flow of the narrative, Joshua 2 is unnecessary; we could have moved from chapter 1 directly to chapter 3. But chapter 2 contributes significantly. The main effect on the reader is to confirm the certainty of God's promise by the unusual technique of having an inhabitant of the land echo God's prediction back to Joshua. So something he should know already is repeated to him from an unlikely source. We raised the question as to why Joshua sent the

---
15 Firth, *The Message of Joshua*, 52.
16 We also see this contrast later in the book, see Joshua 14:8.

spies in the first place; was it because of any lack of faith? We are not told, but we can see God's kindness to him in providing such encouragement. The sixteenth century reformer John Calvin says:

> Although the mere promise of possessing the land ought to have been sufficient, yet the Lord is so very indulgent to their weakness, that, for the sake of removing all doubt, he confirms what he had promised by experience.[17]

This chapter also serves to set up significant features of the battle for Jericho several chapters later, namely the saving of Rahab and her family. The reader is left with a sense of anticipation, waiting to see what will happen to her.

Rahab's faith and salvation
Rahab's response is a key feature. She hears truth about God and responds appropriately. This is what leads to her being cited as an example of faith in Hebrews 11:31: 'By faith the prostitute Rahab, because she welcomed the spies, was not killed with those who were disobedient.' We see some key features of such faith. First, faith comes from hearing, and so here Rahab's hearing of God's actions leads to her belief. Second, Hebrews 11:1 gives the general principle that faith is certainty of something that cannot be seen because it is in the future or is not physically visible. Rahab cannot yet see the defeat of Jericho, but she believes it is coming; she cannot see the LORD as the only true God, but believes that he is. Third, faith is seen in action; this is the feature of Rahab's faith highlighted in James 2:25: 'In the same way, was not even Rahab the prostitute considered righteous for what she did when she gave lodging to the spies and sent them off in a different direction?' Simply believing truth about God is not enough; she also needed to respond to that knowledge. As a result, Rahab stands as a model of faith.

---

[17] John Calvin, *Calvin's Commentaries: Commentary on the Book of Joshua*, Volume 4, trans. Henry Beveridge (Grand Rapids: Baker Book House, 1993), 55.

RAHAB'S FAITH AND GOD'S ENCOURAGEMENT

The scarlet cord

Rahab's faith raises the question of the 'scarlet cord'. This has been cited as a symbol of Jesus's blood; hence, in her hanging it out of the window, Rahab is said to be exercising faith in Jesus. The church father Origen (185–253) says:

> She herself puts the scarlet-coloured sign in her house, through which she is bound to be saved from the destruction of the city. No other sign would have been accepted, except the scarlet-coloured one that carries the sign of blood. For she knew that there was no salvation for anyone except in the blood of Christ.[18]

I would say that is a step too far: I doubt Rahab saw such significance in the cord. However, there is another more plausible route to the same destination. God's destruction will come on Jericho, and Rahab and her family will be saved by sheltering in a house marked with this red cord. For any Israelite reading this there would be an immediate resonance with the events of the Passover: God's destruction passed over those houses marked with blood, meaning the people had to be sure not to leave the house (Exodus 12:1–30). The marking of Rahab's house in this way, and the command for the family to stay within it, looks back to that moment, and the Passover of course looks forward to the death of Jesus. While Rahab would not have known it, her hanging out the red cord does serve to picture the blood of Christ that saves us from God's wrath.[19]

Older commentators often go further than this and see Rahab's house as a picture of the church. The Lutheran minister Johann Gerhard (1582–1637) said:

---

18 Origen, 'Homilies on Joshua', 3.5, in Franke, *Ancient Christian Commentary*, 14.
19 This intertextual interpretation can be found in a variety of commentators, for example, Matthew Henry, *A Commentary on the Holy Bible, Volume 2* (London: Marshall Brothers, 1890), 524. Goldsworthy, *Gospel and Kingdom*, 107–8. For a more in-depth discussion, see Nicholas P. Lunn, 'The Deliverance of Rahab (Joshua 2, 6) as the Gentile Exodus', *Tyndale Bulletin* 65, no. 1 (2014): 11–19.

> The house of Rahab is a type of the church. You see, just as all the citizens of Jericho were struck down with the edge of the sword, and only those who had been taken into Rahab's house were saved, so the Jericho of this world is subject to eternal destruction, but those who come into the church will be saved from that destruction. The rope of scarlet thread that Rahab tied to her window denotes the blood of Christ, which keeps the house of the church safe from destruction.[20]

Certainly, there is truth to this overall picture, as we will see when we look at the destruction of Jericho later in chapter 6. Rahab's house is indeed a picture of a place of shelter for those who trust God, but we may not want to identify it directly with the church.

Rahab's example
We should note that it is a woman, and presumably an underprivileged one, who is at the centre of this story. Someone who might be considered one of the most unlikely candidates both aids God's people to advance his plan and becomes an exemplar of faith. Carolyn Pressler says:

> The story has to do with the difference between human expectations and divine decisions . . . Rahab, a Canaanite, a woman, and a prostitute, is three times 'other', three times despised. Yet she is a deliverer of Israel, the first in the promised land to confess the sovereignty of God.[21]

We can go further in this case and see how God then honoured Rahab in including her in the ancestry of the Lord Jesus (see Matthew 1:5); Dale Ralph David says she became 'a trophy of divine grace'.[22] In many cultures this will challenge our presuppositions of particular people groups and encourage valuing of all people.[23] It also reminds

---

[20] Johann Gerhard, 'Commonplace', 25, in Amos, *Reformation Commentary*, 43.
[21] Carolyn Pressler, *Joshua, Judges and Ruth*, Westminster Bible Companion (Louisville: Westminster John Knox Press, 2002), 25.
[22] Davis, *Joshua*, 29.
[23] So the comment on women often being despised in South Asia, in Jesurathnam, 'Joshua', 268–9.

RAHAB'S FAITH AND GOD'S ENCOURAGEMENT

us of Jesus's challenge to those who were confident of themselves and their identity as God's people: 'Truly I tell you, the tax collectors and the prostitutes are entering the kingdom of God ahead of you' (Matthew 21:31). Equally we can be reassured that Jesus is the one who is known as 'a friend of tax collectors and sinners' (Luke 7:34). Commenting on the description of Rahab as a prostitute in the New Testament, Philippa Carter comments:

> The preservation of this aspect of Rahab's character not only illustrates the sense these writers had of the grace and mercy of God but also their ability to assimilate the possibility that a prostitute, a woman, a pagan, could serve as a witness to the truth and as a moral exemplar.[24]

God and the nations

This episode gives significant nuance to our understanding of God's attitude to the inhabitants of the land. While they are deserving of his punishment and the land must be cleansed of them, Rahab serves as an example of someone who can 'swap sides', commit themselves to the LORD, receive his kindness and so join his people.[25] In this regard, the comment in Hebrews 11 is significant because it says Rahab was not killed 'with those who were disobedient' (Hebrews 11:31). The word used means not to be persuaded, and so denotes disbelief or disobedience.[26] This portrayal of the inhabitants of Jericho sees them as opposed to God, while Rahab is persuaded and so believes/obeys. Donald Guthrie comments, 'This implies that the people of Jericho, having heard of the exploits of God on behalf of his people, should have acknowledged these acts instead of resisting God's people.'[27] It is not, then, that God will punish the people of the land whatever; it is as those who continue to stand opposed to him that they will

---

24 Philippa Carter, 'Joshua', in *The IVP Women's Bible Commentary*, ed. Catherine Clark Kroeger and Mary J. Evans (Downers Grove: InterVarsity Press, 2002), 120.
25 Interestingly, Rahab's daughter-in-law will do the same thing in Ruth 1.
26 It is used earlier in Hebrews of those who disbelieved/disobeyed God's promise to enter the land (Hebrews 3:18).
27 Donald C. Guthrie, *Hebrews*, Tyndale New Testament Commentaries (Leicester: InterVarsity Press, 1983), 242.

receive such destruction. God is not opposed to certain ethnicities but to a certain stance against him.

The nineteenth-century activist Josephine Butler commented on God's purpose in using this episode to teach his people of his desire to bless all nations:

> The great Father of all would teach his chosen and favoured people that, while they were the subjects of his special election, He, their God, was not alone the 'God of all the families of Israel,' but was also the God of families everywhere, in every land, and to the end of time; and that in the family bond, ordained by him, the love and faith of one may draw and gather in many, bringing them all within the saving shelter of the home marked by the symbolic scarlet line.[28]

The ethics of lying

Rahab's example here is often cited within discussions of ethics because of her clear lying.[29] While all agree that lying is wrong in general, the issue here is what to do when two ethical principles are in conflict: here there is the principle of telling the truth versus the responsibility to save life. How such conflicting principles are reconciled depends on the ethical framework in play as well as the reading of the passage.[30] Many commentators have wrestled with this through history. Some have said that Rahab's lie was simply wrong. John Calvin says:

> As to the falsehood, we must admit that though it was done for a good purpose, it was not free from fault. For those who believe that what is called a dutiful lie is altogether excusable do not sufficiently consider how precious truth is in the sight of God.[31]

---

28 Josephine Butler, 'The Lady of Shunem', in *Women of War, Women of Woe: Joshua and Judges through the Eyes of Nineteenth-Century Female Biblical Interpreters*, eds Marion Ann Taylor and Christiana DeGroot (Grand Rapids: Eerdmans, 2016), 51.
29 She is often cited along with the Hebrew midwives of Exodus 1.
30 For an overview of this area, see the excursus in Howard, *Joshua*, 106–12.
31 Calvin, *Joshua*, 4:47.

Others agree that while her lying was wrong, it was understandable because of her pagan background and nascent faith. Others see a hierarchy of principles and so speak of the 'lesser of two evils'; sometimes this sees the lie as a sin (but the lesser one) that requires forgiveness; sometimes it is seen as being made exempt by the greater command. This is often connected with the motive for lying. An alternative reading sees lying as justified because of the evil intent of those who are questioning – they have forfeited their right to the truth.[32]

---

[32] See 'Christian Moral Reasoning' in Arthur F. Holmes and Revd David J. Atkinson (eds.), *New Dictionary of Christian Ethics and Pastoral Theology* (Downers Grove: InterVarsity Press, 1995), 122–7.

3

A Crossing to Remember

Joshua 3–4

Joshua has been appointed to lead the people into the Promised Land and has received encouragement via Rahab as to how the people in the land are feeling. We now come to one of the main events of the book: the actual crossing over the Jordan into the land, which was mentioned as the first phase of entry in Joshua 1:2, 11. The two main action points are the crossing of the Jordan and the setting up of memorial stones. The significance of this section can be seen in the level of detail given. The pace of description slows, the events build to a climax and emphasis is given by recapitulations and summaries. The reader who expects a purely linear description can find this confusing, as events that seem to have happened then recur. In the comments below we will try to appreciate what this style of writing achieves.

This section tells us how Joshua led Israel to enter the Promised Land; more significantly, it teaches us about God and how he is the one who opens the way for his people. It is deliberately set to be reminiscent of the great act of God at the Red Sea as the climax to the Exodus and forms the conclusion to that event. First the waters parted for God's people to escape to freedom; now the waters part for them to enter a new home.

Crossing the Jordan

3 Early in the morning Joshua and all the Israelites set out from Shittim and went to the Jordan, where they camped before crossing over. **2** After three days the officers went throughout the camp, **3** giving orders to the people: 'When you see the ark of the covenant of the LORD your God, and the Levitical priests carrying it, you are to move out from your positions and follow it. **4** Then you will know which way to go, since you have never been this way before.

But keep a distance of about two thousand cubits[a] between you and the ark; do not go near it.'

5 Joshua told the people, 'Consecrate yourselves, for tomorrow the LORD will do amazing things among you.'

6 Joshua said to the priests, 'Take up the ark of the covenant and pass on ahead of the people.' So they took it up and went ahead of them.

7 And the LORD said to Joshua, 'Today I will begin to exalt you in the eyes of all Israel, so that they may know that I am with you as I was with Moses. **8** Tell the priests who carry the ark of the covenant: "When you reach the edge of the Jordan's waters, go and stand in the river."'

9 Joshua said to the Israelites, 'Come here and listen to the words of the LORD your God. **10** This is how you will know that the living God is among you and that he will certainly drive out before you the Canaanites, Hittites, Hivites, Perizzites, Girgashites, Amorites and Jebusites. **11** See, the ark of the covenant of the Lord of all the earth will go into the Jordan ahead of you. **12** Now then, choose twelve men from the tribes of Israel, one from each tribe. **13** And as soon as the priests who carry the ark of the LORD – the Lord of all the earth – set foot in the Jordan, its waters flowing downstream will be cut off and stand up in a heap.'

14 So when the people broke camp to cross the Jordan, the priests carrying the ark of the covenant went ahead of them. **15** Now the Jordan is in flood all during harvest. Yet as soon as the priests who carried the ark reached the Jordan and their feet touched the water's edge, **16** the water from upstream stopped flowing. It piled up in a heap a great distance away, at a town called Adam in the vicinity of Zarethan, while the water flowing down to the Sea of the Arabah (that is, the Dead Sea) was completely cut off. So the people crossed over opposite Jericho. **17** The priests who carried the ark of the covenant of the LORD stopped in the middle of the Jordan and stood on dry ground, while all Israel passed by until the whole nation had completed the crossing on dry ground.

4 When the whole nation had finished crossing the Jordan, the LORD said to Joshua, **2** 'Choose twelve men from among the people, one from each tribe, **3** and tell them to take up twelve stones from the middle of the Jordan, from right where the priests are standing, and carry them over with you and put them down at the place where you stay tonight.'

4 So Joshua called together the twelve men he had appointed from the Israelites, one from each tribe, **5** and said to them, 'Go over before the ark of the LORD your God into the middle of the Jordan. Each of you is to take up a stone on his shoulder, according to the number of the tribes of the Israelites, **6** to serve as a sign among you. In the future, when your children ask you, "What do these stones mean?" **7** tell them that the flow of the Jordan was cut off before the ark of the covenant of the LORD. When it crossed the Jordan, the waters of the Jordan were cut off. These stones are to be a memorial to the people of Israel for ever.'

8 So the Israelites did as Joshua commanded them. They took twelve stones from the middle of the Jordan, according to the number of the tribes of the Israelites, as the LORD had told Joshua; and they carried them over with them to their camp, where they put them down. **9** Joshua set up the twelve stones that had been[a] in the middle of the Jordan at the spot where the priests who carried the ark of the covenant had stood. And they are there to this day.

10 Now the priests who carried the ark remained standing in the middle of the Jordan until everything the LORD had commanded Joshua was done by the people, just as Moses had directed Joshua. The people hurried over, **11** and as soon as all of them had crossed, the ark of the LORD and the priests came to the other side while the people watched.

12 The men of Reuben, Gad and the half-tribe of Manasseh crossed over, ready for battle, in front of the Israelites, as Moses had directed them. **13** About forty thousand armed for battle crossed over before the LORD to the plains of Jericho for war.

14 That day the LORD exalted Joshua in the sight of all Israel; and they stood in awe of him all the days of his life, just as they had stood in awe of Moses.

15 Then the LORD said to Joshua, **16** 'Command the priests carrying the ark of the covenant law to come up out of the Jordan.'

17 So Joshua commanded the priests, 'Come up out of the Jordan.'

18 And the priests came up out of the river carrying the ark of the covenant of the LORD. No sooner had they set their feet on the dry ground than the waters of the Jordan returned to their place and ran in flood as before.

19 On the tenth day of the first month the people went up from the Jordan and camped at Gilgal on the eastern border of Jericho. **20** And Joshua set up at Gilgal the twelve stones they had taken out of the Jordan. **21** He said to the Israelites, 'In the future when your descendants ask their parents, "What do these stones mean?" **22** tell them, "Israel crossed the Jordan on dry ground." **23** For the LORD your God dried up the Jordan before you until you had crossed over. The LORD your God did to the Jordan what he had done to the Red Sea^b when he dried it up before us until we had crossed over. **24** He did this so that all the peoples of the earth might know that the hand of the LORD is powerful and so that you might always fear the LORD your God.'

---

a 4 That is, about 900 metres
a 9 Or *Joshua also set up twelve stones*
b 23 Or *the Sea of Reeds*

1. The instructions and preparation to cross • Joshua 3:1–13

Preparatory instructions (3:1–5)

The people move from Shittim to camp on the banks of the Jordon, and so we should imagine them eyeing the barrier that lies ahead (see map 1). It is unclear how to factor the 'three days' of verse 2 into the overall timing: Joshua 1:11 spoke of three days' time, and the spies were away for three days (Joshua 2:22). These may have been concurrent, or the overall time may have been longer.[1]

The structure of the passage from verse 2 to 13 involves a series of instructions and explanations from and to different people. It begins with the officers giving orders to the people, and Joshua adding to those instructions about what would happen the next day ('tomorrow', verse 5). They are told that the priests will lead the way, carrying the Ark of the Covenant, and the people must follow it, keeping a set distance (verses 3–4). This distance is either because of the holiness of the Ark or to allow everyone to see it clearly; the latter is more indicated by the text.[2] The Ark of the Covenant was the sacred chest containing the Ten Commandments.[3] It was holy, was not to be touched and was only to be carried by the priests. The phrase 'Ark of the Covenant' shows that it pictures God's covenant relationship with his people and hence his presence

---

[1] The phrase 'three days' also does not need to be seen literally. See the discussion in Howard, *Joshua*, 119–20.

[2] This is less clear in the NIV as it changes the order of the verse; The ESV says, 'Do not come near it, in order that you may know the way you shall go, for you have not passed this way before.' Davis, *Joshua*, 33–4.

[3] See instructions for its construction in Exodus 25:10–22. It also contained Aaron's rod and a jar of manna (Exodus 16:32–4; 25:16; Numbers 17:6–11; Hebrews 9:4).

among them. We are told in Numbers what Moses said when the ark was carried and set down:

Whenever the ark set out, Moses said,

'Rise up, LORD!
  May your enemies be scattered;
  may your foes flee before you.'

Whenever it came to rest, he said,

'Return, LORD,
  to the countless thousands of Israel.'
(Numbers 10:35–6)

Adolph Harstad comments, 'Thus *the movement of the ark was the movement of God himself*: when it was lifted up, he arose, and when it was set down, he returned.'[4] In this representative way, the ark forms a central feature of this passage, picturing God himself leading his people.[5]

The day before these events, the people must 'consecrate' themselves (verse 5); that is, to be in a state of purity, ready for a sacred event. This would usually be done by abstaining from sex and by ritual washing.[6] The reason is because the LORD will do 'amazing things' or 'wonders' among them. This word was previously used of the wonders God did in rescuing Israel from Egypt (see Exodus 3:20) and in predicting the events of entering the land (Exodus 34:10–11). Hence expectation is heightened, but it is as yet unclear what will happen.

Instructions to initiate the crossing (3:6–13)

In verse 6 we move to the following day, starting with Joshua calling the priests to initiate the crossing. However, before we read of any actual movement, there is more explanation. First, the LORD

---

[4] Harstad, *Joshua*, 155 (emphasis original).
[5] See the excursus on the ark in Pitkänen, *Joshua*, 6:144–6.
[6] See the parallel instructions for the covenant at Sinai in Exodus 19:10, 14–15.

JOSHUA

promises Joshua that he will be exalted; that is, God will so clearly work through him that the people will know God is with him as he was with Moses (compare Joshua 1:5, 17). He is then told to tell the priests to stand in the water, but at this stage there is still no description of what will happen when they do – the tension is building.

Second, Joshua calls the people to listen to him and so to hear the words of the LORD (verse 9). While never referred to as a prophet, in moments like these Joshua clearly functions in this way in relaying God's word. What is about to happen will be a sign that will reassure them that God is present among them – i.e., he is at work – and that he will go on to drive out the inhabitants of the land. He is called the 'living God' here; that is, the God who is active for them, in contrast to the 'dead' gods of the people groups mentioned.[7] This is the first list given in Joshua of the native inhabitants of the Promised Land. We should be aware that earlier books sometimes refer to them all under the inclusive term of 'Canaanites' or 'Amorites', and within Joshua the lists given are probably not exhaustive and have some flexibility as to which groups are included.[8]

In verses 11–12, Joshua relays the plan of the priests stepping into the river, but the explanation is delayed again by the instruction to select a man from each tribe (the purpose of which will also only made clear later). Then in verse 13 we are finally told what will happen: the river will be cut off. We are reminded for the third time that the priests are carrying the Ark of the LORD, showing that it is God who will act in holding back the river. Joshua also twice elaborates to refer to him as 'the Lord of all the earth', indicating that in doing so he is demonstrating his sovereign power.

We should note the significant use of the word 'know' in this section. The people will 'know' the way to go (verse 4), they will 'know' that God is with Joshua as he was with Moses (verse 7) and they will 'know' that God will drive out the inhabitants of the

---

7 Howard, *Joshua*, 125.
8 See Appendix A: The Tribes of the Promised Land.

land (verse 10).⁹ Knowledge of God here involves understanding but also experience. By the end of the day, the Israelites will truly know these things.

2. The crossing and its remembrance • Joshua 3:14–4:24

The crossing itself (3:14–17)

The passage now moves from talking to acting, and yet the pace slows even further. As David Howard says:

> Here, the narrative slows to a crawl, so that the reader can savour the wonder of the miracle and view it from as many different perspectives as possible. The author, by writing in this way, affirms God's greatness and power and intervention on his people's behalf. The point is not so much that the people were able to cross the Jordan, but the *manner* in which they were able to cross: by a glorious and mighty miracle of God.[10]

The people break camp and the priests lead the way (verse 14), and only at this stage are we told that the River Jordan is in flood.[11] So, as Adolph Harstad says, 'the timing could not be worse for a safe crossing. Yet the timing could not be better for "miracles".'[12] Despite the flood, as soon as the priests' feet hit the water, the river stops flowing. We are given geographical detail to aid picturing this remarkable event: miles upstream at Adam the river is held back, and meanwhile downstream, towards the Dead Sea, the river is cut off.[13] We are simply told that the people cross over opposite Jericho

---

9 Howard, *Joshua*, 122–5.
10 Howard, *Joshua*, 129 (emphasis original).
11 Alert readers will have noticed that the two spies successfully forded the river without a miracle (Joshua 2:23). Presumably it was a different task for a huge convoy, and it may be that God had them cross at a more imposing section of the river.
12 Harstad, *Joshua*, 184.
13 Interestingly, it is known that an earthquake resulted in a blockage of the Jordan in this area in 1927. God may have used such a 'natural' event here (Just as he used a wind to part the Red Sea, Exodus 14:21). See Firth, *Joshua*, 105.

(verse 16), which serves to focus our attention on the miracle rather than the act of crossing itself. Verse 17 then slows down to draw our attention to the actual experience of crossing: we are to see the priests standing stationed firmly in the middle of the dry riverbed while the whole nation walks past them.

We should remember again that the Ark of the Covenant represents God's presence, and thus it is the LORD who leads this procession and who goes into the water first; it is the LORD who is holding back the water while his people cross; and all the people walk past knowing the LORD is opening the door for them to enter.

Memorialising the crossing (4:1–9)

We return to the twelve men, one from each tribe, with the LORD's command to choose them (verse 2). It is hard to know how to put this together with Joshua's instruction in 3:12. Was there previous communication from God not mentioned here? Are the verses out of sequence for literary effect? Whatever the explanation, the task of these men is now made clear: take a stone each from the riverbed to where they will camp (verse 3). The stones are from where the priests stood and hence are representative of the miraculous crossing.

Joshua calls the twelve men already selected, repeats this instruction (verses 4–5) and then elaborates on it (verses 6–7). The repetition focuses our attention on the significance of these stones. The elaboration makes explicit how the stones are to function: they are to serve as a 'sign'. That is a concrete picture that points beyond itself to something more significant. So, when asked about the significance of the stones by their children (who wouldn't know what they represented), the people are to relay how the waters of the Jordan were cut before the Ark of the LORD. The stones are thus to function as a 'memorial . . . for ever'. This emphasises the significance of the event; the previous such 'sign' and 'memorial' was the Passover meal to remember the redemption from Egypt (Exodus 12:14).

Verse 8 then carefully relays how this action is carried out, again giving emphasis to its significance. Verse 9 is debated in translation and meaning: some think it refers to Joshua setting up a different set of stones at the place where the priests were standing. That is certainly possible and is how many translations understand it (such as the ESV). However, it seems unlikely, given these stones would be hidden by the river, and it is unusual to have two identical memorials. The alternative understanding it that it is summarising the section: Joshua set up as a memorial the twelve stones brought from the river (as in the NIV).[14]

Concluding the crossing (4:10–18)

The narrative around the stones has jumped ahead to their erection that evening (assuming the NIV reading). We return in verse 10 to the end of the crossing. The priests remain in their place until everything has been completed, then leave their posts and move to the side of the river while the people watch (verse 11). We are reminded of the trans-Jordanian tribes having crossed first in accordance with Joshua's instructions (Joshua 1:14), and then the total number of armed men they represent. Within this section we are told twice that everything is done 'as Moses had directed'. Hence this is presented as an extended act of obedience on behalf of Joshua and, through him, the people. The result is that Joshua is exalted as God said he would be, and the people are in awe, or fear, of him, just as they were of Moses (see Exodus 14:31).

The priests are then finally commanded to exit the river themselves (verses 15–17). They do so and immediately the river returns to its previous state. Hence the picture is that of God opening the door and holding it open until all have crossed and then closing it behind them.

Enforcement of the need to remember (4:19–24)

The people camp at Gilgal, and that is where the twelve stones are set up as a memorial sign. Gilgal will be the first of three main camps for the Israelites during the first phase of life in the land. We are told the specific date that this happened: the same date as the selection of the Passover lamb (Exodus 12:3). This serves to tie this crossing together with the Exodus, as is made explicit in verse 23.[15]

---

14 See the discussion on translation and meaning by Firth, *Joshua*, 107–8.
15 Firth, *Joshua*, 110.

Joshua then repeats the instruction as to the meaning of the stones but with further elaboration. Again, when their descendants ask about their meaning, they are to be told the story of the crossing. God is identified as the actor here: 'The LORD your God dried up the Jordan before you' (verse 23), and the explicit connection to God's acts at the Red Sea is made.[16] The events of Exodus 14 and Joshua 3–4 form bookends; the first being an act of rescue and deliverance, the second an act of entrance and homecoming. God did not simply want his people out of the land of slavery, but with him in his land of rest.

God has performed these great acts to achieve this entry, but with wider aims in mind (verse 24). All the peoples of the world should know that God is powerful, and his people should always stand in fear of him. Hence, Israel should know her own responsibility to live in the light of God's great acts on her behalf, but also that, through her, he is made known to a watching world.

KEY THEMES AND APPLICATION

God purpose in the crossing
At one level, the purpose of this crossing is to get God's people into the Promised Land; however, we have seen that great significance lies in the way this happens. It is worth listing the different purposes given in the passage:

- To exalt Joshua in the eyes of Israel, so they know God is with him as he was with Moses (3:7; 4:14).
- To assure the Israelites of God's presence such that he will drive out the land's current inhabitants (3:10).
- So all the peoples of the earth would know God's power (4:24).
- So the Israelites would fear God always (4:24).

The creation of the teaching memorial (4:6–7, 21–3) means these purposes are perpetuated for future generations.[17]

---

16 These two events are connected elsewhere in Scripture, such as in Psalm 114.
17 For a slightly different set of purposes, see Creach, *Joshua*, 48–51.

A CROSSING TO REMEMBER

God's gracious work for his people

The emphasis here is on God's actions for his people to enter the land he has promised. The way the people enter leaves them and later readers in no doubt: God got them in. This is seen in the fact of the miracle itself, but also in the movement of the people with respect to the Ark of the Covenant. God went ahead and opened the door. This teaches general truths about God's power: he is indeed the 'living God' and is 'Lord of all the earth'. It more specifically teaches us about how his great acts of salvation are achieved. Along with the Exodus, this shows us that God's people are rescued from slavery and then brought into his land purely by his gracious hand where he does everything needed for his people. This is the Old Testament equivalent of, 'For it is by grace you have been saved, through faith – and this is not from yourselves, it is the gift of God – not by works, so that no one can boast' (Ephesians 2:8–9). The Israelites could, and should, rejoice in their entry into the land, but they could never boast in it.

Some commentators have gone further in seeing the work of Christ more explicitly referenced in this crossing of the river. For example, the Lutheran minister Johann Gerhard (1582–1637) sees the Ark of the Covenant as picturing Jesus who 'stepped into the middle, so that the flood of divine wrath would not suddenly assault us. Instead, by this we many now enter into the promised eternal fatherland.'[18] However, it seems to me that is better to read the events more generally as God's gracious work, which is paralleled in his work in Jesus, rather than pointing to it explicitly (the river never seems to represent God's wrath).

Remembering events of salvation

Much of the passage is about how this act of salvation is to be remembered. The detailing and repetition of the twelve stones underlines this. This is framed in identical terms to the Exodus event and its memorialising through the Passover meal (see Exodus 12:26–7). Within the Exodus, the actual events and the instructions

---

18 Johann Gerhard, 'The Fourth Sunday of Advent', in Amos (ed.), *Reformation Commentary*, 54.

for how they are to be remembered are intermixed such that they blend with each other; the same is true here. We should also notice the way the memorialising includes the listeners in the future. Verse 23 gives the answer to the children as the 'The LORD your God did to the Jordan what he had done to the Red Sea when he dried it up before *us* until *we* had crossed over' (verse 23, my emphasis). When key acts of salvation are relayed, the listeners are often included in the explanation as if they experienced it for themselves. If they are those who enjoy life in the land, this remains something God did *for you*.

The memorial stones and instruction of children connect to the way the Bible presents 'remembering'. Remembering what God has done for you is it not simply remembering that an event occurred, but also what it means; not simply the fact, but also the implications. 'Remembering' what God has done is to live in the light of what God has done. This is foundational to the way biblical religion works: God does not perform repeated acts of salvation in every generation; rather, he performs great acts of salvation and then calls all generations to look back on them and 'remember'.[19] The nineteenth-century author Sarah Smiley puts this very well:

> The lessons to be learned from these stones of memorial are more simple than many others in this history and yet of too much importance to be slighted. The first suggested is the duty of 'remembering well' whatever the Lord has done. There are steps in our Christian course that can never be repeated in act, but need often to be repeated in vivid remembrance. On the other hand, forgetfulness of our past blessings and of the wonderful ways of our God is unspeakable loss. A lively faith will always be blessed with a clear memory, and thus forgetfulness is one of the earliest and surest symptoms of unbelief.[20]

---

19 See Micah 6:4–5 as a call to remember, referencing this crossing.
20 Sarah Smiley, 'The Fullness of Blessing or the Gospel of Christ as Illustrated from the Book of Joshua', in *ESV Church History Study Bible: Voices from the Past, Wisdom for the Present*, ed. Stephen J. Nichols, (Wheaton: Crossway, 2023), 307.

This means we should not look to apply this passage by generalising it to normal Christian life and speaking of how God will 'remove the barriers' in your life, or similar. That is not what later generations in the land would be taught to expect. Rather, we play up the uniqueness of the event and see how it teaches us about the way God brings people into his kingdom. For Christian believers today, the obvious application is then remembering the events of the cross and resurrection and how God achieved their salvation and entry into the kingdom.

Some suggest the use of memory devices, such as crosses, while recognising the long-standing Protestant concern that objects do not become the focus of worship.[21] This passage has also been used by those in the Eastern Orthodox tradition to defend the use of icons as memorials.[22] On this theme, we can also anticipate here some of the later memorials in the book of Joshua, especially those in chapters 22 and 24 which are said to act as 'witnesses' to the people. The sixteenth-century reformer Martin Luther said that the key issue was how such memorials were used:

> If one then can make and set up altars and special stones, so that God's commandment is not trespassed because worship is absent, then my image breakers must also let me keep, wear, and look at a crucifix or a Madonna, yes even an idol's full image, in full accord with the strictest Mosaic law, as long as I do not worship them, but only have them as memorials.[23]

Whatever our view on the use of such self-created memorials, what we all can be very sure of is the appropriateness, and indeed the need, to use the memorials instituted by God himself. For the Israelites that meant the stones; for us it surely means the Lord's Supper. Jesus gave instructions on how his great act of salvation was to be memorialised, and the repeated command is to eat and drink so that we remember (Luke 22:19–20; 1 Corinthians 11:23–6).

---

21 For example, Pitkänen, *Joshua*, 6:142.
22 John of Damascus, 'On Divine Images', 3.23, in Franke, *Ancient Christian Commentary*, 21.
23 Martin Luther, *Church and Ministry II*, Luther's Works (Philadelphia: Muhlenberg Press, 1958), 88.

In some parts of the world, memorialising people and events is common and natural. David Oginde comments that 'perhaps more than any other people, Africans set up all manner of memorials as reminders of significant events'.[24] The challenge in such situations is to channel that instinct appropriately and see God's provision of the Lord's Supper as such a memorial. Elsewhere in the world, where the draw is always to the new, the challenge is to appreciate the need for such memory and inculcate a cherishing of the Lord's Supper as a result. This passage is also suggestive in the way this remembering occurs within the covenant community of God's people. That is, it is through the asking and answering of questions that the history is recited and the remembrance takes place.[25]

Crossing the Jordan and death
It has become common for the crossing of the Jordan to symbolise the death of a believer and their passing into heaven. One of the best-known representations of this is by the eighteenth-century hymn writer William Williams:

> When I tread the verge of Jordan,
> bid my anxious fears subside.
> Death of death, and hell's Destruction,
> land me safe on Canaan's side.[26]

As we saw in the Introduction, this is appropriate because of the symbolism of Canaan: the land is a shadow of the new creation where God will live with his people and give them rest. However, while the land is a picture of the new creation, in the book of Joshua there is a long way to go before 'rest' is granted, and so crossing the Jordan is not simply entering 'heaven'. Teaching this passage today could include this line of application, but probably as an implication rather than the main meaning.

---

[24] Oginde, 'Joshua', 266.
[25] This has been called a 'communal epistemology of remembrance'. Robert L Hubbard, '"What Do These Stones Mean?": Biblical Theology and a Motif in Joshua', *Bulletin for Biblical Research* 11, no. 1 (2001): 11.
[26] William Williams (1717–91), 'Guide Me, O thou Great Jehovah'. Public domain.

Exaltation of Joshua

We have seen how God exalts Joshua through these events of salvation. God often acts through his appointed servants and so the act and the person are connected. That was the case with Moses and will be the case later with people such as King David. This is the moment that Joshua is exalted in the eyes of the people, and they see clearly that God is working through him. It is then supremely true of the Lord Jesus Christ. He was first identified at the Jordan River in his baptism (Matthew 3:16–17). He is then exalted through his death, resurrection and ascension. This is a key element of Peter's explanation of Jesus at Pentecost:

> Exalted to the right hand of God, he has received from the Father the promised Holy Spirit and has poured out what you now see and hear . . . Therefore let all Israel be assured of this: God has made this Jesus, whom you crucified, both Lord and Messiah. (Acts 2:33, 36)

Jesus has been exalted by God and is now looked to as the source of salvation. He is the one we should 'fear' or 'stand in awe of' all the days of our lives.[27] The church father Origen says:

> Certainly, that exaltation of the son of Nun took place in order that the leader of those former people might be held eminent among those whom he ruled. But let us see how our Jesus my Lord, leader and ruler of all this latter people, is 'exalted' in the sight of all the descendants of the sons of Israel. I myself think that he was always exalted and elevated in the presence of the Father. But it is necessary that God exalt him in our sight.[28]

---

[27] See for example Acts 9:31; 2 Corinthians 5:11; Ephesians 5:21.
[28] Origen, 'Homilies on Joshua', 5.3, in Franke, *Ancient Christian Commentary*, 22–3.

4

Identity in the Land

Joshua 5:1–12

The Israelites have just been led by Joshua to cross the Jordan and so enter the Promised Land. We know from God's instructions that battles against the inhabitants lie ahead, but before they engage in those battles, God instructs them to undertake the ritual of circumcision and then they celebrate the Passover meal. This section therefore introduces a pause before the expected action. The principle being articulated is that of 'first things first': having entered the land, there are more important issues to attend to before the invasion proper. Those issues revolve around the covenant identity of Israel. This section therefore shows us the need to be rightly orientated in knowing who we are as God's people. Indeed, such orientation to God comes before any action for God. As Firth says:

> The crossing of the Jordan makes clear that God does indeed have the power to lead Israel into the land, but that power is to be matched with an Israel that lives out the distinctiveness of its calling under covenant.[1]

5 Now when all the Amorite kings west of the Jordan and all the Canaanite kings along the coast heard how the LORD had dried up the Jordan before the Israelites until they[a] had crossed over, their hearts melted in fear and they no longer had the courage to face the Israelites.

Circumcision and passover at Gilgal

2 At that time the LORD said to Joshua, 'Make flint knives and circumcise the Israelites again.' 3 So Joshua made flint knives and circumcised the Israelites at Gibeath Haaraloth.[b]

4 Now this is why he did so: all those

---

1 Firth, *Joshua*, 116.

who came out of Egypt – all the men of military age – died in the wilderness on the way after leaving Egypt. **5** All the people that came out had been circumcised, but all the people born in the wilderness during the journey from Egypt had not. **6** The Israelites had moved about in the wilderness for forty years until all the men who were of military age when they left Egypt had died, since they had not obeyed the LORD. For the LORD had sworn to them that they would not see the land that he had solemnly promised their ancestors to give us, a land flowing with milk and honey. **7** So he raised up their sons in their place, and these were the ones Joshua circumcised. They were still uncircumcised because they had not been circumcised on the way. **8** And after the whole nation had been circumcised, they remained where they were in camp until they were healed.

9 Then the LORD said to Joshua, 'Today I have rolled away the reproach of Egypt from you.' So the place has been called Gilgal[c] to this day.

10 On the evening of the fourteenth day of the month, while camped at Gilgal on the plains of Jericho, the Israelites celebrated the Passover. **11** The day after the Passover, that very day, they ate some of the produce of the land: unleavened bread and roasted grain. **12** The manna stopped the day after[d] they ate this food from the land; there was no longer any manna for the Israelites, but that year they ate the produce of Canaan.

---

[a] 1 Another textual tradition *we*
[b] 3 *Gibeath Haaraloth* means *the hill of foreskins.*
[c] 9 *Gilgal* sounds like the Hebrew for *roll.*
[d] 12 Or *the day*

1. Circumcision and reproach • Joshua 5:1–9

The response of the tribal kings (5:1)

We are first told of the way the local kings responded when they heard how the Israelites had crossed the Jordan.[2] This seems to be an intensification of the fear and lack of confidence that we have seen already in chapter 2. It is particularly significant that 'all' the kings

---

2 Notice here that the variety of tribes are grouped under the two main terms 'Canaanites' and 'Amorites'. See the discussion in Appendix A: The Tribes of the Promised Land.

are specified; that is, the leaders of the inhabitants are trembling, not just the people.

Some commentators and translations place this verse at the end of the previous section, and it can fit there as a conclusion to the crossing. However, it is better placed here as verse 2 refers to it: 'At that time'. In other words, the fragile state of the local kings is the context for what God now commands. One might have thought that such a moment was the best time to strike in battle, but God has other priorities.

Instructions for circumcision (5:2–8)

God speaks directly to Joshua and commands the making of flint knives so that the Israelites can be circumcised.[3] This is referred to as circumcising 'again' and for a 'second time' (although this repetition is avoided in most translations). This is not a second circumcision but rather the reintroduction of the rite of circumcision among the nation. That is what happens, and the place is given an appropriate name as a result (see map 1).[4]

We should remember the significance of circumcision here: it was given in Genesis 17 as a 'sign of the covenant'. The covenant with Abraham included promises of his having descendants, inheriting the land and receiving God's blessing; more fundamentally, it was a promise of relationship, 'to be your God' (Genesis 17:7). Bearing the sign of circumcision showed the inclusion of their children in this covenant; not to be circumcised was to deny the covenant and so be excluded from God's people:

> Any uncircumcised male, who has not been circumcised in the flesh, will be cut off from his people; he has broken my covenant. (Genesis 17:14)

---

[3] Flint knives were unusual and ancient. They may have been commanded to remind people that this was an ancient ceremony, or because they were better than metal. See Harstad, *Joshua*, 225. Circumcision was the cutting of the male foreskin; it was known to be done in other nations (see Jeremiah 9:25–6) but had special significance for Israel.

[4] Gibeath Haaraloth means 'hill of foreskins'. The same place is also called 'Gilgal' in verse 9, which becomes the standard name.

The covenantal significance of circumcision means it is surprising that it has been neglected, and we are given an extended explanation as to why it needed to be reintroduced now (Joshua 5:4–7). We are reminded of the wilderness wandering in which the previous generation died in the desert and told that those born during that time had not been circumcised (verses 4–5). The explanation might end here, but there is further reflection on the previous generation (verse 6): their disobedience meant they were under God's sworn judgment not to enter the Promised Land. It is emphasised that this was those of military age on leaving Egypt; that is, those who did not believe God's promise about entering the land.[5] So it is the next generation that Joshua circumcises, and it is repeated that they were not circumcised during the journey.

While the situation and its background are made clear, there is no explicit explanation. It is not said that the lack of circumcision was an act of disobedience, although it could be viewed as such, and some commentators make this point. It may be better to see this suspension of circumcision as part of the cloud of God's judgment over the nation because of their past disobedience. The sixteenth-century reformer John Calvin says the lack of circumcision is 'a sign of malediction or rejection'.[6] There may have been doubt as to how clearly God's covenant promise applied to this disobedient generation and hence whether they could 'claim' that promise for their children through circumcision. There is a hint of this in verse 6: God had sworn the land to their forefathers but then sworn not to give it to them – so what is the status of this promise now?[7]

The entire male population is now circumcised (verse 8). There is a parallel to verse 6 here: all the previous generation were 'completed' (died); now circumcising all the next generation is 'completed'.[8] One era is over, a new moment begins. Following the circumcision of the whole nation there is a period of healing. This indicates the vulnerability of the Israelites at this moment, which serves to highlight the

---

5 See Numbers 13–14.
6 Calvin, *Joshua*, 4:79.
7 Hess, *Joshua*, 121.
8 Howard, *Joshua*, 150.

IDENTITY IN THE LAND

importance and priority of circumcision in God's eyes: a self-imposed moment of weakness having just entered enemy territory is hardly sound military tactics.

The new start for God's people (5:9)

God then gives his verdict on what has been achieved: he has rolled the reproach of Egypt away from them, leading to the name of Gilgal (from the word 'roll'). The 'reproach' here is disgrace or shame. Israel's time in Egypt was a time of such reproach because they were enslaved and oppressed. God is saying that such reproach has hung over them subsequently. It may be more specific: that the reproach is that of the Egyptians' attitude towards Israel during their wandering in the desert. David Howard says the Egyptians may have been 'concluding that Israel's God has abandoned it and heaping scorn on Israel because of this'.[9]

Whatever the exact nature of the reproach, now comes a new start: God wipes away their shame and reaffirms their identity as his people bearing his covenant sign. The Italian theologian Giovanni Diodati (1576–1649) says:

> [God] caused, as it were, a new people to be born, with whom – by renewing his covenant, and being willing to ratify his promises concerning the bringing of them into the land of promise – he would have the sacrament of the covenant also re-established.[10]

Such a moment is hugely significant for them: as they start a new life in the new land, they are affirmed as to who they are in relation to God.[11]

---

9 Howard, *Joshua*, 152.
10 Giovanni Diodati, 'Annotations on Joshua 5:7', in Amos (ed.), *Reformation Commentary*, 74.
11 While differences exist, there are striking parallels with Moses's circumcision of his son in Exodus 4, prior to the 'showdown' with Pharaoh.

2. Passover and the end of the manna • Joshua 5:10–12

The timing of the entry into the land is such that four days later is the Passover festival (see Exodus 12:6). This was instituted as the memorial of God's rescue from Egypt, both in his judgment 'passing over' them and in freeing them from slavery. It was the most significant festival for them as a nation, marking their 'birth' as God's people.[12] No male who was uncircumcised was allowed to eat the Passover (Exodus 12:48): they needed to have embraced the covenant relationship before celebrating the resulting rescue. Although not stated, this is presumably one reason God commanded the reinstitution of circumcision days earlier.

The Passover here, along with the crossing of Jordan in the previous chapters, forms a connection with the Exodus. In the Exodus, the people celebrated the Passover meal and then escaped through the waters of the Red Sea. That order is now reversed, bringing a sense of closure – their journey is complete. Along with circumcision, this symbolic meal is significant for their identity as God's people, and it is surely part of God's purposes in the timing of the entry that they will remember and affirm who they are so immediately upon entering the land.

We are told that the day after the Passover, the Israelites start eating produce from the land around them. It is harvest time, and they can begin to be provided for through the 'ordinary means' of cultivation.[13] As a result, the miraculous provision of manna which has been sustaining them since early in the Exodus journey, now ceases (see Exodus 16). This sees the start of normal life in the land.

---

12 Prior to the Exodus, the Israelites were God's people in being descendants of Abraham, but this was the moment God brought them out of slavery and into relationship with him (see Exodus 6:6–8).

13 This phrase is used to speak of the way God works and provides through normal processes rather than miraculously.

KEY THEMES AND APPLICATION

Identity of God's people
Both the act of circumcision and eating the Passover reinforce the Israelites' identity. They are the two most significant identity markers of God's people in the Old Testament, often said to be the Old Testament 'sacraments'. They point to an identity that began with God's gracious promise and was then forged through his acts of redemption. God now affirms their status in his covenant by removing the cloud of shame that has been hanging over them. Placing these at the start of their life in the land shows how foundational they are. Rather than pressing on with the task of battle when the enemy is weak and fearful, they make themselves vulnerable. But within that physical vulnerability comes a spiritual strengthening in knowing who they are and affirming their relationship with God.

This shows the importance of knowing and affirming our identity as God's people: such awareness will then shape our ongoing life. In many cultures today, identity is a debated topic, and we should see how a passage such as this speaks into it. It is important to see how our identity within God's people is an identity that is given to us and which we receive, rather than one we create for ourselves. It also an identity we share as God's people and which binds us together, rather than one in which we are unique and distinguished from the rest of God's people. In these ways it counters much contemporary western thinking about identity. But we must also say it is a wonderful identity that gives us dignity and freedom, and in which we can rejoice and celebrate.

While the 'reproach of Egypt' is specific to this context it is wonderfully true that the reproach of our past is rolled away in salvation through Jesus. In him we have a 'new self' to live out. As David Jackman says, 'We know our sin and guilt only too well, but we also know, by God's grace, that every sin and failure has been dealt with, once and for all, in the cross of Christ.'[14] That does not

---

14 David Jackman, *Joshua: People of God's Purpose*, ed. R. Kent Hughes (Wheaton: Crossway, 2014), 62.

mean it is always easy to shake off the shadows of our former life, but it does mean we are not trapped in the shame of our previous experiences, guilt or social status. This might be applied in specific ways for cultures that involve an honour–shame paradigm. In some cultures, this extends to the shame of our ancestors and links with the topic of generational curses.[15] While we cannot rehearse the appropriate arguments here, we do have in this passage an example of God giving people a wonderful 'new start' that is distinct from the previous generation. Such is also ours in Christ.

Old and New Testament sacraments
These two Old Testament 'sacraments' find their New Testament counterparts in baptism and the Lord's Supper: the first as a marker of inclusion in the covenant promises, the second as an ongoing reminder and celebration of God's work of redemption. Teaching this passage will make appropriate connections to passages such as Colossians 2:11–12 and Luke 22:19–20. There will be differences of opinion on the appropriate subjects of baptism and on the regularity and mechanism of the Lord's Supper, but the significance of both as identity markers of God's people can be gladly affirmed. More than that, they should be used.

Baptism gives us a wonderful picture of being washed clean of sin (Acts 22:16), of dying with Christ and rising to new life (Colossians 2:12) and of being united with the body of Christ, the church (1 Corinthians 12:13). While it is a one-off action, we are to think of ourselves as 'baptised' people, looking back to our baptism and what it says about us now (see, for example, Romans 6:1–4).

The Lord's Supper is commanded as a means of remembering Jesus's sacrifice to redeem us (see 1 Corinthians 11:23–6). It also expresses our unity as his people, bound together in him (1 Corinthians 10:17). The physical elements of bread and wine mean it is a 'visible word' to us that proclaims Jesus's death. This connects to the words of promise in the gospel but operates differently from only hearing: it engages our senses and we participate physically, so expressing our need of Christ and trust in him.

---

15 See the discussion in Oginde, 'Joshua', 268–70.

Circumcision of the heart

While being an extension from this passage, we may wish to reflect on the call for the Israelites to circumcise their hearts (Deuteronomy 10:16; Jeremiah 4:4). That is a call to embrace the covenant relationship with God at a heart level, to be committed to him and to trust him. So, in performing the external rite here, the people would be reminded of the call for the internal heart attitude.

We can go further in that God identifies the 'uncircumcision' of his people as an ongoing problem (Jeremiah 9:26; Acts 7:51) and promises to rectify that himself. In fact, God earlier made a specific promise: 'The LORD your God will circumcise your hearts and the hearts of your descendants, so that you may love him with all your heart and with all your soul, and live' (Deuteronomy 30:6). Such an internal work is what is seen in the circumcision performed by Jesus in Colossians 2:11–12.[16] That is what is now celebrated in baptism.

---

16 Some older commentators see this spiritual circumcision alluded to within the command to circumcise the Israelites 'a second time' (Joshua 5:2).

5

The Coming of the Kingdom

Joshua 5:13–6:27

Having been appointed and charged by God, Joshua has led Israel to cross into the land, through God's miraculous intervention. They have then been reminded of their identity as God's people. We now come to one of the best-known events in this book, but also one of the most contested. It is well known because of the exciting drama involved and hence its usual inclusion in children's Bibles. It is contested because of what happened after the walls had fallen – the killing of all the inhabitants. We will consider what is happening in that act both here and in an excursus which follows.[1] What is very clear is that God orchestrates events to show that he is the one doing the fighting and so he is giving his people the city. Jericho is the first of many cities that are conquered and is a paradigm for the later examples.

The fall of Jericho

13 Now when Joshua was near Jericho, he looked up and saw a man standing in front of him with a drawn sword in his hand. Joshua went up to him and asked, 'Are you for us or for our enemies?'

14 'Neither,' he replied, 'but as commander of the army of the LORD I have now come.' Then Joshua fell face down to the ground in reverence, and asked him, 'What message does my Lord[e] have for his servant?'

15 The commander of the LORD's army replied, 'Take off your sandals, for the place where you are standing is holy.' And Joshua did so.

6 Now the gates of Jericho were securely barred because of the Israelites. No one went out and no one came in.

2 Then the LORD said to Joshua,

---

[1] It may also be helpful to refer to 'Holy war' and 'Accusations of genocide' in the Introduction.

JOSHUA

'See, I have delivered Jericho into your hands, along with its king and its fighting men. **3** March round the city once with all the armed men. Do this for six days. **4** Make seven priests carry trumpets of rams' horns in front of the ark. On the seventh day, march round the city seven times, with the priests blowing the trumpets. **5** When you hear them sound a long blast on the trumpets, make the whole army give a loud shout; then the wall of the city will collapse and the army will go up, everyone straight in.'

6 So Joshua son of Nun called the priests and said to them, 'Take up the ark of the covenant of the LORD and make seven priests carry trumpets in front of it.' **7** And he ordered the army, 'Advance! March round the city, with an armed guard going ahead of the ark of the LORD.'

8 When Joshua had spoken to the people, the seven priests carrying the seven trumpets before the LORD went forwards, blowing their trumpets, and the ark of the LORD's covenant followed them. **9** The armed guard marched ahead of the priests who blew the trumpets, and the rear guard followed the ark. All this time the trumpets were sounding. **10** But Joshua had commanded the army, 'Do not give a war cry, do not raise your voices, do not say a word until the day I tell you to shout. Then shout!' **11** So he had the ark of the LORD carried round the city, circling it once. Then the army returned to camp and spent the night there.

12 Joshua got up early the next morning and the priests took up the ark of the LORD. **13** The seven priests carrying the seven trumpets went forwards, marching before the ark of the LORD and blowing the trumpets. The armed men went ahead of them and the rear guard followed the ark of the LORD, while the trumpets kept sounding. **14** So on the second day they marched round the city once and returned to the camp. They did this for six days.

15 On the seventh day, they got up at daybreak and marched round the city seven times in the same manner, except that on that day they circled the city seven times. **16** The seventh time round, when the priests sounded the trumpet blast, Joshua commanded the army, 'Shout! For the LORD has given you the city! **17** The city and all that is in it are to be devoted[a] to the LORD. Only Rahab the prostitute and all who are with her in her house shall be spared, because she hid the spies we sent. **18** But keep away from the devoted things, so that you will not bring about your own destruction by taking any of them. Otherwise you will make the camp of Israel liable to destruction and bring trouble on it. **19** All the silver and gold and the articles of bronze and iron are sacred to the LORD and must go into his treasury.'

20 When the trumpets sounded, the army shouted, and at the sound of the trumpet, when the men gave a loud shout, the wall collapsed; so everyone charged straight in, and they took the city. 21 They devoted the city to the LORD and destroyed with the sword every living thing in it – men and women, young and old, cattle, sheep and donkeys.

22 Joshua said to the two men who had spied out the land, 'Go into the prostitute's house and bring her out and all who belong to her, in accordance with your oath to her.' 23 So the young men who had done the spying went in and brought out Rahab, her father and mother, her brothers and sisters and all who belonged to her. They brought out her entire family and put them in a place outside the camp of Israel.

24 Then they burned the whole city and everything in it, but they put the silver and gold and the articles of bronze and iron into the treasury of the LORD's house. 25 But Joshua spared Rahab the prostitute, with her family and all who belonged to her, because she hid the men Joshua had sent as spies to Jericho – and she lives among the Israelites to this day.

26 At that time Joshua pronounced this solemn oath: 'Cursed before the LORD is the one who undertakes to rebuild this city, Jericho:

'At the cost of his firstborn son
   he will lay its foundations;
at the cost of his youngest
   he will set up its gates.'

27 So the LORD was with Joshua, and his fame spread throughout the land.

---

e 14 Or *lord*

a 17 The Hebrew term refers to the irrevocable giving over of things or persons to the LORD, often by totally destroying them; also in verses 18 and 21.

1. The commander of the Lord's army • Joshua 5:13–15

Joshua is near Jericho and appears to be on his own when he is suddenly confronted with a mysterious figure.[2] The drawn sword implies a readiness for battle and so Joshua questions which side

---

2 A more literal rendering is, 'he lifted up his eyes, and looked, and behold, a man standing in front of him . . .'

he is fighting on.[3] The reply, 'Neither,' might suggest he is not for the Israelites; it is more literally, 'No.' Joshua is asking the wrong question, or asking from the wrong stance. This figure does not take sides; rather, he is the one who determines or sets the sides. He is the 'commander of the army of the LORD', hence he is superior to Joshua and Joshua must align himself with him. As David Jackman says, 'He has not come to take sides, but to take charge.'[4] The phrase 'commander of' is used of figures of supreme authority over armies but under that of a king. So here is someone over God's armies but under the LORD himself.[5]

This figure says that as commander he has 'now come': hence he is to lead the battle that is about to commence. Joshua responds appropriately in reverence or worship, and in ready submission for what he is to do. The first command is to remove his shoes because of the holiness of the ground – so echoing Moses in Exodus 3. The best preparation for battle is a smaller view of yourself and a greater reverence for God.

This figure has often been identified as the 'angel of LORD' who has appeared multiple times in the biblical story so far, most significantly in Exodus 3. This angel is distinct from God but represents him, and, as the narrative goes on, the identity often blurs so that it becomes the LORD himself speaking (so for example, Exodus 3:4). That is exactly what happens in this passage (see chapter 6:2). Many commentators have seen the 'angel of the Lord' and this 'commander' as Christophanies; that is, pre-incarnation appearances of Jesus. This is particularly common among older commentators. For example, the Baptist minister John Gill (1697–1771):

> This is not a mere man, not a created angel in an human form, but a divine person in such a form, even the Son of God, who frequently appeared in this manner to the patriarchs – as is clear from the worship paid unto him by Joshua by calling him Lord

---

3 See other uses of the 'drawn sword' in Numbers 22:23 and 1 Chronicles 21:16.
4 Jackman, *Joshua: People of God's Purpose*, 64.
5 Howard, *Joshua*, 156–7.

and owning himself to be his servant, and by the ground on which he stood being holy through his presence, as well as by his title, the captain of the Lord's host.[6]

This figure may be assumed to be speaking in chapter 6 but is not referred to again. What is achieved through his appearance is the clear picture that in the battle to come it is not Joshua or the Israelites who are really doing the fighting. In fact, it is not so much that God aids them in their battle as that they join him in his.[7]

2. *The circling of the city* • *Joshua 6:1–14*

The instructions for the battle (6:1–5)

We are told that Jericho is 'securely barred because of the Israelites' (verse 1): the words used indicate the sealing of the city to prevent any movement in or out rather than suggesting great fortifications.[8] What is clear is a sense of barricade and that there is no obvious way into the city. Despite this, Joshua is simply told, 'I have delivered Jericho into your hands' (verse 2).[9] Joshua is to look beyond appearances and see Jericho as defeated. The battle instructions from the LORD follow here and are then carried out as the passage develops, with extra detail being given as events unfold. We have seen this sort of pattern before in the crossing of the Jordan.

The key instruction is the marching round the city each day for seven days; on the first six days this is with the trumpets blowing but the people staying silent (this is clarified in later verses), and then on the seventh day the people finally shout. This will result in the collapse of the city walls and the opening of the city to the advance of the Israelites. Most prominent in this is the Ark, in a very similar

---

[6] John Gill, 'An Exposition of the Old Testament', in Nichols (ed.), *ESV Church History Study Bible*, 309.
[7] Firth, *Joshua*, 128.
[8] Firth, *Joshua*, 128–9.
[9] Howard suggests this verse functions similarly to 3:15, presenting a problem only for a divine solution; Howard, *Joshua*, 168–9.

way to the crossing of the Jordan. The LORD himself, represented by the Ark, will parade around the city with trumpets announcing his presence, and his people following. The mention of trumpets and rams' horns would be reminiscent of the people's experience of God at Sinai (see Exodus 19:10–19). So here they are reminded of God's awesome presence and they represent that to the people of Jericho.

The period of seven days may connect to the seven days of the Feast of Unleavened Bread which followed the Passover. In Exodus, the first Passover meal ended with the destruction of the Egyptian army (although not on the seventh day). Some see this combination of factors adding to make a link back to the Passover celebration of chapter 5. Richard Hess argues:

> The combination of the march around Jericho and the Passover of Joshua 5 recalls the first Passover. God will destroy Israel's enemies and consecrate the nation to himself. The battle becomes part of the Passover celebration, a memorial to the first exodus and a victory over enemies in the Promised Land.[10]

Instructing the people and the first six days (6:6–14)

Joshua relays the instructions to the priests to carry the Ark and to carry trumpets ahead of it; then he commands the 'people' (NIV 'army') to march around the city (verse 7). The importance of these commands, and of following them precisely, is emphasised by their repetition in verses 8–9. The priests and the people do as Joshua said, and we start to picture this procession circling the city. There is an additional comment in verse 10 stressing the silence of the people until the final day. We have a summary of the first day (verse 11), and then the order of events for the second day (verses 12–13). That too is summarised, and we are told it continued for a total of six days (verse 14). The repetition and slow pace here serve to draw out the narrative so that the reader starts to enter into the experience of the day-by-day circling of the city.

We should also note the repeated use of the number seven (priests,

---

10 Hess, *Joshua*, 130.

trumpets, days, circuits on the seventh day). Seven is the number of perfection and totality in the Bible and so is associated with God and his holiness.[11] These are not randomly chosen instructions but a sacred act.

3. The destruction of the city and the saving of Rahab • Joshua 6:15–25

The instructions for the seventh day (6:15–19)

The seventh day begins with a repeat circling of the city except that it is now done seven times. The key action seems to arrive in verse 16, with the final trumpet sound and the instruction for the people to shout, but there is then a pause to hear further instruction from Joshua. This was almost certainly delivered earlier but is placed here to emphasise its significance.

The key instruction is that the city and everything and everyone in it are to be 'devoted to the LORD', apart from Rahab and her family (verse 17). This is the first use of the key word 'devoted' in this passage, but it is then used multiple times in the following verses.[12] This sees the city in its entirety being dedicated to God either by being killed (in the case of people), being burnt (in the case of flammable materials) or being brought into the treasury (in the case of precious metals). God is exercising his sovereign claim on this city and all in it. That is why is the Israelites must not claim any of it for their own (verse 18); if they do, they will become subject to this 'devotion' themselves (which is what we will see happen in the next chapter). This is significant in showing that the concept is not about ethnicity but about God's claim.[13] For further discussion of the term 'devotion' and its theological significance, see the excursus which follows.

---

11 Doug Johnson, *Teaching Joshua: From Text to Message* (Fearn, Ross-shire: Christian Focus, 2019), 182.
12 This is the word *herem* which we have mentioned earlier. See 'Holy war' in the Introduction and also Excursus: Devoting to the LORD, which follows.
13 Firth, *Joshua*, 136.

The actions of destruction and salvation (6:20–25)

In verse 20 we return to the moment of verse 16: the trumpets sound, the people shout. This is then repeated in reverse to emphasise that it is what brought about the resulting collapse of the walls.[14] The people then charge straight in as the LORD had promised (verse 5). Rather than any description of fighting, we are simply told that they devoted the city to the LORD. The list in verse 21 stresses the totality of the destruction; none escapes. None, that is, apart from Rahab and her extended family. Joshua instructs the two spies, who would know where her house was, to bring her and her family out as they promised. Their actions are reported in verse 23, stressing the completeness of the family grouping. They are placed somewhere outside the camp of Israel, presumably reflecting their uncertain status: they are not 'Jericho' because they are spared, but nor are they yet 'Israel' (although that will be seen to change).

After the killing of the inhabitants and the rescue of Rahab's family, the final acts of 'devotion' are the burning of the city and bringing precious metal items into the LORD's treasury. This 'treasury' is probably linked with the Tabernacle, given the mention of the 'LORD's house'; it is unknown before this passage but appears with the building of the Temple (e.g., 1 Kings 7:51). The saving of Rahab is repeated in verse 25, which is the third mention within this passage (previously in verses 17 and 23). This underlines both their salvation and the destruction of everyone else. The comment that Rahab lives among the Israelites to this day shows that, despite their initial uncertain status, she and her family were absorbed into the people of Israel.

4. *The curse on Jericho* • *Joshua 6:26–7*

No instruction from God is mentioned regarding this curse so this may have been at Joshua's initiative; however, it certainly fits with what has happened to Jericho and its symbolic status in the land.

---

14 The reversed order of trumpets and shout is less clear in the NIV's rendering.

Anyone who undertook to rebuild the city would be seeking to reverse God's judgment on it and so would be under a curse. The reformer John Calvin says that God wished that 'the ruins and devastation should exist forever as a kind of trophy; because the rebuilding of it would have been equivalent to an erasure effacing the miracle'.[15] The specific nature of the curse was that the builder's oldest and youngest child would die. This is exactly what is reported later in Israel's history (see 1 Kings 16:34).

The section concludes with the statement that the Lord was with Joshua: as we saw in chapter 1, God's presence was the key element in all his success, so here his presence in seen in what is achieved at Jericho. The result is the Joshua's 'fame' (literally 'name') spreads through all the land.

KEY THEMES AND APPLICATION

God's power and the Israelites faith
The way the battle is won at Jericho demonstrates God's sovereign power and his 'giving' his people victory. This is shown in different ways through the book of Joshua: many battles will be won in 'ordinary ways' (see chapter 8), but this first battle is designed to emphasise God's work. All the people do is march round the city – a curious military tactic – and God 'gives' them the city.

God's power and promise go hand in hand with the people's faith and obedience.[16] This is seen in their meticulous observation of God's commands and so their trust that he will do what he has promised. The New Testament comment on this event is, 'By faith the walls of Jericho fell, after the army had marched around them for seven days' (Hebrews 11:30). As we saw with Rahab, this is an example of trusting God for something that they could not yet see, believing his word over against the evidence of their eyes (see Hebrews 11:1).

We should see this as an example of faith that all of God's people are called to imitate. Hebrews 11 lists examples such as these to encourage the same faith in those reading. However, in encouraging

---

15 Calvin, *Joshua*, 4:100.
16 See 'God's action and the people's response' in the Introduction.

such faith, we must be clear both on the *object* of faith – that is, what we have faith in – and on the *content* of faith; that is, what we are trusting God for. There are two issues here. First, western culture has made faith an irrational 'leap in the dark', where one simply chooses to have faith. Calls to imitate faith from this passage could be heard as calls to make such 'leaps' by summoning up feelings of confidence from within. That is not biblical faith at all, but rather wishful thinking or even self-delusion; biblical faith is a reasonable trust *in God* even though we cannot yet see the reality of what is promised.[17] The story of Jericho must be taught in this way.

Second, we are only to trust God for what he has promised. Some applications of this passage speak of conquests in our personal life paralleled with that of Jericho and give assurance of victory against all 'strongholds'. That is both to domesticate what is described here and to assume that God has made direct promises over such areas in our lives as he did to Joshua. The application in Hebrews 11 is to believe God's promises to his people – in that context, the promises of a future homeland we cannot yet see and so live by faith now (see Hebrews 11:39–12:3).

The 'foolishness' of God's tactics

The tactics God commands to defeat Jericho might have appeared rather foolish; indeed, one wonders how the Israelites felt after a few days of circling the city. We might ask why God commanded such a drawn-out and curious process. Yet this was the God-ordained method, and the people's faith was shown in trusting him and obeying his commands, rather than doing whatever they thought wise.

This illustrates a general point about trusting God's commanded approach, which has sometimes been applied specifically to the 'foolishness' of preaching the gospel today (1 Corinthians 1:18; 2 Corinthians 10:4). The seventeenth-century English reformer, Arthur Jackson states:

---

[17] For a discussion of how faith is understood today, see Christopher Watkin, *Biblical Critical Theory: How the Bible's Unfolding Story Makes Sense of Modern Life and Culture* (Grand Rapids: Zondervan Academic, 2023), 256–8.

Yes, and in this we have as well a figure of God's subduing the world to Christ our Joshua, or Jesus, in these days of the gospel. For by trumpets of ram's horns – that is by 'the foolishness of preaching' (for so carnal men judge it) – does the Lord beat down all the strongholds and fortifications of Satan raised in human hearts.[18]

The arrival of God's kingdom and destruction
As explained in the Introduction, the land is seen as the place of God's kingdom in the Old Testament: it is where God is setting up his rule and presence with his people. Therefore, as his kingdom comes in the land, his rule is brought. That is seen by the 'devotion' of the city to the LORD: everything is brought under his sovereign rule; no rebellion remains. That means the most direct parallel for Christian believers today is the arrival of the kingdom with the return of Jesus. That is when God's rule will be established, this time over the whole world, not one small section of it. His rule will be brought by his appointed king, the commander of the LORD's army, the Lord Jesus (see Revelation 19:11–21). That will be the day when the trumpet will sound and the Lord will descend (1 Thessalonians 4:16). At the sounding of that trumpet, it will be said that, 'The kingdom of the world has become the kingdom of our Lord and of his Messiah, and he will reign for ever and ever' (Revelation 11:15). That is when God's punishment on those who resist him will come, and when every knee will be brought to bow before him (Philippians 2:9–11).

God's kingdom does of course come now – and has been advancing since Jesus's life, death and resurrection. However, currently his kingdom comes as people voluntarily recognise Jesus as King and bow to him. Currently, rebellion against Jesus is still 'allowed'. What we see in Jericho is a moment where such lordship is 'enforced'. The Lutheran commentator Paul Kretzmann said:

---

18 Arthur Jackson, 'Annotations on Joshua', 6:3, in Amos, *Reformation Commentary*, 86–7.

But in the fall of Jericho we also see a type of the final overthrow of all the powers of the world, death, and hell. At the end of the world the Lord will come with the voice of the archangel and with the trumpet of God (1 Thess. 4:16), and the whole world will fall down in ruins as he proceeds to carry out his judgment upon his enemies.[19]

This passage gives the sobering but reassuring reminder that God will not allow a rebellious world to rebel forever, and that sin will be punished. It also refocuses our picture of God as the true King who will rule in triumph over his enemies. The church is virtually always in need of such reminders as our consciousness of Jesus's return fades all too easily.

The offer of salvation
The repeated mention of Rahab and her family shows that their salvation is a key theme: Richard Hess says, 'The salvation of Rahab was as important as the destruction of Jericho'.[20] Within the certainty of destruction is the possibility of salvation. We should remember that the Lord takes 'no pleasure in the death of the wicked' but rather calls people to 'turn from their ways and live' (Ezekiel 33:11). Within Jericho, Rahab and her family 'turned' and lived as result.

This shows us that the issue at stake was not people's ethnicity but their stance towards God. We note again that the citizens of Jericho are referred to as 'disobedient' (Hebrews 11:31). This theme of salvation for all is emphasised for us by Rahab's inclusion, along with other non-Israelites, in the genealogy of Matthew 1. Matthew demonstrates a 'Jewish' gospel that is for all nations (see also Matthew 28:19–20). In Jericho, those who turned to God before judgment fell were 'spared'. The same applies today in the light of Jesus's coming. The nineteenth-century writer Charlotte Maria Tucker wrote movingly of the reassurance that the 'scarlet cord' would have been provided to Rahab amid falling judgment. She says of the Church on the

---

19 Paul Kretzmann, 'Popular Commentary of the Bible: Old Testament', in Nichols (ed.), *ESV Church History Study Bible*, 311.
20 Hess, *Joshua*, 134.

day of judgment, 'She has nothing to fear in that day: the blood of Christ is her salvation – the angel of destruction will see the token of living faith, and not touch the redeemed of the Lord.'[21] Hence, in teaching this passage, we might call others to turn and so be spared, we might encourage God's people to call others to turn; and we might rejoice in God's mercy of sparing us.

---

21 Charlotte Maria Tucker, 'The Sign of the Cord', in Taylor and DeGroot, *Women of War, Women of Woe*, 40.

Excursus: Devoting to the LORD

We have noted the significance of the phrase 'devoted to the LORD'. The Hebrew word used is *herem*.[1] This word is occasionally used of total destruction (e.g., 2 Chronicles 20:23; Daniel 11:44), but the theological weight of this term comes when something is devoted *to the LORD*. The verb is usually translated 'devoted' but can also be 'completely destroyed' or 'devoted to destruction' or similar; the noun is usually the 'devoted things' or 'things devoted for destruction'.

The background for this term is found in Leviticus 27:28–9. The key point here is that anything devoted to the LORD cannot be redeemed; it is 'most holy to the LORD' (Leviticus 27:28). This is why the NIV translation gives an explanatory footnote saying the term 'refers to the irrevocable giving over of things or persons to the LORD'. Regarding physical objects, this means they cannot be sold or bought back; with regard to people, this means they must be put to death. It indicates a strong element of God's sovereign claim over people and things.

In Joshua, the verb is used in 2:10 as a description of what Israel did to the Amorite kings east of the Jordan. It is then the key description of what is done to Jericho, and Jericho then becomes paradigmatic for other cities. The rationale given in Deuteronomy 20 for such total destruction of the cities in the Promised Land is so that the people who previously lived there would not teach them to follow other gods.

There is therefore a strong element of purification of the land associated with this term. There is also the theme of judgment on

---

[1] For an overview of this area, see J. P. U. Lilley, 'Understanding the Herem', *Tyndale Bulletin* 44, no. 1 (1993): 169–77. Also see Howard, *Joshua*, 180–87.

people for their false worship and sinful living. This is seen in the use of the verb in Exodus 22. That passage contains a list of sins, many of which are punished by death, but the only one that is punished by 'devotion' to the LORD is that of sacrificing to another god (Exodus 22:20). Another key text in this regard is Deuteronomy 13:12–18, which gives the example of people in the land turning away to worship other gods. Such people are to be devoted to the LORD by being destroyed completely, and the city is to remain a ruin forever, never to be rebuilt. This clearly has strong echoes in the Jericho narrative.

This term, 'devoted to the LORD', then, refers to God's sovereign claim over someone or something, particularly where his purifying judgment is exercised on it for worship of other gods. When we combine this with biblical theology and see the land as a picture of God's kingdom, we can draw the conclusions reached in the Introduction: this is a picture of God's judgment coming as he brings his rule on earth.

6

Placing Yourself on the Wrong Side: Achan's Sin

Joshua 7

Joshua's leading of the people into the land has so far been a success. He and the people have followed God's commands and so known his blessing. However, after the high points of crossing the Jordan and the battle of Jericho comes the first 'failure' in Joshua. This shows that the Israelites cannot disregard God's instructions; they are privileged but not immune, and so can place themselves on the wrong side of God. Indeed, while Rahab and her family can be saved from 'devotion to the LORD', Achan and his family can become liable to it. She became an Israelite; he became a Canaanite.

So far, we have seen the positive side of God's promising his people success and their response of faith and obedience; now we see the inverse relationship.[1] Such an event stands as a sobering reminder to God's people not to presume on God but to revere him.

Achan's sin

7 But the Israelites were unfaithful in regard to the devoted things[a]; Achan son of Karmi, the son of Zimri,[b] the son of Zerah, of the tribe of Judah, took some of them. So the LORD's anger burned against Israel.

2 Now Joshua sent men from Jericho to Ai, which is near Beth Aven to the east of Bethel, and told them, 'Go up and spy out the region.' So the men went up and spied out Ai.

3 When they returned to Joshua, they said, 'Not all the army will have to go up against Ai. Send two or three thousand men to take it and do not weary the whole army, for only a few people live there.' **4** So about three thousand went up; but they were routed by the men of Ai, **5** who killed about thirty-six of them. They chased the Israelites from the city

---

[1] See 'God's action and the people's response' in the Introduction.

JOSHUA

gate as far as the stone quarries and struck them down on the slopes. At this the hearts of the people melted in fear and became like water.

6 Then Joshua tore his clothes and fell face down to the ground before the ark of the LORD, remaining there till evening. The elders of Israel did the same, and sprinkled dust on their heads. **7** And Joshua said, 'Alas, Sovereign LORD, why did you ever bring this people across the Jordan to deliver us into the hands of the Amorites to destroy us? If only we had been content to stay on the other side of the Jordan! **8** Pardon your servant, Lord. What can I say, now that Israel has been routed by its enemies? **9** The Canaanites and the other people of the country will hear about this and they will surround us and wipe out our name from the earth. What then will you do for your own great name?'

10 The LORD said to Joshua, 'Stand up! What are you doing down on your face? **11** Israel has sinned; they have violated my covenant, which I commanded them to keep. They have taken some of the devoted things; they have stolen, they have lied, they have put them with their own possessions. **12** That is why the Israelites cannot stand against their enemies; they turn their backs and run because they have been made liable to destruction. I will not be with you any more unless you destroy whatever among you is devoted to destruction.

13 'Go, consecrate the people. Tell them, "Consecrate yourselves in preparation for tomorrow; for this is what the LORD, the God of Israel, says: there are devoted things among you, Israel. You cannot stand against your enemies until you remove them.

14 ' "In the morning, present yourselves tribe by tribe. The tribe that the LORD chooses shall come forward clan by clan; the clan that the LORD chooses shall come forward family by family; and the family that the LORD chooses shall come forward man by man. **15** Whoever is caught with the devoted things shall be destroyed by fire, along with all that belongs to him. He has violated the covenant of the LORD and has done an outrageous thing in Israel!" '

16 Early the next morning Joshua made Israel come forward by tribes, and Judah was chosen. **17** The clans of Judah came forward, and the Zerahites were chosen. He made the clan of the Zerahites come forward by families, and Zimri was chosen. **18** Joshua made his family come forward man by man, and Achan son of Karmi, the son of Zimri, the son of Zerah, of the tribe of Judah, was chosen.

19 Then Joshua said to Achan, 'My son, give glory to the LORD, the God of Israel, and honour him. Tell me what you have done; do not hide it from me.'

20 Achan replied, 'It is true! I have sinned against the LORD, the God of Israel. This is what I have done: **21** when I saw in the plunder a beautiful robe from Babylonia,[c] two hundred shekels[d] of silver and a bar of gold weighing fifty shekels,[e] I coveted them and took them. They are hidden in the ground inside my tent, with the silver underneath.'

22 So Joshua sent messengers, and they ran to the tent, and there it was, hidden in his tent, with the silver underneath. **23** They took the things from the tent, brought them to Joshua and all the Israelites and spread them out before the LORD.

24 Then Joshua, together with all Israel, took Achan son of Zerah, the silver, the robe, the gold bar, his sons and daughters, his cattle, donkeys and sheep, his tent and all that he had, to the Valley of Achor. **25** Joshua said, 'Why have you brought this trouble on us? The LORD will bring trouble on you today.'

Then all Israel stoned him, and after they had stoned the rest, they burned them. **26** Over Achan they heaped up a large pile of rocks, which remains to this day. Then the LORD turned from his fierce anger. Therefore that place has been called the Valley of Achor[f] ever since.

---

[a] 1 The Hebrew term refers to the irrevocable giving over of things or persons to the LORD, often by totally destroying them; also in verses 11, 12, 13 and 15.
[b] 1 See Septuagint and 1 Chron. 2:6; Hebrew *Zabdi*; also in verses 17 and 18.
[c] 21 Hebrew *Shinar*
[d] 21 That is, about 2.3 kilograms
[e] 21 That is, about 575 grams
[f] 26 *Achor* means *trouble*.

1. The defeat at Ai • Joshua 7:1–9

The statement of the problem (7:1)

The opening verse reveals to the reader what has happened and therefore Israel's state before God, but the story proceeds with its protagonists ignorant of this. The issue is stated in general terms first: 'the Israelites were unfaithful in regard to the devoted things'. To be unfaithful here is to act treacherously or to go against someone. It can be used of unfaithfulness in marriage but also, as in this case, to be disloyal to God (see, for example, Numbers 5:12; Deuteronomy 32:51). The 'devoted things' are those that God had specified to be destroyed, and that taking them would make Israel 'liable to destruction' in the previous chapter (Joshua 6:18). The actual act is then specified: Achan took some of these things God had reserved for himself when they were 'sacred' or 'set apart' for God (Joshua 6:19). We are given Achan's family line which identifies him as a true Israelite, and which will become significant later. The result is God's anger burning against his people; what that anger looks like will now become clear.

The resulting defeat (7:2–5)

Joshua sends men to spy out the next town to attack, which is Ai, west of Jericho.[2] They do as they are told and return with a report stressing the small size of the town and hence the smaller number of fighters required to take the city. Joshua clearly agrees, and three thousand go to attack. Some suggest that this shows overconfidence following the success of Jericho; it is also pointed out that there is no consultation with God on the matter. The nineteenth-century Anglican bishop, J.C. Ryle, said:

> Like Israel, puffed up with the fall of Jericho, we are ready to say to ourselves, 'The men of Ai are but few' (Josh vii.3); 'There is no need to put forth all our strength.' Like Israel, we often learn by bitter experience, that spiritual battles are not to be won without hard fighting.[3]

There is no explicit statement of this in the passage, but it might be inferred from chapter 8, where God instructs Joshua to take the whole army (Joshua 8:1). However, we should see that their fate is already determined by the pronouncement of verse 1; it wouldn't have mattered how many of the army were sent if God was against them.[4] The three thousand 'flee' before the men of Ai (NIV 'routed by'), and some are

---

[2] It is not stated why Ai is chosen; many commentators believe it is in a strategic position.
[3] John Charles Ryle, *Expository Thoughts on the Gospel of Matthew* (London: Hodder and Stoughton, 1910), 213.
[4] It is, of course, possible that God's opposition to his people meant he led them to be proud and self-sufficient and so become the means of their own downfall.

PLACING YOURSELF ON THE WRONG SIDE: ACHAN'S SIN

killed. What is stressed here is their desperate retreat: they run from 'the city gate as far as the stone quarries'.[5] It is then that the Israelites tremble in fear: they are reduced to the state of the Canaanites earlier (see Joshua 2:11; 5:1).

Joshua's lament (7:6–9)

Joshua and the elders of Israel respond appropriately in lament before God's presence (represented in the Ark), shown in the physical acts of tearing clothes, falling on the ground and putting dust on their heads. That lament is then expressed in words questioning God (verses 7–9).[6] Joshua asks, 'Why?' Why has God brought them into this land only to give them into the hands of the Amorites? This reverses the language of Joshua 6:2, where God gave Jericho into Joshua's hand. Joshua questions whether God's purpose is to 'destroy' them.[7]

Joshua expresses his confusion: 'What can I say?' The key issue is that Israel has been 'routed'. David Howard says this uses a rare expression 'capturing the shame and turmoil involved for Israel'.[8] There is a God-honouring perplexity to Joshua's words: he doesn't understand what has happened and so questions God's purposes. Joshua foresees the result of the other inhabitants hearing, being emboldened and wiping out the Israelites' name. But ultimately the question is what will happen to God's name; God's reputation is on the line in what will happen to his people.

2. God's diagnosis and instructions • Joshua 7:10–15

God responds in verse 10. It is not so much a rebuke of Joshua, who has responded appropriately given what he knew, as a call to act. The answer to Joshua's question comes in verse 11 in increasing levels of

---

5 A distance of about three and half miles; Hess, *Joshua*, 147.
6 The NIV uses 'Sovereign LORD' to convey the Hebrew for 'Lord' plus God's covenant name 'Yahweh'.
7 There are parallels in Numbers 14:2–4 and 20:3–5; Hess, *Joshua*, 148.
8 Howard, *Joshua*, 192. It is a different word from that which was also translated 'routed' by the NIV in verse 4.

specificity. Most generally, 'Israel has sinned'; it is Israel that is at fault, not God. The nature of that sin is violation (or transgression) of the covenant relationship with God. The specific nature of this covenant breaking is in taking some of the 'devoted things'. God then details three actions involved in this: they have 'stolen' the items in question, 'lied' about it (or better would be 'deceived') and 'put them with their own possessions' – i.e., taken them as their own. The explanation lands in verse 12: that is why Israel has been defeated in battle; they themselves have become 'liable to destruction', using the key word from chapter 6.[9] This means the vital promise of God's presence is suspended until destruction is executed on what has become 'devoted'. Verse 12b is the crux of the matter and the hinge of the passage.[10]

This explanation results in God's commands of verse 13: the people are to be consecrated because God will act among them the following day (see the parallel with Joshua 3:5). There are now 'devoted things' among them (either items or persons or both) and they must be removed. This sees the threat of Joshua 6:18 brought into reality. Unfaithfulness with what is 'devoted' to God makes them 'devoted' themselves, which is only resolved by destroying what is 'devoted'.

God will act by selecting the appropriate tribe, clan, family and man (verse 14). Whoever is selected in this way and found with the 'devoted' things will themselves be destroyed by fire. Verse 15 forms a bracket with verse 11 but with a change: rather than Israel, it is now, 'He has violated the covenant'; they are looking for an individual. This is described as an 'outrageous thing in Israel'; that is, a thing that should never happen.[11]

3. The enactment of God's judgment • Joshua 7:16–26

The note that Joshua rises early in the morning connects this day with other days where God's work would be done (see Joshua 3:1; 6:12; 8:10).[12] In the selection process we see the family line of Achan,

---

9 Hebrew *herem*.
10 As pointed out in the structure of the passage by Davis, *Joshua*, 58, 62–3.
11 Previous examples are only Genesis 34:7 and Deuteronomy 22:21.
12 Howard, *Joshua*, 152.

which was given in verse 1, now in reverse order. The reader knows what is coming but feels the increasing tension as the group gradually narrows to leave Achan standing alone. Some commentators have seen in this process an opportunity for Achan to step forward and confess, and that not doing so shows his hardness of heart.[13] Joshua confronts him in gentle ('my son') but firm terms, calling on him to act rightly before God: he should 'give glory' and 'honour him' by now revealing the truth, so 'tell me' and 'do not hide it'.[14] Some commentators think this a call to a confession that will result in forgiveness, but that is clearly not what happens, and does not seem likely.[15]

Achan confesses with a general statement – 'I have sinned' – and then details what happened with three key verbs: 'I saw', 'I coveted' and 'took'. What he saw was both valuable and beautiful, meaning he wanted them for himself, resulting in taking. There are strong echoes of Genesis 3 here with key words being repeated: the woman 'saw' something 'good' (translated 'beautiful' in Joshua 7) that was 'desired' (translated 'coveted' in Joshua 7), and she 'took' it. When we remember that the Promised Land is like a new Eden, we can read this as a repeat of the fall. God graciously gave his people all that they needed in a paradise and gave a command as a test of loyalty – and they fail.

Achan concludes with his hiding place and Joshua sends for the items to be fetched. The discovery is detailed for the reader to experience: 'and there it was . . .' They are brought back to the assembly and spread out 'before the LORD', acknowledging that these are God's belongings. So Achan and all that belongs to him is gathered – the stolen goods, family, possessions, livestock – and they are stoned and then burnt. There is some debate over the translation and references in verse 25 which raises a query as to whether Achan's family were included in his punishment or not.[16]

---

13 For example, Arthur Jackson, 'Annotations on Joshua 7:14', in Amos, *Reformation Commentary*, 109.
14 A similar call to glorify God by speaking truthfully is seen in John 9:24.
15 Goldingay, *Joshua*, 172.
16 The majority of commentators think they were; see discussion by Harstad, who concludes that it is an open question, Harstad, *Joshua*, 328–9.

If we assume that Achan's family are included, that understandably raises questions and protestations: why should they be punished for his sin? Elsewhere God prohibits the punishment of the innocent on the basis of familial connection (see Deuteronomy 24:16; Ezekiel 18:1–20). This means we can presume that something more is happening here. We can see an inverse parallel with the saving of Rahab's family. In that instance her family had to 'join' her in her profession of faith by coming to and staying in her house. There may be a parallel here in Achan's family joining him in his sin.

This is all summarised in terms of 'trouble': Achan brought trouble on Israel, so God brings trouble on him, and the place is named Valley of Trouble. This term is again a repeat of the warning of Joshua 6:18. The pile of stones (NIV 'rocks') marking Achan's grave is 'there to this day'. This looks ahead to the burial of the king of Ai and so places Achan with him (Joshua 8:29). It also echoes the memorial stones of chapter 4 (Joshua 4:9): one set of stones remembers God's grace, the other his justice. With this resolution, the Lord turns from his 'burning' anger (NIV 'fierce'), so resolving the issue raised at the start in verse 1.

KEY THEMES AND APPLICATION

God's expectation of obedience
God's relationship with his people is shaped by the covenant.[17] That covenant is always gracious, but it is not unconditional: God expects covenant loyalty. This passage gives an example of covenant transgression and subsequent punishment. God's people are therefore being taught what it means to live within the covenant. As Trent Butler explains:

> Covenant means more than simply accepting the promises of God to multiply the nation and extend its power in the land. It meant more than going through the ritual of circumcision and the celebration of the yearly festivals. Being the people of God meant accepting certain obligations set down by God. It

---

17 See 'Covenant relationship' in the Introduction.

meant adopting the divinely ordered lifestyle. It meant making each decision of life in the light of divine leadership, not in the light of personal self-confidence.[18]

Under the Mosaic covenant, transgression had certain consequences, and the more severe the transgression, the greater the consequences, as seen here. Believers today do not live under the same covenant and so we cannot, and should not, make a connection between disobedience and misfortune in life. However, the principle that God expects his people to obey remains the same.

Comparison might be drawn with 1 Peter 1:13–21: we live in reverent fear because we know God judges our lives impartially. God's people do not get a free pass on obedience. Hence, we might warn people against presumption: being part of God's people does not mean we can act as we wish, and we certainly cannot sin with impunity; rather, there is a greater obligation to honour God. We may want to link this with God's loving discipline of his people (Hebrews 12:4–11). In making these points we will need to be careful: a believer's relationship with God is to be one of confidence in their loving Father, but also one of reverence.

A warning for God's people
This passage, then, gives a sobering warning against taking God and his warnings lightly. The number of terms used to describe what was wrong, the strength of language used and the severity in the passage all combine to show God's depth of feeling. What has happened is wrong; God hates it and will not tolerate it; his people should beware of it and its effects on the community. Mention of this incident later in Joshua certainly functions in that way (Joshua 22:20).[19]

Within this is the theme of God's knowledge of our sin, even when it is hidden from others, which should cause us to revere him. The sixteenth-century reformer John Calvin says:

---

18 Butler, *Joshua 1–12*, 7A:418.
19 Goldingay, *Joshua*, 174.

> Though God does not bring all guilty actions to light at the very moment, nor always employ the casting of lots for this purpose, he has taught us by this example that there is nothing so hidden as not to be revealed in its own time. The form of disclosure will, indeed, be different, but let every one reflect for himself that things that escape the knowledge of the world are not concealed from God, and that to make them public depends only on his pleasure.[20]

We should also note that this particular revelation and punishment happens early in their time in the land – it is not clear whether such acts would always result in this strength of discipline and punishment. We might draw a parallel with Ananias and Saphira in Acts 5: God acts to enforce the purity of his church in its early existence. Both examples serve to warn God's people for the future. He may do the same in pioneer situations as the church is first established or at crucial moments in the church's life if he so wishes.

The nature of sin
We noted the progression of sin in Achan's confession: seeing, coveting, taking. So we might reflect on how sin works in us: we see something desirable or beautiful, then long for it for ourselves and then break God's command in reaching for it. There is a madness to it because in doing so we are turning away from the God who promises us what is truly good. We could see a parallel in James 1:13–18.

The Swiss theologian Ludwig Lavater (1527–1586) helpfully hypothesises what Achan should have said to himself in that moment:

> What benefit will these things bring you? You must not dare to keep on like this. Likewise, God will grant you spoils of other cities. He has wealth enough who possesses a God who is pleased with him.[21]

---

20 Calvin, *Joshua*, 4:113.
21 Ludvig Lavater, 'Homily 32 on Joshua 7:20–23', in Amos, *Reformation Commentary*, 112.

PLACING YOURSELF ON THE WRONG SIDE: ACHAN'S SIN

As Lavater intimates, the foolishness of Achan is shown in that God would go on to allow plunder from later cities. A key dynamic in fighting covetousness is to be convinced of the goodness of God and the good things he will give us.

Punishment of sin

We should make clear that God does not respond to all acts of disobedience in the way he responds to Achan. That is clearly not the case, because the sacrificial system gives provision for confession and forgiveness (for the Christian today, see 1 John 1:9). Achan's sin is an act of disobedience that shows covenant disloyalty, and in doing so Achan places himself under the destruction reserved for the Canaanites. We see another example of such repudiation of God in later uses of the same word 'unfaithful' later in Joshua, which is paralleled with Achan's sin (see Joshua 22:16–20).

Application to believers today must take this nature of 'unfaithfulness' into account. While it does give a general warning against sin, it should be applied specifically to acts that show someone to be rejecting the gospel message and so repudiating God. One might refer to passages to such as Hebrews 6:4–8 and 10:26–31.

The parallel response in the church today to such rejection of God is seen in church discipline (see, for example, 1 Corinthians 5). This passage has been commonly cited as an example and basis for such excommunication, especially in older commentators. Dirk Philips (1504–1568), an early Anabaptist theologian, wrote:

> It is clearly demonstrated how necessary excommunication or separation from the church is, without which no church of God can subsist, which all true ministers of the Word must teach and exhort so that the entire church not be polluted and guilty of the sins of others. We have evident examples and assured witnesses in the book of Joshua: to wit, that Israel is become totally soiled by the sin and transgression of Achan so that the Lord would not combat for Israel.[22]

---

22 Dirk Philips, 'Evangelical Excommunication', in Amos, *Reformation Commentary*, 108.

We should also note that in this incident Israel are punishing one of their own – Achan's Israelite pedigree is well established. This means that familial or tribal proximity counts for nothing when set against disloyalty to God. In many cultures in the world, certain tribes, ethnic groups or classes of people are given preferential treatment and may be immune from such punishment because of how they are regarded. Achan teaches us that it should not be so.

The consequences of sin
It is very clear in this chapter is that sin has consequences. First, that is so for the nation as a whole: they lose the battle and people are killed. The idea of 'corporate solidarity' has been used here: Achan and the nation are joined such that God can say, 'Israel has sinned,' and Achan can say, 'I have sinned.'[23] This solidarity means Achan's sin affects the entire community. While that solidarity is seen in a specific way in this moment, there is a general point here about the effect of our sin on others. As Adolf Harstad says:

> Sin always harms others as well as the perpetrator. There is no such thing as a victimless sin. Even if an evil behaviour does not appear to affect anyone else, it incurs God's wrath and has consequences for the transgressor that will affect all those who live, work, and interact with the perpetrator.[24]

That corporate solidarity also means the community must then act. As John Goldingay says, 'Because of the interrelationship between individual and corporate, it is then the entire people's responsibility to take action when one person goes wrong (1 Cor. 5:4–6).'[25]

The future of God's people in the land
We noted how Achan's action were a replay of those by Eve in the Garden of Eden. This should sober us regarding the loyalty of the Israelites. Having entered the Promised Land and been assured of

---

23 See discussion in Howard, *Joshua*, 193–4.
24 Harstad, *Joshua*, 304.
25 Goldingay, *Joshua*, 176.

PLACING YOURSELF ON THE WRONG SIDE: ACHAN'S SIN

God's provision for them, it takes no time at all for this failure to come. While this does not result in a wholescale fall as in Genesis 3, it is an ominous note and raises questions as to the future. This theme will develop through the book and so would probably only be noted briefly in teaching this section.

7

Obedience and Success: The Battle Against Ai

Joshua 8:1–29

Having entered the land, the battle against its inhabitants began with the triumph over Jericho, quickly followed by the failure at Ai. The determining factor was whether God was for or against his people, which turned on their covenant faithfulness to him. God led his people, through Joshua, to deal with the unfaithfulness of Achan, and now the military campaign can resume. God assures Joshua of success against Ai second time round. This time, however, the victory is not won through a miracle, as with Jericho, but through a God-given strategy. Much of the narrative is given over to describing this.

Despite the difference in military tactics there are repeated themes to Jericho: God is one who gives them the city and they 'devote' it and its inhabitants to the LORD. With this success at Ai, the conquest is gradually gaining ground. Some details in this section are debated, especially in terms of the movements of the armies, but the overall picture it paints remains clear.[1]

Ai destroyed

8 Then the LORD said to Joshua, 'Do not be afraid; do not be discouraged. Take the whole army with you, and go up and attack Ai. For I have delivered into your hands the king of Ai, his people, his city and his land. **2** You shall do to Ai and its king as you did to Jericho and its king, except that you may carry off their plunder and livestock for yourselves. Set an ambush behind the city.'

3 So Joshua and the whole army moved out to attack Ai. He chose thirty thousand of his best fighting men and sent them out at night **4** with these orders: 'Listen carefully. You are to set an ambush behind the city. Don't go very far from it. All of

---

[1] For discussion of chronology and movement, see Howard, *Joshua*, 200–201.

JOSHUA

you be on the alert. **5** I and all those with me will advance on the city, and when the men come out against us, as they did before, we will flee from them. **6** They will pursue us until we have lured them away from the city, for they will say, "They are running away from us as they did before." So when we flee from them, **7** you are to rise up from ambush and take the city. The LORD your God will give it into your hand. **8** When you have taken the city, set it on fire. Do what the LORD has commanded. See to it; you have my orders.'

9 Then Joshua sent them off, and they went to the place of ambush and lay in wait between Bethel and Ai, to the west of Ai – but Joshua spent that night with the people.

10 Early the next morning Joshua mustered his army, and he and the leaders of Israel marched before them to Ai. **11** The entire force that was with him marched up and approached the city and arrived in front of it. They set up camp north of Ai, with the valley between them and the city. **12** Joshua had taken about five thousand men and set them in ambush between Bethel and Ai, to the west of the city. **13** So the soldiers took up their positions – with the main camp to the north of the city and the ambush to the west of it. That night Joshua went into the valley.

14 When the king of Ai saw this, he and all the men of the city hurried out early in the morning to meet Israel in battle at a certain place overlooking the Arabah. But he did not know that an ambush had been set against him behind the city. **15** Joshua and all Israel let themselves be driven back before them, and they fled towards the wilderness. **16** All the men of Ai were called to pursue them, and they pursued Joshua and were lured away from the city. **17** Not a man remained in Ai or Bethel who did not go after Israel. They left the city open and went in pursuit of Israel.

18 Then the LORD said to Joshua, 'Hold out towards Ai the javelin that is in your hand, for into your hand I will deliver the city.' So Joshua held out towards the city the javelin that was in his hand. **19** As soon as he did this, the men in the ambush rose quickly from their position and rushed forward. They entered the city and captured it and quickly set it on fire.

20 The men of Ai looked back and saw the smoke of the city rising up into the sky, but they had no chance to escape in any direction; the Israelites who had been fleeing towards the wilderness had turned back against their pursuers. **21** For when Joshua and all Israel saw that the ambush had taken the city and that smoke was going up from the city,

OBEDIENCE AND SUCCESS: THE BATTLE AGAINST AI

they turned round and attacked the men of Ai. **22** Those in the ambush also came out of the city against them, so that they were caught in the middle, with Israelites on both sides. Israel cut them down, leaving them neither survivors nor fugitives. **23** But they took the king of Ai alive and brought him to Joshua.

24 When Israel had finished killing all the men of Ai in the fields and in the wilderness where they had chased them, and when every one of them had been put to the sword, all the Israelites returned to Ai and killed those who were in it. **25** Twelve thousand men and women fell that day – all the people of Ai. **26** For Joshua did not draw back the hand that held out his javelin until he had destroyed[a] all who lived in Ai. **27** But Israel did carry off for themselves the livestock and plunder of this city, as the LORD had instructed Joshua.

28 So Joshua burned Ai[b] and made it a permanent heap of ruins, a desolate place to this day. **29** He impaled the body of the king of Ai on a pole and left it there until evening. At sunset, Joshua ordered them to take the body from the pole and throw it down at the entrance of the city gate. And they raised a large pile of rocks over it, which remains to this day.

---

[a] 26 The Hebrew term refers to the irrevocable giving over of things or persons to the LORD, often by totally destroying them.
[b] 28 *Ai* means *the ruin*.

1. The plan to attack Ai • Joshua 8:1–9

God's reassurance and instruction (8:1–2)

God now takes the initiative in speaking to Joshua to reassure him that they have returned to 'normal operations' following the transgression of Achan. Joshua is not to fear or be dismayed, both of which he may have felt from chapter 7, which might have resulted in hesitation rather than boldness. He is now to attack Ai again, this time with the whole army.[2] God gives a series of four commands to action: 'Take', 'Go up', 'Attack', 'See'. The first three all flow from the fourth, 'See I have delivered . . .' (translated as 'For' in the NIV). Joshua is to realise that Ai is already given to them and therefore they are to attack in this way. The listing of 'king', 'people', 'city'

---

2 The 'whole army' is 'all the people of war', which may mean 'an entire division' rather than every fighting man, Harstad, *Joshua*, 334.

and 'land' shows the completeness of this. This reassurance from God echoes instructions given at the start of the book and before Jericho (Joshua 1:9; 6:2).

The connection with Jericho is tightened in verse 2 as they will repeat what they did there; the only difference is that they are allowed plunder this time. Hence, we should see the city as being 'devoted' to the Lord as Jericho was, but God is at liberty to release what is his if he wishes, so here he grants plunder.[3] God gives one specific tactic: to set an ambush. The details of this are unclear at this stage but, as with earlier passages, the details are filled out as the narrative unfolds.

Joshua's instructions (8:3–9)

Joshua's obedience to God's commands is clear in the immediate repetition of key words in verse 3: he 'goes up' to 'attack'. Joshua selects thirty thousand choice troops (literally 'men of valour') and sends them to hide behind the city as the ambush party. He explains that he, leading the rest of the army, will advance on Ai, and when attacked by them will flee. He anticipates the response of the inhabitants thinking it is a repeat of the previous battle. Then the ambush party will attack, with the confidence that 'the LORD your God will give it into your hand' (verse 7). Then they are then to set the city alight. The importance of doing as the LORD has commanded according to his word is stressed – this battle must be fought in obedience to God.

2. The attack and destruction of Ai • Joshua 8:10–29

The initial attack and deception (8:10–17)

Joshua and the elders lead the main army to Ai. The sequence of movement here is debated, with some seeing verses 11–13 as a 'flashback'.[4] They approach the city itself and then move a little way to

---

[3] The 'devotion' to the LORD is made explicit with the use of the word *herem* later in verse 26.
[4] Howard, *Joshua*, 205.

the north with a valley between them and the city. It may be that a detachment remains 'in front' of the city while the main force sets up camp on the north side. Verse 12 probably refers to the previously mentioned ambush group as their location is the same as verse 9. The oddity is that the number of men is different. Some think this is a second ambush party; alternatively, it is the same group, and the smaller number is a subset who attacked the city. The latter is more likely, as verse 13 summarises the Israelites' positions and only refers to two groups. Joshua's whereabouts that night is referred to again (as in verse 9), showing that the focus is very much on him as leader.[5]

The unfolding of the plan is described in verses 14–17: the king of Ai comes out with his army to fight but he is unaware of the ambush group lying in wait. The battle starts at an 'appointed place' (NIV 'certain place'); this probably isn't an agreed battleground but rather shows God's sovereign governing of the engagement. The Israelites fall back, as if being defeated, and then flee. The remaining soldiers in Ai are called to help with the pursuit and the city is left defenceless. The neighbouring town of 'Bethel' is mentioned for the first and only time here; it provides some men for the pursuit, but it is hard to know if it is also included in the defeat.

The ambush and defeat of Ai (8:18–23)

Now the Israelite plan swings into action. God tells Joshua to point his javelin towards Ai. This seems to be symbolic of God's giving them the city and acts as a sign to the ambush party who rush forward, capture the city and set it on fire. There is repeated use of the word 'hand' here: Joshua is told to raise the javelin in his hand, the city will be given into his hand, Joshua raises the javelin in his hand and the men attack when he raises his hand. This emphasises Joshua's instrumentality in the ensuing victory.

This now results in disaster for the army from Ai. They look over their shoulders and see the devastation of their city, and on turning back around they see the Israelites they have been pursuing now

---

[5] This is probably a different 'valley' from the one referred to in verse 11 as a different word is used.

attacking them, quickly followed by the ambush party from the city attacking their rear. The description is deliberately slow and detailed, allowing the reader to picture and absorb what is happening. The Israelites kill the army, leaving no survivors except the king of Ai.

The final victory (8:24–9)

The total annihilation of the army and the inhabitants is related in verses 24 and 25. The explanation comes in verse 26: Joshua continued to hold out his javelin until this total 'devotion' by death was complete.[6] Hence Joshua's holding out his hand with the javelin acts as a sign of God's judgment over Ai, and it is not withdrawn until judgment has fully fallen. The parallels with Moses reinforce Joshua's position as successor (see Exodus 14:16; 17:8–16). David Howard says that the use of the singular 'he' in verse 26 'reminds us of the uniqueness and importance of [Joshua's] position'.[7] This is written a way that is deliberately reminiscent of Jericho, but with the contrast in verse 27 of being allowed to take plunder from the city along with the reminder that this has been 'commanded' (NIV 'instructed') by God (see verse 2).

Ai, like Jericho, is burned and becomes desolate. We are told specifically of the execution of the king, who is hung on a tree or a pole.[8] It is explained in Deuteronomy that this is a sign of God's curse and so again shows that this is not an ordinary battle but a bringing of God's judgment (see Deuteronomy 21:22–3). That same passage commands the removal of someone hanging on a pole in this way before nightfall so as not to desecrate the land – hence Joshua's command here. The wording of the burial and of the stones remaining reminds the reader of Achan (Joshua 7:26). It is significant that the king is buried at the city gate: rather than being the place he would have sat to exercise judgment, it is now a memorial to the judgment exercised on him.

---

6 Using the key word *herem*. See Excursus: Devoting to the LORD.
7 Howard, *Joshua*, 210.
8 The word can mean a 'tree' or a piece of 'wood'.

OBEDIENCE AND SUCCESS: THE BATTLE AGAINST AI

KEY THEMES AND APPLICATION

God's use of ordinary means
The way victory over Ai is achieved provides a striking contrast with Jericho. At Jericho, the victory came through a miracle, and consequently the people had to have faith that the walls would fall as God has promised. At Ai, victory comes through use of military tactics and use of deception. But we are still told at the start that God has delivered the city into Joshua's hands (verse 1), and that is repeated at the key moment within the plan (verse 18). Hence the victory over Ai is as much a gift from God as that over Jericho, but it is achieved through 'ordinary means'.[9] That will, in fact, be the normal pattern from this point on.

There is a significant lesson here for us in how God works. He can and does work supernaturally. More commonly he works 'ordinarily', but both are equally his work. This is true of everything, from his provision of food to his advance of the kingdom through the gospel. It means we must not divide activities into those that we do and those that God does for us, but rather see God working through our efforts. It also means that while we of course admire the spectacular moments of God's working, we do not despise the ordinary.

A repeated picture of God's judgment
We noted the similarity to Jericho – specifically verses 2 and 26. We also noted the symbolism of Joshua's javelin, and the hanging of the king of Ai on a pole. All this points to God's judgment falling on Ai. This is a repeat of what we saw at Jericho.[10] Hence, we can point people to God's judgment of this world and the final judgment that will come when Jesus returns. There is a sense in which he, Jesus, will not withdraw his sword of judgment until it is complete. Some older commentators relate the burning of the city to the final fire of judgment. The church father Origen said of this passage:

---

9 This is common phrase for God's use of natural processes as opposed to supernatural.
10 For more on the theology behind this, see Excursus: Devoting to the LORD.

For it is not so much that a piece of land is forever uninhabitable, but that the place of demons will be uninhabitable when no one will sin and sin will not rule in anyone. Then the devil and his angels will be consigned to the eternal fire with our Lord Jesus Christ sitting as ruler and judge . . .[11]

The success of obedience
Following the disastrous attempt to attack in Ai in chapter 7, this chapter provides a contrasting success. Such success is clearly because of God's being with them rather than his anger burning against them (Joshua 7:1). It is also clear that God's blessing relies on their having dealt appropriately with Achan's sin and now following God's instructions obediently. God gives the commands and Joshua complies (verses 1–3, 18); Joshua commands the people and they comply (verses 8–9, 19). The picture being built through these events is that when Israel obeys God, they are successful, which is of course what God had promised (see Joshua 1:7–9). Marten Woudstra says that 'the object of the present chapter, therefore, is to show what can be done (and what *was* done) when God's people act in accordance with his will'.[12]

We should encourage people that following God's ways will bring God's blessings. There is usually an ongoing need among believers to be convinced that obedience will never be to our detriment. However, we need to be careful in applying this because we know that 'success' and 'blessing' may look very different from how we imagine; indeed, obedience to God may bring suffering (see, for example, 2 Timothy 3:12). In addition, as we have already mentioned, the trajectory of Joshua is towards increasing disobedience with a concomitant concern over the people's future. Their success at this stage is because of a leader who is obedient to God; our confidence is ultimately in Jesus and his obedience for us.

---

11 Origen, 'Homilies on Joshua', 8.5, in Franke, *Ancient Christian Commentary*, 48–9.
12 M. H. Woudstra, *Book of Joshua* (Grand Rapids: Eerdmans, 1981), 134 (emphasis original).

OBEDIENCE AND SUCCESS: THE BATTLE AGAINST AI

The curse of hanging on a tree
We saw that the king of Ai is seen as under God's curse, and as a representative of the city we can see this is true of the people at large as well. They suffer the consequences of that curse in their destruction. We may wish to draw a line to Jesus who takes our curse for us; this connection is made tighter because the curse of being hung on a pole is specifically applied to him:

> Christ redeemed us from the curse of the law by becoming a curse for us, for it is written: 'Cursed is everyone who is hung on a pole.' He redeemed us in order that the blessing given to Abraham might come to the Gentiles through Christ Jesus, so that by faith we might receive the promise of the Spirit. (Galatians 3:13–14)

This is ultimately how the blessing of the nations, which God promised through Abraham, can come to us.

The ethics of deception in war
This passage has been a source of debate as to whether deception is allowed within a war. The church father Augustine believed it teaches us that it is, if the war itself is just in nature:

> In as much as God ordered Joshua to plant an ambush in their rear, that is to plant warriors in hiding to ambush the enemy, we can learn that such treachery is not unjustly carried out by those who wage a just war.[13]

The sixteenth-century reformer John Calvin agreed:

> If war, then, is lawful, it is beyond all controversy that the usual methods of conquering may be lawfully employed, always provided that there be no violation of faith once pledged either by truce or in any other way.[14]

---

13 Augustine, 'Questions on Joshua 10–11', in Franke, *Ancient Christian Commentary*, 46.
14 Calvin, *Joshua*, 4:125.

8

The Shaping of the Relationship

Joshua 8:30–35

Having entered the land and seen the initial battles, we now pause in Israel's interactions with the native inhabitants of the land for them to perform a ceremonial enactment of their covenant relationship with God. This is usually referred to as a covenant 'renewal', although it is not called that in the passage. This ceremony was commanded previously through Moses, and so we will consider the relevant passages below.

We are not told why the Israelites enact this ceremony now, but it is significant in coming early in their time in the land and at a moment that does not make military sense (they would have had to travel some distance from Ai – see map 1).[1] It may be that the battles with Jericho and Ai are seen as one combined event which marks Israel's entry into the land and in that sense this is placed directly after the first victory.[2] At the heart of this ceremony is the shape of their relationship with God: how they will live with him as their God in the land he has given.

The covenant renewed at Mount Ebal

30 Then Joshua built on Mount Ebal an altar to the LORD, the God of Israel, **31** as Moses the servant of the LORD had commanded the Israelites. He built it according to what is written in the Book of the Law of Moses – an altar of uncut stones, on which no iron tool had been used. On it they offered to the LORD burnt offerings and sacrificed fellowship offerings. **32** There, in the presence of the Israelites, Joshua wrote on stones a copy of the law of Moses. **33** All the Israelites, with their elders, officials and judges, were standing on both sides of the ark of the covenant of

---

1 Howard, *Joshua*, 212.
2 Biddle, 'Literary Structures', 196–7.

the LORD, facing the Levitical priests who carried it. Both the foreigners living among them and the native-born were there. Half of the people stood in front of Mount Gerizim and half of them in front of Mount Ebal, as Moses the servant of the LORD had formerly commanded when he gave instructions to bless the people of Israel.

34 Afterwards, Joshua read all the words of the law – the blessings and the curses – just as it is written in the Book of the Law. **35** There was not a word of all that Moses had commanded that Joshua did not read to the whole assembly of Israel, including the women and children, and the foreigners who lived among them.

1. *The background in Deuteronomy*

This ceremony was commanded in Deuteronomy 27 and involved two key physical components. First, there was the use of stones covered with plaster on which the Law was to be written (Deuteronomy 27:2–3). Second, an altar was to be built and sacrifices were to be offered (Deuteronomy 27:5–7). All of this was to be on Mount Ebal. The altar was specifically to be made of stones on which no iron tool had been used. This use of uncut stones comes from an earlier command applying to all altars (see Exodus 20:25) and may be to avoid any 'shaping' of an altar which could betray the second commandment. The German theologian Johannes Brenz (1499–1570) comments that 'shaping stones with iron is instituting some work by human intelligence for the worship of God'.[3] These two sets of stones form a joint monument combining worship and law-keeping.

There was then to be a recital of the Law of Moses with its blessings and curses. This was to be done with six tribes standing on Mount Ebal and six on Mount Gerizim, one group pronouncing the blessings, and the other the curses (Deuteronomy 27:12–13). These two hills are very close to each other and form a natural amphitheatre. In Deuteronomy, this ceremony acts as a summary and enforcement of the covenant relationship between the Israelites and

---

3 Johannes Brenz, 'Commentary on Joshua 8:30–31', in Amos, *Reformation Commentary*, 122.

the LORD. We should note, though, that Deuteronomy foresees the disobedience of later generations and so their experience of God's curses. It then looks beyond that to a time when 'The LORD your God will circumcise your hearts and the hearts of your descendants, so that you may love him with all your heart and with all your soul, and live' (Deuteronomy 30:6). So even as this ceremony is conducted and the Law is read, the participants (and later readers) would know of their need for this internal work of God for them ever to obey. This background is very significant for our understanding of the enactment in Joshua 8.

2. The building of the altar and offering of sacrifices • Joshua 8:30–31

We are told first of the building of the altar. As soon as Mount Ebal is mentioned as the location, Deuteronomy 27 would be in the reader's mind. It is said to be built specifically in fulfilment of what God has commanded through Moses, emphasised by saying it is 'according to what is written in the Book of the Law of Moses'.

On this altar, two types of offerings are then made: burnt offerings and fellowship offerings, which are those specified in Deuteronomy 27. These are the same offerings as performed within the formation of the covenant at Sinai (Exodus 20:24; 24:5). They are later detailed in Leviticus. The burnt offering is God's provision to deal with sin: the sacrifice makes atonement for the people (Leviticus 1:4). The fellowship offering (or peace offering) gives thanks to God and is seen to express or establish harmonious relationship (Leviticus 3).[4] These sacrifices both allow and express ongoing relationship between a sinful people and a holy God. In Deuteronomy, these offerings also involve the people 'rejoicing in the presence of the LORD your God' (Deuteronomy 27:7). God has made a way for us to know him and be close to him, and this is a reason for celebration. This is therefore both a solemn and a joyful occasion.

---

4 Harstad, *Joshua*, 362.

3. The writing and reading of the Law • Joshua 8:32–5

The Law is written on stones covered in plaster, as commanded in Deuteronomy. The Law of Moses in its fulness is the entire Torah, the first five books of the Old Testament, and so it is not simply law as the form of 'command', but more broadly 'instruction'. Sections of Deuteronomy summarised the 'commands' of this Law, which could be summed up even further in the Ten Commandments.[5] We do not know the extent of the Law written out here.

We are then told of the arrangement of the people. First, this is with respect to the Ark and the Levitical priests who stand in the centre, so God's presence is at the heart of this ceremony; they are gathered around him. Second, this is with respect to the two hills, with half the Israelites in front of Mount Ebal and half in front of Mount Gerizim. Then Joshua read all the words of the Law out loud. This is where the enactment appears to deviate from the commands in Deuteronomy, which said that the tribes were to read the Law to each other. However, Deuteronomy only indicates the tribes as having a responsive role, and they may have played that part in this ceremony. The emphasis here is on Joshua completing the ceremony as commanded.

Two elements are especially stressed in this section. First, that *all of the Law* is read. This is stated positively – 'Joshua read all the words of the law' – and negatively – 'There was not a word of all that Moses had commanded that Joshua did not read.' Second, all of the Law is read to *all of the people*. Verse 33 says all the Israelites are present and clarifies that this includes both foreigners living among them as well as the native-born. Then verse 35 refers to the whole assembly, including women, children and foreigners. The category of foreigners shows that Israel is not ethnically bounded but is open to people joining. In Joshua we have already seen Rahab and her family; earlier examples include Egyptians who come up with Israel (Exodus 12:38).

This Law will shape the people's relationship with God and their experience of him in the land. That was the drum beat in

---

[5] Exodus 20:1–17; Deuteronomy 5:6–21.

Deuteronomy which lies behind this enactment. If Israel obeys, they will know God's blessing in the land in prosperity and harmony, but if they disobey, they will know God's curse in defeat and exclusion.

KEY THEMES AND APPLICATION

God determines how we relate to him
The writing and reading of the Law here reinforce who is in charge within the covenant relationship. God gives his Law to his people; they receive it, write it and read it, all with the purpose of obeying it. Jerome Creach expresses it like this:

> The community of faith is not to be an autocracy, in which one person exercises dominion. Nor is it to be a democracy, with all parties deciding together their common will. Rather the covenant community is to be a theocracy, every person seeking God's intention and being shaped by a divine purpose.[6]

We can go further and see not just that God commands through his Law, but that God decides the entire shape of the relationship with his people. God, being God and being the one who has rescued his people, determines how we now relate to him. There is no negotiation over the terms, and there is no different track to choose. God writes the covenant; we only sign it. If God's people are to live in relationship with God in the land he has given, it will be on his terms.

This connects to the emphasis on enacting exactly what Moses commanded and repeating exactly what he said. In that sense, this covenant ceremony involves a significant posture from Joshua and the people of Israel: that of submission and acceptance before God. We will consider the new covenant below but should recognise that we too should adopt that posture. God has graciously made it possible to relate to him; we respond with grateful acceptance of his terms rather than questioning them.

In many cultures, such an asymmetrical relationship, with such submission to the will of another, is anathema. It is commonly

---

6 Creach, *Joshua*, 83.

thought that we need to break free from precisely such subservience, which is limiting and restrictive of us. In teaching this passage, we will need to lead people to see that such a desire for autonomy is actually at the heart of sin; attitudes of dictating to God the basis on which we will relate to him are seeking to elevate ourselves above him. More positively, we will need to show people the graciousness of God in bringing us into relationship with him, the rightness that he determines the nature of that relationship and, above all, the true freedom and delight we can know in that relationship.

The inclusion of all the people
We noted the stress on all of Israel being present; the groups of leaders and priests are mentioned, but so are the women, children and foreigners. This shows us several things. First, the equality of all people: all these groups are considered part of the assembly as much as any other group; none is pushed to the margins.[7] Second, the responsibility of all people: everyone is to hear the Law and live within its commands. Third, the dignity of all people: everyone is addressed and is responsible to hear, listen and obey. Philippa Carter says:

> That women, children and aliens are specifically mentioned here illustrates their membership in Israel and, more important, their responsibility and accountability under the terms of the covenant.[8]

We could see a parallel with New Testament letters being written to whole churches and all members being expected to hear and respond.

Relationship with God involves grace and obedience
The Mosaic covenant re-enacted here is often presented as a covenant of 'works'. That is, the people's experience of God is determined by their level of obedience; they will know his blessings or curses depending on how they live. The conditionality of this covenant is inescapable and is fundamental to the ceremony itself. However, we

---
7 Firth, *Joshua*, 170.
8 Carter, 'Joshua', 123.

must beware casting the Mosaic covenant as purely conditional on their works. First, we must remember that this covenant relationship has only come about because of God's gracious rescue from Egypt: his deliverance came before his demands. The Ten Commandments themselves reflect this in the opening statement: 'I am the LORD your God, who brought you out of Egypt, out of the land of slavery' (Exodus 20:1). Second, the Law itself contains remedy for sin, seen here in the burnt offerings which make atonement. In giving the Law, and this recital of it, God is not asking for perfection but loyalty within the covenant. Third, obedience is not a condition of blessing in a mechanistic way, but rather is the means by which blessing flows. As David Jackman says:

> Obedience, then, is not the price that God demands in order to dispense his blessings from his otherwise reluctant grasp. Rather it is the means by which the channels of overflowing grace are kept open, so that all the blessings of the covenant faithfulness of Yahweh can be experienced by a dependent people who trust and obey.[9]

We have already mentioned the prediction of disloyalty seen in Deuteronomy, and so in reading this passage now we are led to be doubtful as to how the people will go on to live. But we also know God has promised to change people's hearts so that they will love him fully. This leads to our next point.

We live under the new covenant
Our understanding of how the covenants through Scripture relate to each other is a matter of debate and will depend on the individual's overall theological position. It is common to see the covenant with Abraham as the overarching covenant of salvation which brings blessing to all nations as fulfilled in the gospel.[10] The covenant with Moses is then a temporary dispensation within that, and is what is in view when we speak of the old covenant as opposed to the new

---

9 Jackman, *Joshua: People of God's Purpose*, 101.
10 See Genesis 12:1–3 and Galatians 3:8.

covenant.[11] Whatever overall schema is held, however, in applying this passage to Christian believers today, we must make clear that we are no longer under the Mosaic covenant.

This results in two significant differences. First, because of people's inability to keep the Law, Jesus comes as the perfect Israelite. He keeps the Law on our behalf and then takes the curse of the Law in his death (see Galatians 3:10–14). So rather than trying to deserve God's blessing through our works, we receive God's blessing through Jesus's work; rather than receiving God's curse because of our disobedience, Jesus takes it on our behalf. This is what changes our experience now from that described in the blessings and curses here. As the sixteenth-century reformer Martin Luther said of the old and new covenants (referred to as 'Testaments'):

> There is this difference between the two: the New is founded wholly on the promise of the merciful and faithful God, without our works; but the Old is founded also on our works. Therefore Moses does not promise beyond the extent to which they keep the statues and judgments. For this reason the Old Testament finally had to become antiquated and be put aside; it had to serve as a figure of that New and eternal Testament which began before the ages and will endure beyond the ages.[12]

Second, the work of God that was predicted in Deuteronomy 30:6 has come about. The circumcising of people's hearts spoken of there is elaborated later in the Old Testament. A new covenant is promised in Jeremiah 31:31–4 precisely because of the people's inability to keep the Law. One of the elements of the new covenant God promises is that his Law will be written on people's hearts rather than on stones. In other words, God will work in people to move them to obey, rather than simply having external commands. This is linked with the work of the Holy Spirit in renewing us, a work that starts at conversion but is not complete until the new creation.[13]

---

11 Hebrews 8:7–13.
12 Martin Luther, *Lectures on Deuteronomy, Volume 9*, trans. Richard R. Caemmerer, Luther's Works (Saint Louis: Concordia Publishing House, 1960), 63.
13 Also see Ezekiel 36:24–8; Joel 2:28–9.

In reading this passage, we should therefore be reminded and rejoice that God's Law is not simple written externally for us to read as it was for the Israelites. Rather, it is now written internally so that we will obey. And that is a good thing, because this is a good Law! Older commentators sometimes linked this idea with that of believers now forming the Temple or altar. The German reformer Konrad Pellikan wrote:

> Christ our Lord writes on living and perfect stones the second law, namely he writes the gospel and the commandment of love toward God and our neighbour onto the hearts of the faithful, which are stones suitable for the building on an altar.[14]

We should finish this passage rejoicing in the new covenant relationship, which God has brought about for us, and desiring to live loyally within it.

---

14 Konrad Pellikan, 'Commentary on Joshua 8:33–5', in Amos, *Reformation Commentary*, 123.

9

Salvation by Deception

Joshua 9

With Israel having established their covenant relationship with God, we now expect a renewed military engagement against the native inhabitants of the land. However, before that resumes, we are told of Joshua and Israel interacting with a particular group of the native inhabitants, the Gibeonites. Their approach to Israel is in stark contrast to the other tribal groups who prepare to fight; the Gibeonites seek a treaty but resort to deception to gain it. As a result, they become part of Israel, albeit as slaves. The definition of who forms God's people is being refined so that we see it revolves around people's response to God, not their ethnicity. While Joshua and Israel are portrayed as making a mistake here, there is still an overall positive feel to the inclusion of this tribe. As Adolph Harstad expresses it, 'God mercifully granted them a place in his covenant people, even if his acceptance of them came about through Israel's negligence.'[1]

The Gibeonite deception

9 Now when all the kings west of the Jordan heard about these things – the kings in the hill country, in the western foothills, and along the entire coast of the Mediterranean Sea as far as Lebanon (the kings of the Hittites, Amorites, Canaanites, Perizzites, Hivites and Jebusites) – **2** they came together to wage war against Joshua and Israel.

3 However, when the people of Gibeon heard what Joshua had done to Jericho and Ai, **4** they resorted to a ruse: they went as a delegation whose donkeys were loaded[a] with worn-out sacks and old wineskins, cracked and mended. **5** They put worn and patched sandals on their feet and wore old clothes. All the bread of their food supply was dry and mouldy. **6** Then they went

---

1 Harstad, *Joshua*, 373.

to Joshua in the camp at Gilgal and said to him and the Israelites, 'We have come from a distant country; make a treaty with us.'

7 The Israelites said to the Hivites, 'But perhaps you live near us, so how can we make a treaty with you?'

8 'We are your servants,' they said to Joshua.

But Joshua asked, 'Who are you and where do you come from?'

9 They answered: 'Your servants have come from a very distant country because of the fame of the LORD your God. For we have heard reports of him: all that he did in Egypt, 10 and all that he did to the two kings of the Amorites east of the Jordan – Sihon king of Heshbon, and Og king of Bashan, who reigned in Ashtaroth. 11 And our elders and all those living in our country said to us, "Take provisions for your journey; go and meet them and say to them, 'We are your servants; make a treaty with us.' " 12 This bread of ours was warm when we packed it at home on the day we left to come to you. But now see how dry and mouldy it is. 13 And these wineskins that we filled were new, but see how cracked they are. And our clothes and sandals are worn out by the very long journey.'

14 The Israelites sampled their provisions but did not enquire of the LORD. 15 Then Joshua made a treaty of peace with them to let them live, and the leaders of the assembly ratified it by oath.

16 Three days after they made the treaty with the Gibeonites, the Israelites heard that they were neighbours, living near them. 17 So the Israelites set out and on the third day came to their cities: Gibeon, Kephirah, Beeroth and Kiriath Jearim. 18 But the Israelites did not attack them, because the leaders of the assembly had sworn an oath to them by the LORD, the God of Israel.

The whole assembly grumbled against the leaders, 19 but all the leaders answered, 'We have given them our oath by the LORD, the God of Israel, and we cannot touch them now. 20 This is what we will do to them: we will let them live, so that God's wrath will not fall on us for breaking the oath we swore to them.' 21 They continued, 'Let them live, but let them be woodcutters and water-carriers in the service of the whole assembly.' So the leaders' promise to them was kept.

22 Then Joshua summoned the Gibeonites and said, 'Why did you deceive us by saying, "We live a long way from you," while actually you live near us? 23 You are now under a curse: you will never be released from service as woodcutters and water-carriers for the house of my God.'

24 They answered Joshua, 'Your

servants were clearly told how the LORD your God had commanded his servant Moses to give you the whole land and to wipe out all its inhabitants from before you. So we feared for our lives because of you, and that is why we did this. **25** We are now in your hands. Do to us whatever seems good and right to you.'

26 So Joshua saved them from the Israelites, and they did not kill them. **27** That day he made the Gibeonites woodcutters and water-carriers for the assembly, to provide for the needs of the altar of the LORD at the place the LORD would choose. And that is what they are to this day.

---

a 4 Most Hebrew manuscripts; some Hebrew manuscripts, Vulgate and Syriac (see also Septuagint) *They prepared provisions and loaded their donkeys*

1. The response of the kings of the land • Joshua 9:1–2

We first are told of the reaction of 'all the kings' in the Promised Land (clearly except for the Gibeonites).[2] The list of tribes is the same as in Joshua 3:10 except that the Girgashites are missing.[3] The response of these kings is prompted by hearing, but what is heard is not specified; it is presumably of the fall of Jericho and Ai. The kings in question and their territories are listed to convey the extensiveness of the area covered. Then we are ominously told that they gather to fight against Joshua and Israel. Whereas previously their hearing resulted in trembling in fear – see Joshua 5:1 – they are now galvanised into opposition. Their unity in this endeavour is emphasised: they 'gathered together' and were 'as one' (not translated by the NIV). Hence the scene is set for such a battle, but before that occurs, we are told of a different reaction.

---

2 The term describing the kings' location is 'beyond' the Jordan, which here means 'west of'. For this and discussion of geography, see Howard, *Joshua*, 220–21.
3 See comment in Appendix A: The Tribes of the Promised Land.

2. The response of the Gibeonites • Joshua 9:3–15

The Gibeonite plan (9:3–6)

When the people of Gibeon hear the same news (now with explicit reference to Jericho and Ai), they respond differently and act with 'cunning' or 'deception' (NIV 'ruse'). This word can be used positively or negatively depending on the context, so here we might simply say they acted 'cleverly'.[4] We are talked through their plan before knowing exactly what they hope to achieve by it, and so the reader is drawn into the story as experienced by the Israelites, except that we know things are not as they appear.

They send a delegation with food and clothing that give the appearance of having made a long journey. The text carefully lists their 'evidence', then we are told they go to Joshua ask to make a treaty with them. This is a 'covenant', such as between God and Israel, but also as established between people.[5] It is formal promise that shapes the relationship and commitments on both sides.

The Israelite response (9:7–15)

Israel has been explicitly warned by God not to make covenants like this with the inhabitants of the land (see Deuteronomy 7:2), and so they ask where the Gibeonites have come from. The Gibeonites are called 'Hivites' here, who were included in the list of opposing groups in verse 2. They are probably a subset of this larger group, but this name may be used here to remind the reader that they are one of the groups to be eliminated from the land.[6] They respond with the lie of having come from a distant country, but this is allied with the partial truth of having heard about Israel's God. Their speech in verses 9–10 is reminiscent of Rahab in chapter 2: they too have heard what God has done in the Exodus and the conquest of Sihon and Og. They omit to

---

4 Firth, *Joshua*, 176–7.
5 For example, as in Genesis 21:22–34.
6 Woudstra, *Joshua*, 157–8.

say that they have also heard of what God did to Jericho and Ai, which is what has prompted their delegation (presumably this would have given the lie to the location of their homeland, as this news could not have travelled so quickly). However, while not as explicitly stated as it was by Rahab, there is a right recognition of God in their thinking. They present themselves as 'your servants' (verses 8 and 11), meaning they are happy to be in a subservient relationship to Israel.

This leads into their presentation of the false evidence in the form of the previously listed items (verses 12–13). The Israelites 'sampled' their possessions, meaning they examined them, but, significantly, we are told they did not 'enquire of the LORD'. We are not told how this would have been done, but we do know that the high priest and the Urim and Thummim were provided for seeking God's guidance.[7] The Israelites are convinced by the Gibeonites' story and evidence, and so Joshua makes peace with them, formalised by a covenant. This covenant is 'to let them live', meaning they will live in harmony together and will not attack them. This again is reminiscent of Rahab and her family where the same word (to live) is used (see Joshua 2:13 and 6:17, 25).

> *3. The revealing of the truth and
> its consequences • Joshua 9:16–27*

Discovery and abiding by their oath (9:16–21)

We are not told how, but the Israelites soon discover they have been misled and so set out to meet the Gibeonites again in their cities. Their oath means they do not attack the Gibeonites, to the complaint of the people at large. The leaders hold their ground, saying they have sworn by the LORD and so are bound not to harm them. Breaking their oath would make them liable to punishment by God. The 'oath' made in verse 15 is referred to three times in verses 18–20, emphasising that they are bound by it. Instead, the proposal

---

7 See Numbers 27:21.

is to make the Gibeonites woodcutters and watercarriers serving the wider people. These are tasks that were specified for foreigners within Israel (see Deuteronomy 29:11).

Discussion with Joshua (9:22–7)

Joshua calls the Gibeonites to question them regarding their actions and declares that they will be under the curse of perpetual service to the Israelites. This service is specifically for the 'house of my God', which probably refers to the Tent of Meeting but anticipates the Temple.[8] The Gibeonites' answer gives us a more detailed insight into their understanding: they know of the command through Moses to destroy the inhabitants of the land and so they knew they would die. This is why they resorted to deception. They admit this and entrust themselves into Joshua's hands: the request to do what is 'good and right' is a call for what is just in the eyes of God.[9]

The summary at the end repeats this conclusion but with an interesting angle. First, Joshua is said to have 'saved' the Gibeonites from the Israelites. This looks back to verses 18–19 and the insistence of the leaders that they keep their oath, and means Joshua was key within this. Second, they are made servants, as previously mentioned, but it is now detailed to be for the 'altar of the LORD at the place the LORD would choose'. This refers to the place of worship God would designate in the land (see Deuteronomy 12:4–7).

KEY THEMES AND APPLICATION

Failing to consult God
The comment on the Israelites in verse 14 is damning. It is not that they were gullible, because they asked questions, examined the evidence and drew a conclusion. The issue is that they were self-reliant; they relied on their own judgment and failed to seek God. As Dale Ralph Davis puts it, 'It is not that they were sloppy

---

8 Firth, *Joshua*, 184.
9 Howard, *Joshua*, 230.

in their investigation but that they were alone in their decision.'[10] Applying this today is harder because we do not have the direct access to God's answers that Joshua appeared to have. However, we can see that there is an attitude towards God we should desire, of dependence and seeking, versus an attitude towards self, of confidence and presumption. Leaders and churches as a whole should be very mindful of this, especially when making significant decisions, and our dependence and seeking will surely be expressed in prayerfulness.

Keeping oaths
While the Israelites' oath was poorly made, it was still made, and once made it needed to be honoured. There is no verdict from God on this issue, but the clear picture is that they were right to stick to their oath and let the Gibeonites live. Interestingly, today we might say that they made this oath under false pretences and so it would be void.[11] However, the leaders say they made their oath 'by the LORD, the God of Israel'; his character overshadows their oath and so it must be kept. This is reiterated later in the biblical story when king Saul goes against Joshua's oath and tries to eliminate the Gibeonites and David makes recompense for this (see 2 Samuel 21:1–3).

Inclusion of the Gibeonites with God's people
While the Gibeonites are deceptive and the Israelites are seen to be at fault, the result is inclusion within Israel. They are included as 'servants' but are servants of the 'house of . . . God', serving the 'needs of the altar'. One of the great concerns regarding the inhabitants of the land was that they would lead Israel to worship false gods. Instead, the move here is that the people of the land will aid Israel in their worship of the true God. David Jackman reads the Gibeonites' deception as Satanic in nature, seeking to undermine Israel from within, and then sees this outcome as God's sovereign ruling and protection.[12] We might not read the Gibeonites so negatively but can still see God's gracious providence at work.

---

10 Davis, *Joshua*, 77.
11 Commentators have debated whether this oath was required to be kept, with differing opinions being argued.
12 Jackman, *Joshua: People of God's Purpose*, 110.

While different in their deception, the Gibeonites are often seen as a parallel to Rahab – and we have seen the similarities in the text. They stand as an example of those who recognise the true God and lay down their arms before him. The English reformer John Mayer (1583–1664) said:

> It was not unlawful to save such as submitted themselves, and yielded to become proselytes, as did Rahab and her house, and as these Gibeonites did. For the command to destroy all was doubtless to be understood with this exception: that in some extraordinary case, when any of them should voluntarily yield from their possessions and religion, and be at their disposing.[13]

As a result of this treaty the Gibeonites are now bound together with Israel. We will see this confirmed in the next passage where an attack on the Gibeonites means Israel comes to their defence. Later we are told that the Gibeonites are the only city that made peace with Israel, and it is portrayed as a positive thing that other cities could have done if they had wanted to (Joshua 11:18–19). This again shows us that the relationship with the people of the land is nuanced. The majority will be killed as God's judgment falls on them through Israel, but there is the possibility of siding with Israel instead and so being saved. We later read of individual Gibeonites being part of Israel (see 1 Chronicles 12:4; Nehemiah 3:7; 7:25).

This is particularly significant in our understanding of God and his command to kill the inhabitants. William Ford argues that the Gibeonites (along with Rahab) show that God's command still leaves room for people's response, and he 'can and will respond with acceptance and mercy when people respond appropriately to him'.[14] Similarly, John Goldingay says, 'In principle Canaanites must be eliminated, but Canaanites who behave like Israelites may take their place within the people of God. Israel's nation boundaries are critically important, but flexible.'[15]

---

13 John Mayer, 'Commentary on Joshua 9:3', in Amos, *Reformation Commentary*, 126.
14 William Ford, 'What About the Gibeonites?', *Tyndale Bulletin* 66, no. 2 (2015): 216.
15 John Goldingay, *Old Testament Theology: Israel's Gospel, Volume 1* (Downers Grove: IVP Academic, 2003), 511.

So, while their methods are condemned as deceptive, the stance the Gibeonites take is commended. This raises the question as to whether there was a more honest way they could have been saved. The English minister Charles Simeon (1759–1836) said, 'Their better way would certainly have been to declare the whole truth and to implore Joshua's intercession with God to spare their lives and instruct them in the knowledge of his ways.'[16]

---

16 Charles Simeon, *Horae Homileticae, Volume 2* (London: H. G. Bohn, 1855), 588.

10

Having God on Your Side

Joshua 10:1–15

After the initial battles with Jericho and Ai there was a pause for the covenant affirmation and then the interaction with the Gibeonites. But now the focus shifts back to the native inhabitants of the land and the expected battles against them. We have previously been told that many kings gathered to fight Israel (Joshua 9:1–2), but now the treaty with Gibeon has a further effect: the surrounding tribes perceive an increased threat against them and band together to fight. They target Gibeon itself, but this draws in Israel and leads to a climactic battle. With God fighting for them, Israel is victorious. But the focus is not so much on the fact of victory as on the manner of it; the nature of the battle, and especially Joshua's role within it, teaches Israel, and us, about God and how he works.

The sun stands still

10 Now Adoni-Zedek king of Jerusalem heard that Joshua had taken Ai and totally destroyed[a] it, doing to Ai and its king as he had done to Jericho and its king, and that the people of Gibeon had made a treaty of peace with Israel and had become their allies. **2** He and his people were very much alarmed at this, because Gibeon was an important city, like one of the royal cities; it was larger than Ai, and all its men were good fighters. **3** So Adoni-Zedek king of Jerusalem appealed to Hoham king of Hebron, Piram king of Jarmuth, Japhia king of Lachish and Debir king of Eglon. **4** 'Come up and help me attack Gibeon,' he said, 'because it has made peace with Joshua and the Israelites.'

5 Then the five kings of the Amorites – the kings of Jerusalem, Hebron, Jarmuth, Lachish and Eglon – joined forces. They moved up with all their troops and took up positions against Gibeon and attacked it.

6 The Gibeonites then sent word to Joshua in the camp at Gilgal: 'Do not abandon your servants. Come up to us quickly and save us! Help us, because all the Amorite kings from the hill country have joined forces against us.'

⁷ So Joshua marched up from Gilgal with his entire army, including all the best fighting men. ⁸ The LORD said to Joshua, 'Do not be afraid of them; I have given them into your hand. Not one of them will be able to withstand you.'

⁹ After an all-night march from Gilgal, Joshua took them by surprise. ¹⁰ The LORD threw them into confusion before Israel, so Joshua and the Israelites defeated them completely at Gibeon. Israel pursued them along the road going up to Beth Horon and cut them down all the way to Azekah and Makkedah. ¹¹ As they fled before Israel on the road down from Beth Horon to Azekah, the LORD hurled large hailstones down on them, and more of them died from the hail than were killed by the swords of the Israelites.

¹² On the day the LORD gave the Amorites over to Israel, Joshua said to the LORD in the presence of Israel:

'Sun, stand still over Gibeon,
    and you, moon, over the Valley
        of Aijalon.'

¹³ So the sun stood still,
    and the moon stopped,
    till the nation avenged itself
        on[b] its enemies,

as it is written in the Book of Jashar.

The sun stopped in the middle of the sky and delayed going down about a full day. ¹⁴ There has never been a day like it before or since, a day when the LORD listened to a human being. Surely the LORD was fighting for Israel!

¹⁵ Then Joshua returned with all Israel to the camp at Gilgal.

---

a 1 The Hebrew term refers to the irrevocable giving over of things or persons to the Lord, often by totally destroying them; also in verses 28, 35, 37, 39 and 40.

b 13 Or *nation triumphed over*

1. The coalition against Gibeon and their call for help • Joshua 10:1–6

The last chapter began with the tribal kings hearing of Israel's exploits and joining together to fight. Now Adoni-Zedek, the king of Jerusalem, hears both of victory at Ai and of the treaty with Gibeon and this sparks him into action. The news causes fear because of Gibeon's status. It is like a royal city, which means it is influential over other neighbouring cities, it is large, and its men are known as warriors.

This results in an appeal to four other kings to join in attacking Gibeon because of her alliance with Israel. We see here the nature of Gibeon's covenant: it means siding with Israel and so becoming an enemy within her own land. The coalition of five kings are all called 'Amorites' here, possibility meaning they are part of one larger tribal group, as opposed to the Hivites to which Gibeon belonged, but these terms can used more loosely.[1] The cities are listed a second time (verse 5), showing the overpowering nature of this combined force. There is an ominous feel to the second half of verse 5 which describes their movements with four verbs: they 'gathered' their forces, 'went up', 'laid siege' and 'attacked'.

The Gibeonites, despite their size and warriors, are clearly outnumbered and so send to Joshua for help. Their call is for Joshua not to 'loosen his hand' from them – i.e., not to give up or let go of them (NIV 'abandon').[2] This is an understood implication of their covenant arrangement: Joshua should not now abandon them, but rather should come to their rescue.

2. Israel's victory and God's action • Joshua 10:7–15

Israel's victory (10:7–11)

Joshua responds immediately, taking with him the whole army, including his best warriors. God's encouragement is given after Joshua's initial reaction, so affirming him in it. As with previous battles, Joshua is told not to fear (see Joshua 8:1) and is assured of victory as God has given the enemy into his hands (see Joshua 6:2; 8:1). The reassurance here is made more emphatic with the addition that not one of them will 'withstand you' (literally 'stand before you', echoing Joshua 1:5). David Firth says of this, 'God's speech thus brings together earlier promises that Joshua knew had been fulfilled to assure him of the certainty of success against these kings.'[3] We should note that this is directed to Joshua in the singular, highlighting his role as God's leader.

---

[1] Firth, *Joshua*, 194. See Appendix A: The Tribes of the Promised Land.
[2] This echoes God's promise not to let go of Joshua in chapter 1:5.
[3] Firth, *Joshua*, 196.

The action is then described in a breathless rush: Joshua comes on the Amorite kings 'suddenly' (NIV 'by surprise') following an all-night march. The battle itself is described very briefly with two components: the confusion brought about by God and the defeat inflicted by Israel. This sudden effective strike is followed by a slower description of the pursuit and elimination of the army. The Amorites are chased and killed by the pursuing Israelites: the places listed let us view them fleeing north-west (to Beth Horon) and then towards the south to Azekah, and further south to Makkedah), being cut down all the way. On top of this, God sends large hailstones, which kill even more of them.[4] The combination of divine and human action is blurred as the subjects of some verbs are unclear: the Amorites may have been struck by, and fled before, God or the Israelites.[5] Such blurring may be deliberate in that God is the one at work, but through his people.

Joshua's prayer and its results (10:12–15)

The narrative pauses in verse 12 to reflect on an unexpected element; it will pick up on the fleeing kings again in verse 16. These events do not necessarily follow chronologically from verses 9–11; rather, they give a complementary perspective on them. They focus on Joshua's prayer, specified to be on this day. His words are semi-poetic and they call for the sun and moon to stand still. The prayer is said to be recorded in the Book of Jashar, which is also referred to in 2 Samuel 1:18 but is otherwise unknown.

The most common understanding is that Joshua sees that more time is needed for the pursuit and elimination of the enemy – which would have been hindered by nightfall – and so calls for the sun to stand still. Verse 13b then describes this again in prose: that the sun stopped and delayed going down, extending the daylight by another day. Alternatively, Joshua is asking for the sun to cease in its shining rather than its movement and so is asking for an extension of

---

[4] The word used is not the usual word for hailstones; it simply means 'stones', and so some believe this isn't a meteorological phenomenon. However, this word is used occasionally elsewhere referring to hail (e.g., Ezekiel 13:11).
[5] Firth, *Joshua*, 196.

darkness.[6] There are several other interpretations, the most convincing of which is that Joshua is calling on cosmic forces, represented by sun and moon, to fight for Israel.[7] This sees the words as figurative, and there is a similar reference in Habakkuk 3:11. While such a figurative interpretation is possible, it involves stretching the usual meaning of some words and overall is unconvincing.[8]

The narrator then comments that there has never been a day like it, before or after. His amazement, though, seems to be less about the miraculous stopping of the sun as that it occurs in response to Joshua: it is the day God listens to a human. The comment that God is fighting for Israel is seen by the NIV as a climatic conclusion drawn from these events ('Surely . . .'). Alternatively, it is an explanation of the previous statements ('For . . .').

That God listened to a human is not a surprise, as there are many examples of answered prayer prior to this in Scripture. There is a difference here in the strength of statement: the words used present God as 'obeying' the voice of a person, but while rare, this is not unique.[9] What is unique here is the combination of God's response and the nature of the miracle involved. The result is to highlight the role Joshua plays: God listens to him.

Verse 15 is odd in that it describes a return to the Israelite base camp, while the next section will continue to describe the pursuit of the kings; the words of verse 15 are repeated in verse 43. There are several potential explanations.[10] What is clear is that this verse serves to end this section and so we will read the continuation of the events of the five kings with the remainder of the chapter.[11]

---

[6] Davis, who argues for this view, suggests it would have delayed the sapping heat of the day. Davis, *Joshua*, 84–6.
[7] For this argument, see Firth, *Joshua*, 199–200.
[8] For an overview of interpretations, see Howard, *Joshua*, 241–8.
[9] See Numbers 21:3 and 1 Kings 17:22.
[10] Howard, *Joshua*, 251.
[11] The start of verse 16 and the link in verse 28 also suggest this division.

KEY THEMES AND APPLICATION

God is the one fighting
While Israel engages in the battle, it is very clear that God is the one doing the fighting and giving the victory. We see this is in the confusion of verse 10, the hailstones of verse 11 and the miracle of verses 12–14. It is a repeat of what we saw at Jericho and Ai, but with a variation in presentation which stresses that God is fighting for Israel. The Israelites would know that victory was only because of God, not because of them. This points us to a general truth in the Christian life and ministry: God is the one at work, and things of substance will only be achieved if he is at work. We might point to passages such as Matthew 16:18, 1 Corinthians 3:6–7; Philippians 3:13.

This also contributes to our picture of God. We have seen this previously in Joshua, but it is particularly pointed in this passage: God is a warrior who fights. This is an underemphasised presentation of God in many parts of the world today, being seen as too harsh or unloving. We must say that such a picture is not at odds with God as a father who listens to us (Matthew 7:11) or as a mother who has compassion on us (Isaiah 49:15). Rather, it puts steel into such images: the very one who listens and who has compassion is mighty and will fight for us. In some contexts, perhaps where the idea of opposing spiritual forces is accepted, this picture of God will be reassuring: no other power can stand against him. In other contexts, perhaps more secular settings, it will challenge the temptation to domesticate God to fit cultural expectations or our preferences. Such a neutered God will end up being no use to us. As Dale Ralph Davis says:

> No mild God or soft Jesus can give his people hope. It is only as we know the warrior of Israel who fights for us (and sometimes without us) that we have hope of triumphing in the muck of life.[12]

---

12 Davis, *Joshua*, 84.

God fights through his leader

While the battle is fought by Israel as a whole, we have noted the key role Joshua plays. God's reassurance is to him specifically in verse 8; he leads the people in battle, and then, most significantly, God responds to his prayer. God grants victory through his anointed leader. We have seen this already in Joshua, but it is particularly prominent here. For the Christian, this must point us to Jesus and the victory God gives through him. We can speak of God's promise to be with and work through Jesus, and of God hearing Jesus's prayer and responding.

God is for his people

God fights for his people and so he is on their side. God's people can be assured of God's commitment to them. This could take us to passages such Romans 8:31–9: 'If God is for us, who can be against us?' This passage shows a God who is for us.

This is to encourage us in prayer. The sixteenth-century reformer Martin Luther makes the point from this passage that God responds to Joshua's prayer, and goes on to say:

> Thus this account serves to rouse and spur us on to prayer in all our dangers, since God wants to do what we want, provided that we humbly prostrate ourselves before him and pray . . . And in Scripture there are more evidences of this kind; they prove that God allows Himself to be prevailed upon and subordinates His will to ours. Why then are we so remiss in regard to prayer?[13]

We might strengthen this point by considering the failure of Joshua and the people in chapter 9 in not consulting God over the treaty with the Gibeonites. Despite that failure, God is still for them and honours their treaty. Hence, we are not trapped in past mistakes. Oginde draws a sharp contrast with traditional African religions in which the gods respond badly to any failure, and so worshippers must always walk in trepidation.[14]

---

13 Martin Luther, *Lectures on Genesis: Chapters 15–20, Volume 3*, trans. George V. Schick, Luther's Works (Saint Louis: Concordia Publishing House, 1961), 289.
14 Oginde, 'Joshua', 281.

The experience of believers in the world
While not the main point of the passage, many commentators see the Gibeonites and Israel as illustrating elements of the experience of believers today. There are often three points made. First, the Gibeonites suffer persecution for aligning themselves with God. Having allied themselves with Joshua in the previous chapter, this now brings them into trouble with the surrounding tribes. This illustrates the new battles we may face on allying ourselves with Christ and his church in the world. The church father Origen said, 'There is no doubt that when a human soul associates itself with the Word of God, it is immediately going to have enemies, and that those it once considered friends will be changed into adversaries.'[15]

Second, the Gibeonites illustrate prayer: they call on Joshua, and so on God, in their moment of trouble. Many commentators have seen here a picture of how we call on Jesus. The Anglican minister Charles Simeon says, 'Such is the way in which Christians also must obtain deliverance. If they attempt to resist their enemies in their own strength, they will infallibly be vanquished, but if they take themselves to prayer, they cannot but succeed.'[16]

Third, the Israelites stand together with the Gibeonites, illustrating how we should help Christian brothers and sisters who are under attack. Adolph Harstad says:

> The entire church militant must rush to the aid whenever any members of the body of Christ are under attack . . . Even if persecuted Christians are on the other side of the globe, we may instantly support them in prayer to the Lord, who alone is able to defend and preserve them unto life everlasting.[17]

---

15 Origen, 'Homilies on Joshua', 11.2 in Franke, *Ancient Christian Commentary*, 56–7.
16 Simeon, *Horae Homileticae*, 2:594.
17 Harstad, *Joshua*, 408.

11

Symbolising and Realising Victory

Joshua 10:16–43

We previously have seen battles against Jericho and Ai and then, following the Gibeonite treaty with Israel, in rescuing Gibeon. That rescue involved fighting against five kings and their armies. The previous passage detailed their defeat and the flight of their armies, and we now return to the five kings and see their demise. They act as a worked example of what will happen with the other cities in the Promised Land, and we are then taken on a whirlwind tour of the victories in the southern region. Six cities and their rulers are described in brief sketches with repeated themes, plus one extra king and city is involved, albeit differently. These form part of one campaign where the victory is because 'the LORD, the God of Israel, fought for Israel' (verse 42). The overall effect is to enforce to the reader that God will give his people the victory he has promised.

Five Amorite kings killed

16 Now the five kings had fled and hidden in the cave at Makkedah. **17** When Joshua was told that the five kings had been found hiding in the cave at Makkedah, **18** he said, 'Roll large rocks up to the mouth of the cave, and post some men there to guard it. **19** But don't stop; pursue your enemies! Attack them from the rear and don't let them reach their cities, for the LORD your God has given them into your hand.'

20 So Joshua and the Israelites defeated them completely, but a few survivors managed to reach their fortified cities. **21** The whole army then returned safely to Joshua in the camp at Makkedah, and no one uttered a word against the Israelites.

22 Joshua said, 'Open the mouth of the cave and bring those five kings out to me.' **23** So they brought the five kings out of the cave - the kings of Jerusalem, Hebron, Jarmuth, Lachish and Eglon. **24** When they had brought

JOSHUA

these kings to Joshua, he summoned all the men of Israel and said to the army commanders who had come with him, 'Come here and put your feet on the necks of these kings.' So they came forward and placed their feet on their necks.

25 Joshua said to them, 'Do not be afraid; do not be discouraged. Be strong and courageous. This is what the LORD will do to all the enemies you are going to fight.' 26 Then Joshua put the kings to death and exposed their bodies on five poles, and they were left hanging on the poles until evening.

27 At sunset Joshua gave the order and they took them down from the poles and threw them into the cave where they had been hiding. At the mouth of the cave they placed large rocks, which are there to this day.

Southern cities conquered

28 That day Joshua took Makkedah. He put the city and its king to the sword and totally destroyed everyone in it. He left no survivors. And he did to the king of Makkedah as he had done to the king of Jericho.

29 Then Joshua and all Israel with him moved on from Makkedah to Libnah and attacked it. 30 The LORD also gave that city and its king into Israel's hand. The city and everyone in it Joshua put to the sword. He left no survivors there. And he did to its king as he had done to the king of Jericho.

31 Then Joshua and all Israel with him moved on from Libnah to Lachish; he took up positions against it and attacked it. 32 The LORD gave Lachish into Israel's hands, and Joshua took it on the second day. The city and everyone in it he put to the sword, just as he had done to Libnah. 33 Meanwhile, Horam king of Gezer had come up to help Lachish, but Joshua defeated him and his army – until no survivors were left.

34 Then Joshua and all Israel with him moved on from Lachish to Eglon; they took up positions against it and attacked it. 35 They captured it that same day and put it to the sword and totally destroyed everyone in it, just as they had done to Lachish.

36 Then Joshua and all Israel with him went up from Eglon to Hebron and attacked it. 37 They took the city and put it to the sword, together with its king, its villages and everyone in it. They left no survivors. Just as at Eglon, they totally destroyed it and everyone in it.

38 Then Joshua and all Israel with him turned round and attacked Debir. 39 They took the city, its king and its villages, and put them to the sword. Everyone in it they totally destroyed. They left no survivors. They did to Debir and its king as they had done to Libnah and its king and to Hebron.

40 So Joshua subdued the whole region, including the hill country, the Negev, the western foothills and the mountain slopes, together with all their kings. He left no survivors. He totally destroyed all who breathed, just as the LORD, the God of Israel, had commanded. **41** Joshua subdued them from Kadesh Barnea to Gaza and from the whole region of Goshen to Gibeon. **42** All these kings and their lands Joshua conquered in one campaign, because the LORD, the God of Israel, fought for Israel.

43 Then Joshua returned with all Israel to the camp at Gilgal.

1. Defeat of the Amorite kings • Joshua 10:16–27

The continuation of the pursuit (10:16–21)

The five kings listed earlier in the chapter now hide in a cave at Makkedah, which was their destination in fleeing in verse 10. We should picture the change from their confident gathering together of their armies to go to war, to their helpless hiding together at the back of a cave. It sums up their defeat and the futility of fighting against God. On hearing of them, Joshua's tactic is to trap them in the cave so they cannot escape while the pursuit of the regular soldiers continues. Joshua commands this ongoing pursuit to take full advantage of their enemies' vulnerability outside their cities.

The summary in verse 20 is that the Amorite armies are defeated completely. This is clearly a hyperbolic overstatement, as the same verse goes on to speak of survivors who did reach the safety of the cities. What is to be envisaged is a crushing, but not entire, defeat. With this, the Israelites return to camp at Makkedah. The comment that 'no one uttered a word against the Israelites' speaks of the lack of opposition: no one dares speak against them, let alone act against them.[1]

The execution of the kings (10:22–7)

The kings are then brought out at Joshua's command and listed for the third time. Rather than proceeding immediately with execution, Joshua draws the people and the commanders into a symbolic act. The people

---

[1] See the only other use of this phrase in Exodus 11:7.

are gathered and the commanders are told to put their feet on the kings' necks, and the narrative slows to describe their doing so. This act, which is known of in Ancient Near East pictures, symbolises subjection of these kings under the Israelites.[2] We should picture the scene and then hear Joshua's words in verse 25. He calls for confidence using two negatives (not being afraid or discouraged) and two positives (being strong and courageous). This repeats God's words to Joshua in chapter 1.[3] The call to confidence is because this is what God will do to all the enemies they will now face. Placing their feet is therefore not only symbolic of this present victory, but also prophetic, anticipating future victory.

Dale Ralph Davis says of this action:

> The leaders' feet upon the necks of these prostrated kings was an acted parable, an assuring sign, of how Yahweh would certainly place all their enemies beneath them. The symbolic action is intended as a visible encouragement to the people of God.[4]

Having been executed, the kings are hung on poles (or trees). As we saw with the king of Ai, this demonstrates God's curse and, once again, in accordance with the Law, they are taken down at sunset (see Joshua 8:29).[5] Their previous place of safety, having become a prison, now becomes their tomb. This is the third mention of burial stones which are 'there to this day', all of which have symbolised God's judgment (previously in Joshua 7:26; 8:29).

2. Defeat of the southern cities • Joshua 10:28–43

The southern campaign (10:28–39)

There now comes the list of defeated cities. We will not discuss each in detail but rather make some comments on the whole section. In terms of activity, each city involves a victorious battle which is described

---

2 Hubbard, 'What Do These Stones Mean?', 20.
3 See Joshua 1:9; identical words are used apart from that for 'afraid'.
4 Davis, *Joshua*, 87.
5 Deuteronomy 21:23.

as putting the inhabitants to the sword. We see the repeated use of the key word 'totally destroyed' – previously translated as 'devoted' in chapter 6. This word comes in verses 28, 35, 37 and 39 and is then used in summary in verse 40. While it is not used explicitly of every city, it is the term that describes the entire activity and so shows God's sovereign judgment, as we have seen before.[6] There is also a common use of the formula, 'he did to city X as he had done to city Y', where a previous city serves as a template for a later one. This starts in verse 28 with reference back to Jericho and comes again in verses 30, 32, 35, 37 and 39. This again serves to emphasise the similarity between the cities.

There is a repeated reference to there being no survivors, although this is not used in every case. That will be repeated in the summary section, and we will comment on it below. The only battle that is slightly different is that in verse 33. Instead of attacking a city, Joshua fights against Horam king of Gezer who has come to help Lachish. While Horam and his army are defeated, Gezer itself is not attacked. With the mention of Gezer there are seven cities in all. This is only a representative list as other cities are mentioned later in chapter 12 as being defeated which are not listed here, and two of the five cities from earlier in the chapter are not included. Choosing seven cities may be deliberate to give the picture of completion.[7]

Summary of southern campaign (10:40–43)

The NIV summarises, saying Joshua 'subdued' the whole region; it is more specifically 'striking' the whole region. The result would have been that it was subdued, but the focus is on the action of attacking. The region in question is then outlined, and the action of striking is more fully described, saying he 'totally destroyed' all who were alive and left no survivors. This last phrase must be seen as a statement of overall victory, as later chapters will refer to natives of these cities who are still alive (for example Hebron in Joshua 14:12–13). That may be because some of the population left in the face of war and returned later, or because the statement itself is hyperbolic.

---

6 See Excursus: Devoting to the LORD.
7 The number seven often indicates completeness.

The totality of victory is emphasised in verse 41, repeating that Joshua 'struck' them all and reiterating the geography in question, this time using key geographical markers that lie within the areas previously listed. The point is driven home again in verse 42, this time referring to the kings and saying they were conquered within this one campaign, with the explanation that the Lord fought for Israel. This phrase ties this section together with 10:1–15. We will read in the next chapter that Joshua 'waged war . . . for a long time' (Joshua 11:18), and so we must not overemphasise the speed of this conquest; rather, the emphasis is on its totality. We should also note that at the end of this campaign Joshua returns with all Israel to Gilgal. This is an act of initial conquering, not occupying, which will come later.

KEY THEMES AND APPLICATION

The anticipation of God's judgment and victory
The killing of the five kings and the symbolic gesture of placing the commanders' feet on their necks anticipates what will happen next. The commanders are assured of future victory because of God's promise. When we connect this with the theme of God's kingdom coming, we can see a parallel for the believer today. We are assured that our enemies of sin, death and Satan are defeated by Jesus, but we wait for the completion of that victory. We are reassured that God 'will soon crush Satan under your feet' (Romans 16:20). We might say that Jesus tells us to put our feet on their necks and so symbolise the victory that will be ours. We, like the commanders, are then called to press on in confidence that it will be so; we are not to be afraid or discouraged but rather strong and courageous because we know Jesus will conquer.

Seeing Joshua as a type of Jesus here is common among older commentators. Tthe German Lutheran theologian David Chytraeus (1531–1600) said that the victories over the five kings:

> . . . are images and types of the victories and triumphs of the true Joshua, the Son of God, our Lord Jesus Christ, who by his suffering and dying and rising from the dead by his divine

power, crushed the head of the serpent and trod Satan under our feet and removed the devil, death, sin and the law (which accuses and damns us) . . . he triumphed over them by himself and imparted this victory of his to us.[8]

This is not to lead to a 'name it and claim it' version of the Christian life where we believe we will win every battle. Rather, it is to say that in the victory of Jesus we are guaranteed ultimate victory; even in our sufferings we are 'more than conquerors' (Romans 8:37–9), and 'God gives us the victory through our Lord Jesus Christ' (1 Corinthians 15:57). This is especially needed at times when the church can feel as if it is losing ground and so is discouraged; we need to be assured of Jesus's victory, that he will win, and we will reign with him.

If we ask what the 'anticipatory sign' is for Jesus's coming victory, then we would look to the resurrection and ascension. The apostles see Jesus as raised and exalted and so are confident that every enemy will be brought under his feet (see Acts 2:33–5; 1 Corinthians 15:25; Ephesians 1:22).

The totality of God's judgment

We have argued previously that the entry into the Promised Land pictures God's kingdom coming; it is God bringing his rule to bear in that region. What is emphasised here is the totality of that judgment through his people. We wait for God's kingdom to come when Jesus returns, but we are told that when he does, he will have 'coming out of his mouth . . . a sharp sword with which to strike down the nations' (Revelation 19:15). This section of Joshua gives us a picture of that total 'striking down'. That is sobering for us to consider, as we know many who currently oppose Jesus; it is also reassuring for us to consider because Jesus will rule this world one day.

---

8 David Chytraeus, 'Commentary on Joshua 10:16–27', in Amos, *Reformation Commentary*, 144.

The spread of the gospel now

While primarily referring to our confidence in Jesus's future victory, we may also want to relate this campaign to the growth of the kingdom now as the gospel message spreads and people bow to Jesus as Lord. That connection can be seen in the mission of the seventy-two sent out by Jesus in Luke 10. They go as Jesus's representatives so that whoever listens to them listens to him, and whoever rejects them rejects him (Luke 10:16). They return full of joy at what has happened through them, and Jesus comments:

> I saw Satan fall like lightning from heaven. I have given you authority to trample on snakes and scorpions and to overcome all the power of the enemy; nothing will harm you. (Luke 10:18–19)

Tremper Longman and Daniel Reid list a series of connections between this mission and Old Testament battles and conclude, 'The effect of this evidence, taken as a whole or in part, forms a strong suggestion that the seventy-two are sent on an eschatological mission that is set in the context of divine warfare.' In particular, trampling on snakes and scorpions may be seen as exercising authority over the forces of evil, and there is a parallel with Joshua's encouragement of his commanders.[9]

---

9 Longman and Reid, *God Is a Warrior*, 106.

12

The Final Victory

Joshua 11

We have seen the entry into the land, the initial battles against Jericho and Ai, and then the more sustained campaign against the kings in the south. We now move to further military campaigns in the north. This section works as a pair with chapter 10: in that previous chapter a king, hearing about the Israelites, created a coalition to fight against Israel, resulting in the conquest of the southern cities. In chapter 11, another a king hears about these events and creates a new coalition, resulting in the conquest of the northern cities. What is different between the chapters is the scale of the challenge facing Israel, which increases significantly. This is the greatest military challenge Joshua has faced, and the greatest in the whole book. But God grants Joshua success. There is then a moment of summary, looking at what has been achieved so far.

Northern kings defeated

11 When Jabin king of Hazor heard of this, he sent word to Jobab king of Madon, to the kings of Shimron and Akshaph, ²and to the northern kings who were in the mountains, in the Arabah south of Kinnereth, in the western foothills and in Naphoth Dor on the west; ³to the Canaanites in the east and west; to the Amorites, Hittites, Perizzites and Jebusites in the hill country; and to the Hivites below Hermon in the region of Mizpah. ⁴They came out with all their troops and a large number of horses and chariots - a huge army, as numerous as the sand on the seashore. ⁵All these kings joined forces and made camp together at the Waters of Merom to fight against Israel.

⁶The LORD said to Joshua, 'Do not be afraid of them, because by this time tomorrow I will hand all of them, slain, over to Israel. You are to hamstring their horses and burn their chariots.'

⁷So Joshua and his whole army came against them suddenly at the Waters of Merom and attacked them,

8 and the Lord gave them into the hand of Israel. They defeated them and pursued them all the way to Greater Sidon, to Misrephoth Maim, and to the Valley of Mizpah on the east, until no survivors were left. **9** Joshua did to them as the Lord had directed: he hamstrung their horses and burned their chariots.

10 At that time Joshua turned back and captured Hazor and put its king to the sword. (Hazor had been the head of all these kingdoms.) **11** Everyone in it they put to the sword. They totally destroyed[a] them, not sparing anyone that breathed, and he burned Hazor itself.

12 Joshua took all these royal cities and their kings and put them to the sword. He totally destroyed them, as Moses the servant of the Lord had commanded. **13** Yet Israel did not burn any of the cities built on their mounds – except Hazor, which Joshua burned. **14** The Israelites carried off for themselves all the plunder and livestock of these cities, but all the people they put to the sword until they completely destroyed them, not sparing anyone that breathed. **15** As the Lord commanded his servant Moses, so Moses commanded Joshua, and Joshua did it; he left nothing undone of all that the Lord commanded Moses.

16 So Joshua took this entire land: the hill country, all the Negev, the whole region of Goshen, the western foothills, the Arabah and the mountains of Israel with their foothills, **17** from Mount Halak, which rises towards Seir, to Baal Gad in the Valley of Lebanon below Mount Hermon. He captured all their kings and put them to death. **18** Joshua waged war against all these kings for a long time. **19** Except for the Hivites living in Gibeon, not one city made a treaty of peace with the Israelites, who took them all in battle. **20** For it was the Lord himself who hardened their hearts to wage war against Israel, so that he might destroy them totally, exterminating them without mercy, as the Lord had commanded Moses.

21 At that time Joshua went and destroyed the Anakites from the hill country: from Hebron, Debir and Anab, from all the hill country of Judah, and from all the hill country of Israel. Joshua totally destroyed them and their towns. **22** No Anakites were left in Israelite territory; only in Gaza, Gath and Ashdod did any survive.

23 So Joshua took the entire land, just as the Lord had directed Moses, and he gave it as an inheritance to Israel according to their tribal divisions. Then the land had rest from war.

---

a 11 The Hebrew term refers to the irrevocable giving over of things or persons to the Lord, often by totally destroying them; also in verses 12, 20 and 21.

THE FINAL VICTORY

1. The defeat of Hazor and the northern cities • Joshua 11:1–15

The new threat against Israel (11:1–5)

The chapter begins, as with previous sections, with a king hearing of Israel's exploits (see Joshua 5:1; 9:1; 10:1). The king in question, Jabin, calls together a large coalition of forces.[1] They are described either by name and/or city (three kings), by region (four regions) and by tribal group (six tribes). While the main grouping is from the north, the Jebusites are from Jerusalem in the south. The overall impression is that the rest of the country now joins forces against Israel. The coalition of chapter 10 suddenly looks like a preliminary skirmish in comparison. This impression is reinforced in verse 4 as their combined troops are described as a 'huge army' and 'as numerous as the sand on the seashore'.[2] They are not only numerous, but they are also well equipped with horses and chariots. Moreover, they are united: verse 5 describes their joining together, ready to fight Israel. They gather at a wadi, suggesting they chose suitable open ground for their horses and chariots.[3] The reader should therefore sense that the challenge to Israel is now overwhelming. David Howard says the description casts 'a dark cloud of impending doom over the Israelites'.[4]

God's reassurance and Israel's victory (11:6–9)

In the face of this overwhelming opposition, God reassures Joshua. The call is not to fear them, but the focus is the promise of what will happen in the next twenty-four hours. The prediction is that God will deliver them all, killed, to Joshua. In reality, the Israelites

---

1 There is a later reference to a Jabin in Judges 4; this is different incident and so it may have been a hereditary title. Woudstra, *Joshua*, 187–8.
2 Potentially echoing the promise to Abraham regarding his descendants in Genesis 22:17. There may be a deliberate comparison: these forces in the Promised Land occupy the position promised to Israel and so stand in their way.
3 Firth, *Joshua*, 220. Although Harstad disagrees on the suitability of the terrain, Harstad, *Joshua*, 454.
4 Howard, *Joshua*, 265.

did the actual killing, but this emphasises that it is God at work. The command to disable the horses and chariots is probably so that the Israelites then wouldn't utilise them for themselves. Hamstringing horses would incapacitate them for warfare but not necessarily for domestic use; the chariots would be burnt as they could not be repurposed.[5] Israel is not to arm itself as other nations would, but rather continue to trust in their God.[6]

We are given little detail of the battle itself, only that Joshua and the army attack them 'suddenly' (as with the five kings in 10:9) at their base camp and the Lord gives them into their hand. As a result, they defeat them there and they scatter in different directions (to the north-west and to the north-east) and over a great distance. Another pursuit is described, in which they inflict huge losses (as in 10:10–11). Joshua is then obedient to God's commands regarding the horses and chariots, despite their potential military value to Israel.

Wider destruction in accordance with Moses's command (11:10–15)

The scene now widens from the battle at the Waters of Merom to engagements with the tribes represented and their home cities. Rather than the twenty-four hours of the first devastating strike, we should now envisage a more protracted campaign. It begins with Hazor, as the leading city of the coalition, with the expected formula of putting everyone in it to the sword and 'totally destroying' it (using the key idea of 'devoting to the LORD').[7] But then, unlike chapter 10, we do not get a city-by-city account but a broader summary, where Joshua does the same to 'all these royal cities' (verse 12). It is clarified that they burn Hazor but not the others, and that they are permitted to take plunder.

Within this there is great stress on the obedience of Joshua to what Moses commanded. That comes in a general statement in verse 12,

---

5 Firth, *Joshua*, 221.
6 See Psalm 20:7.
7 See Excursus: Devoting to the LORD.

THE FINAL VICTORY

and then is reinforced positively and negatively in verse 15, which can be laid out as follows:

> As the LORD commanded Moses
> > Moses commanded Joshua
> > > Joshua did it
> > Joshua left nothing undone
> Of all the LORD commanded Moses

Hence, as the battle section of the book draws to a close, it stresses Joshua's obedience to God via Moses, so drawing a connection with chapter 1 (see Joshua 1:7–8) and implicitly signalling the basis for Joshua's success.

2. Summary and comment on the conquest • Joshua 11:16–23

Summary of land and explanation (11:16–20)

The land that Joshua 'took' in both northern and southern campaigns is now summarised. It is described in terms of broad regions and then the southernmost and northernmost points (Mount Halak and Baal Gad). The victory is summed up in the capturing and killing of the kings who ruled these territories. We should note the focus on Joshua here: David Howard says, 'He alone is identified as the agent in almost all the activities.'[8] Verse 18 comments on the length of time this took, which means we should not read chapters 10 and 11 as a lightning strike across the region but a more protracted campaign; the account we are given is condensed and probably partial. While it may have taken time, though, there was never any doubt about its outcome.

Verses 19–20 are particularly significant in explaining what has happened. The Gibeonites were the only city to seek peace, which, despite their deception, is viewed positively here. No other city did so because God had hardened their hearts, which led to them fight

---

8 Howard, *Joshua*, 271.

against God's people. Hardening of hearts has been seen previously in Exodus with Pharaoh and the Egyptians (we will discuss this further below).[9] We should note that the 'heart' is the centre of the person in their thinking, desiring and acting; it is not simply a place of emotion as in much contemporary speech. This hardening is so that God might bring his judgment on them (using the expected term 'devoted to destruction'). Again, we are reminded this is in accordance with what was commanded via Moses.

Destruction of the Anakites and conclusion (11:21–3)

We are given an additional note that Joshua also destroyed the Anakites. What is unusual is that this is mentioned after the summary statements already given and includes cities already listed as conquered. Hence this additional note seems out of place. The reason is the significance of the Anakites. They were a tribe mentioned when Israel first spied out the land and who terrified them (see Numbers 13:22, 28, 33; Deuteronomy 1:28). They were famously strong and tall and fearsome fighters: 'Who can stand up against the Anakites?' (Deuteronomy 9:2). They are placed out of sequence here as a climatic finale to say that even the Anakites were included in the conquering of the land.[10]

This is the last time we see the term 'totally destroyed' (or 'devoted') in Joshua. While further battles still lie ahead, they are not of this nature; God's judgment has now fallen. Even here, though, is there is a slightly sour note in detailing the places where some Anakites survived – again showing that 'totally destroyed them' should not be read literally.

We finish with a summary and an anticipation. The summary is that Joshua took 'all' the land, according to 'all' that God had said to Moses – again connecting the victory with obedience. The anticipation is that Joshua gave the land as an 'inheritance' to Israel. The theme of inheritance was mentioned in the introduction in Joshua

---

9 A similar phrase is also used of Sihon, although using a different verb (Deuteronomy 2:30).
10 The introductory phrase 'at that time' does not need to place these events after the summaries of previous verses, but simply at the time of these battles.

THE FINAL VICTORY

1:6 but has not been mentioned since, until now. It is the theme that will dominate the second half of the book. Having 'taken' the land they are now poised to 'inherit' the land.

The last comment is that the land has 'rest from war'; this is a different word from the promises of 'rest' in the land (as in Joshua 1:13) and only means that warfare has ceased, at least for now.[11] This means we should not jump to concluding that God's promises of rest are fulfilled; that needs to wait until Joshua 21:44. True rest in the land is not simply the cessation of war but rather requires the enjoyment of inheritance in possessing the land.[12]

MAIN THEMES AND APPLICATIONS

Final victory against united resistance
We saw the details of the northern coalition army in its size, equipment and unity, then the promise of God of victory within twenty-four hours, and then the crushing defeat by Joshua. This repeats earlier themes in Joshua but on a higher register: it is now clear that nothing can stop God and so his people. More than that, it pictures a last desperate attempt of the enemy to band together to resist God, but then the ease of their overthrow.

This points us to broader biblical themes: the rebellion and resistance of the world against God and yet his sovereign judgment and victory over them. We might think of Psalm 2 where:

> The kings of the earth rise up,
>   and the rulers band together
>   against the LORD and against his anointed
> (Psalm 2:2)

In response, the Lord laughs at them and grants victory to his anointed (Psalm 2:4–6). While speaking of the king in Israel, we can read this as a picture of Joshua as God's anointed leader, and it

---

[11] It is a common term in Judges where it also means a temporary rest from warfare. Firth, *Joshua*, 230.
[12] This point is sometimes missed by commentators and fulfilment is claimed too early.

points forward to Jesus. This rising up against Joshua and the 'final battle' can then be seen as an anticipation of the final battle when Jesus returns. The gathering of forces against God and his people are also described as numerous – 'like the sand on the seashore' – but are quickly destroyed (Revelation 20:8–9). We are also told that, in that final battle, the 'kings of the earth and their armies gathered together to wage war against the rider on the horse and his army', but that this rider, Jesus, wins with the sword coming out of his mouth (Revelation 19:19–21). Joshua's victory against those opposing God anticipates that final battle. Hence, this passage should both warn us of opposition to Jesus and reassure us of his final victory.

Victory through God's obedient leader
We noted the emphasis on Joshua having obeyed all that God commanded through Moses (verses 12, 15, 20, 23), which looks back to chapter 1. In chapter 1 we saw the need for Joshua to obey so that he would be prosperous and successful, and that this was what the Israelites needed to successfully enter the land. This forms a moment of closure on that theme: Joshua did indeed obey all that God said through Moses, and so here they are, having successfully taken the land.

As previously in the book, we can apply this to the Christian believer: God calls us all to obedience, and there is a sense in which we will be 'successful' as a result – as long as success is defined in God's terms. We might more pointedly apply it to Christian leaders. The description of Joshua here exemplifies the instruction for kings in Deuteronomy 17:18–20: their great concern is to be for their own obedience to the Law. Trent Butler says of Joshua, 'His faithfulness thus stands as a goal for all future leaders of Israel. Rather than being lawmakers, the kings of Israel are law takers and law keepers.'[13] So Christian leaders today are to be most concerned about their own close following of God through his word.

But, despite the validity of those applications, the larger point is

---
13 Butler, *Joshua 1–12*, 7A:516.

THE FINAL VICTORY

to say that God works by appointing his leader who obeys and so wins success for his people. In that way, this looks forward to Jesus, the obedient servant who wins victory for his people. This is the way in which Joshua encourages us with gospel truth, not simply exhorts us in Christian living.

Reminder of God's gracious faithfulness
The highlighting of the Anakites in verses 21–2 has several effects on the reader. Assuming they know of the significance of the Anakites earlier in Israel's history, there will be a sense of finality and closure: Israel finally even defeated the Anakites. They will also be sobered because this will remind them of Israel's failure to trust God's promises precisely because of the Anakites; that was why they did not enter the land at the first time of asking. But this should then lead to rejoicing in God's gracious faithfulness: he promised to get them into the land and defeat its inhabitants, and now here they are. God has been faithful to his promises, and has been so despite his people, not because of them.

God's sovereign purposes
We noted the significance of verses 19–20 as an explanation of the previous chapters. God sovereignly hardened the inhabitants of the land so that they would fight rather than ask for peace, in order that God might bring his judgment on them. One's understanding of this passage will depend on the position taken over God's sovereignty. It fits most comfortably with a Reformed view that God can and does turn people's hearts as he pleases. That should not be taken to mean he made people resist when they did not want to – his sovereignty never reduces us to puppets in Scripture. But it does mean there is no zone of 'freedom' in the human heart where we make decisions apart from him. The Dutch theologian Abraham Kuyper said of this passage and other passages:

> With these passages before us, it is impossible to deny that the Scripture reveals God as the Author of the hardening. And he who says that the God whom he worships can not harden any

man's heart, ought to see that he does not worship the God of the Scripture.[14]

We should remember the background of Pharaoh in the Exodus here. God hardened Pharaoh's heart (e.g., Exodus 4:21), and Pharaoh also hardened his own heart (e.g., Exodus 8:15); how these two actions interplay is never fully explained. Certainly Pharaoh, and by implication the nations here, bear responsibility for their response to God. In that sense the comparison with the Gibeonites is instructive, as the implication is that other tribes could have heard and responded likewise. But they chose to resist. God confirms or even initiates people's stance against him so that he might bring deserved punishment. We might connect this with New Testament passages such as John 12:37–41 and Romans 9:14–24. The reformer John Calvin comments on this passage:

> In the first place, then, stands the will of God which must be regarded as the principal cause. For seeing their iniquity had reached its height, he determined to destroy them. This was the origin of the command given to Moses, a command, however, that would have failed in its effect had not the chosen people been armed to execute the divine judgment, by the perverseness and obstinacy of those who were to be destroyed. God hardens them for this very end, that they may shut themselves out from mercy. Hence that hardness is called his work, because it secures the accomplishment of his design.[15]

---

14 Abraham Kuyper, *The Work of the Holy Spirit*, trans. Henri De Vries (London: Funk & Wagnalls Company, 1900), 593.
15 Calvin, *Joshua*, 4:174–5.

13

The Roll Call of Victory

Joshua 12

We have seen Joshua appointed as leader of Israel and the successful entry into and conquering of the Promised Land. We might then have expected to move from the end of chapter 11 straight into the inheriting of the land, which will dominate the second half of the book. But before that, there is a pause to look back over what has been achieved in terms of the Israelites gaining land and defeat of the kings whose territories they have conquered. This survey means we draw back to a time before Joshua's leadership, looking at Moses and the land east of the Jordan, and then recount what has happened within the book of Joshua itself. The result is a roll call of Israelite victories. This functions to make the reader slow down and absorb the magnitude of what God has done. It also paints a picture of a united Israel in land gained by Moses and then by Joshua, and which is separated by the Jordan, but is all given by the same God.

List of defeated kings

12 These are the kings of the land whom the Israelites had defeated and whose territory they took over east of the Jordan, from the Arnon Gorge to Mount Hermon, including all the eastern side of the Arabah:

² Sihon king of the Amorites, who reigned in Heshbon.

He ruled from Aroer on the rim of the Arnon Gorge – from the middle of the gorge – to the River Jabbok, which is the border of the Ammonites. This included half of Gilead. ³ He also ruled over the eastern Arabah from the Sea of Galilee[a] to the Sea of the Arabah (that is, the Dead Sea), to Beth Jeshimoth, and then southward below the slopes of Pisgah.

JOSHUA

4 And the territory of Og king of Bashan, one of the last of the Rephaites, who reigned in Ashtaroth and Edrei.

5 He ruled over Mount Hermon, Salekah, all of Bashan to the border of the people of Geshur and Maakah, and half of Gilead to the border of Sihon king of Heshbon.

6 Moses, the servant of the LORD, and the Israelites conquered them. And Moses the servant of the LORD gave their land to the Reubenites, the Gadites and the half-tribe of Manasseh to be their possession.

7 Here is a list of the kings of the land that Joshua and the Israelites conquered on the west side of the Jordan, from Baal Gad in the Valley of Lebanon to Mount Halak, which rises towards Seir. Joshua gave their lands as an inheritance to the tribes of Israel according to their tribal divisions. **8** The lands included the hill country, the western foothills, the Arabah, the mountain slopes, the wilderness and the Negev. These were the lands of the Hittites, Amorites, Canaanites, Perizzites, Hivites and Jebusites. These were the kings:

9 the king of Jericho — one
the king of Ai (near Bethel) — one
10 the king of Jerusalem — one
the king of Hebron — one
11 the king of Jarmuth — one
the king of Lachish — one
12 the king of Eglon — one
the king of Gezer — one
13 the king of Debir — one
the king of Geder — one
14 the king of Hormah — one
the king of Arad — one
15 the king of Libnah — one
the king of Adullam — one
16 the king of Makkedah — one
the king of Bethel — one
17 the king of Tappuah — one
the king of Hepher — one
18 the king of Aphek — one
the king of Lasharon — one
19 the king of Madon — one
the king of Hazor — one
20 the king of Shimron Meron — one
the king of Akshaph — one
21 the king of Taanach — one
the king of Megiddo — one
22 the king of Kedesh — one
the king of Jokneam in Carmel — one
23 the king of Dor (in Naphoth Dor) — one
the king of Goyim in Gilgal — one
24 the king of Tirzah — one
thirty-one kings in all.

---

a 3 Hebrew *Kinnereth*

THE ROLL CALL OF VICTORY

1. Territory and kings east of the Jordan • Joshua 12:1–6

Whereas chapter 11 summarised the conquests within the Promised Land itself, we now back up to remember previous conquests under Moses and which are placed alongside those under Joshua. This section is structured primarily as a listing of the kings who were defeated. East of the Jordan this only numbers two: Sihon and Og. The description is carefully constructed with the use of the key words 'defeated' and 'possession' at the start in verse 1 which are repeated at the end in verse 6. This is somewhat hidden in the NIV, which uses 'defeated' and 'took over' in verse 1 and then 'conquered' and 'possession' in verse 6. This repetition shows the key actions: defeating so that land can be possessed.

The territory itself is described in broad terms in verse 1, and then more precisely for each king in turn, for Sihon in verses 2–3 and then for Og in verses 4–5. Their territory is adjoining and so forms the land occupied east of the Jordan. The battles against these two kings were previously detailed in Numbers 21:21–35, and Joshua referred to their allocation in chapter 1.

In verse 6, Moses is said to be the agent of these victories: he defeated them (with the Israelites), and he gave their land as a possession to the two and a half tribes.[1] Moses is twice called 'the servant of the LORD' here. We will see in a moment how his role is paralleled with that of Joshua, and so one effect is to highlight Joshua's significance.

2. Territory and kings west of the Jordan • Joshua 12:7–24

The second section details the kings and territory west of the Jordan. It begins as the first section ended, focusing on the agent of victory, Joshua instead of Moses. It also uses the key terms again in verse 7 – defeat and possession – emphasising that the same process is happening (this time the NIV uses 'conquered' and 'inheritance'). The reference to the giving of the land by the tribal divisions anticipates

---

[1] See their request in Numbers 32.

what is to come in the following chapters, but here it is presented as already done. The effect is to sandwich Moses and Joshua in adjacent verses having achieved identical things for God's people.

As in verse 1, there is a broad description of the land in north–south terms (reversed in order from 11:17), but the pattern then changes from the first half. Rather than list the kings and their territory, there is a more general description of territory and tribes (verse 8), and then a list of kings by their cities (verses 9–24). Not all of these have been mentioned previously, so confirming that the earlier narratives were selective and partial.[2] The order of the list is roughly along the flow of the book from chapters 6–11: entry into the land, southern regions and then northern regions.[3] The word 'one' is used after each king, to indicate counting, and then the total is given at the end: 'thirty-one kings in all'. There is therefore a celebratory recounting of each victory. For readers today, such a list feels very dry, but if we were listing the previous rulers of areas we now lived in, and against whom we or our ancestors had fought, we would probably feel very differently about reading or hearing such a list.

KEY THEMES AND APPLICATION

The unity of God's people
Having summarised Joshua's campaigns in chapter 11, this chapter draws in Moses and the eastern tribes. In that vein it also places Moses and Joshua together as the ones through whom God has achieved the key actions of defeating and possessing. Gordon McConville says:

> The present chapter therefore not only resumes the victories of Joshua and Moses, but insists that they together form a single action of Yahweh in fulfilment of his promise to gift the land of Canaan to Israel. It also has the effect of determining that the two areas, east and west of the Jordan, together form the full extent of the given land. Transjordan is not secondary to the western territory in this respect . . .[4]

---

2 Firth, *Joshua*, 233–4.
3 Hess, *Joshua*, 228.
4 McConville and Williams, *Joshua*, 60.

Therefore, all Israel is presented in this chapter on equal terms: they have all taken part in the defeat of kings and been granted land as their possession. This connects back to chapter 1:12–15 and the commands to the two and a half tribes to aid their fellow Israelites until they have taken possession of their land. It also looks ahead to the chapter 22 and the return of the eastern tribes. What is important in all this presentation is the unity of God's people. There was a very real threat that their different histories in taking possession of their land and the geographical boundary of the River Jordan could divide Israel (as chapter 1 was concerned about and as 22 anticipates). This chapter affirms Israel as one.

For the church today, we might speak of our unity in Christ. There are different angles on this: for example, our unity as one body (1 Corinthians 12:12–14), or the reconciliation Christ brings between people (Ephesians 2:11–22). A more specific route from this passage would be to speak of our shared enemies being defeated and enjoying equal share in Jesus's victories.

Reflection and praise for God's victories
There is also a meditative and doxological purpose in this chapter. Meditative, because it makes the reader review and absorb once again the scope of what has been achieved. Doxological, because such reflection would lead to praise and thanksgiving for all that God had done. Rather than seeing the list of kings at the end as a boring administrative list, they should be read as a celebration of victories. If read corporately one might imagine a growing shout of 'One!' following each king listed. Perhaps the comparison of a sports fan listing the victories of their team in an unbeaten championship winning season might start to give the appropriate feel. Marten Woudstra says that 'this list is a song of praise to the Lord's honour'.[5] Or Dale Ralph Davis suggests it constitutes 'the stanzas for Israel's version of "Great is Thy Faithfulness"'.[6]

For Christian believers, this points us to the appropriate reviewing, reflection and celebration of God's victories through Jesus. There is

---
5 Woudstra, *Joshua*, 200.
6 Davis, *Joshua*, 105.

a place for listing God's triumphs for us, not to learn something new but to be reminded of something old. The Lutheran theologian George Stoeckhardt (1842–1913) said of these verses:

> Israel was never to forget how miraculously the Lord fought for his people, as he himself led them into the land of promise. We too at all times are to remember the great deeds of God, through which God has made room for his church on earth, and gave them peace.[7]

We might think of the various enemies we have faced – our own sin, entrapment in the world, the deception of Satan, the looming fear of death. Jesus has defeated each one through his death and resurrection and won for us a new kingdom, his kingdom of light, to live in. For each enemy we can shout, 'One!' We might reflect on verses such these:

> ... giving joyful thanks to the Father, who has qualified you to share in the inheritance of his holy people in the kingdom of light. For he has rescued us from the dominion of darkness and brought us into the kingdom of the Son he loves, in whom we have redemption, the forgiveness of sins. (Colossians 1:12–14)

> When you were dead in your sins and in the uncircumcision of your flesh, God made you alive with Christ. He forgave us all our sins, having cancelled the charge of our legal indebtedness, which stood against us and condemned us; he has taken it away, nailing it to the cross. And having disarmed the powers and authorities, he made a public spectacle of them, triumphing over them by the cross. (Colossians 2:13–15)

We recount victories, we celebrate and we give praise.

---

7 George Stoeckhardt, 'The Biblical History of the Old Testament', in Nichols, *ESV Church History Study Bible*, 321.

PART TWO

JOSHUA 13–21

14

Introduction to Possessing the Land

Now that we have seen the battles to conquer the land, chapters 13 to 19 focus on the allocation of the land to the different tribes and their exploits in then taking possession of it. We will make a few comments here on our overall approach to this section.

1. *Conquering and possessing*

The reader might be surprised to read of the land that remains to be possessed. The previous few chapters have described a total conquering of the inhabitants and the taking of the 'entire' land (for example, Joshua 11:23). Why is such a total victory now spoken of as partial?

The answer lies in a few key areas. First, the aim of the last chapters has been to portray God giving the land to Israel and so they have emphasised totality. This was an overall victory such that you can truly say they defeated the 'whole land' while still recognising significant pockets that had not yet been defeated.

Second, this was an initial strike that inflicted 'defeat' but not an elimination of the inhabitants of the land. We have noted how cities that are said to have been captured and destroyed are later said to still be occupied by the native inhabitants. One example is Debir, which is said to be conquered in 10:38–9 but then needs to be recaptured in 15:15–17. This is probably because of the use of hyperbole in describing the elimination of the inhabitants, and/or that some of the population may have fled and then later returned to reoccupy the city.

Third, we must distinguish between some key words describing the conquest. It is regularly said that Israel has 'taken' or 'captured' a city (the NIV varies in its translation). For example, it 'took' Jericho, Ai and the cities of chapters 10 and 11.[1] In addition, a different word is used in chapter 11 to summarise Israel 'taking' the whole land and

---

[1] This is the word *lakhad*; Joshua 6:20; 10:1, 28, 32, 35, 37, 39, 42; 11:10, 12, 17.

all the cities.² However, both of these are different from the idea of 'possessing' the land; that is, where Israel 'move in', as it were, to make a place their home.³ While language of 'taking' mainly comes in the first half the book, the language of possessing dominates the second half. Having been 'taken', now the land needs to be 'possessed'.⁴ This is sometimes hidden in translation; unfortunately, in the opening verse of chapter 13 we read 'there are still very large areas of land to be taken over' (NIV), whereas the word used here is that for 'possess', and so the apparent contradiction with chapter 11 evaporates.

2. The boundaries of the inheritances

The general picture we receive in these chapters is a description of each tribe's inherited land, usually given in terms of its boundary lines and key cities. Some of these are well known today; many are unknown or debated. In the commentary that follows, we will not describe these geographical issues in any detail. While we must recognise the importance of the concrete geography of Israel's inheritance and recognise that accuracy would have been crucial to the first readers – this is describing *their* inheritance – the message of the book is not found in these geographical details. As the sixteenth-century reformer John Calvin says of this, 'Great labour would produce little fruit to the reader.'⁵ Map 2 gives the generally accepted territories. Readers who wish to examine this in more detail are referred to the appropriate commentaries.

We should remember that while reading such boundary outlines is rather dull to a modern reader, it would not have been so for the first audiences. That is so for at least three reasons. First, these were places they knew: hearing the description of somewhere you can picture is very different from a list of unknown names. In teaching this material, one might try describing an area known to the audience using road

---

2 This is the word *laqah*; Joshua 11:16, 19, 23.
3 This is the word *yarash* which can be used of possessing a place, or dispossessing others so as to possess it yourself; Joshua 1:11, 15; 3:10; 8:7; 12:1; 13:1, 6, 12, 13; 14:12; 15:14, 63; 16:10; 17:12–13, 18; 18:3; 19:47; 21:43; 23:5, 9, 13; 24:4, 8.
4 See the comments in Davis, *Joshua*, 89–90.
5 Calvin, *Joshua*, 4:200.

INTRODUCTION TO POSSESSING THE LAND

names and local landmarks to make this point; your listeners can track the boundary line in their mind's eye as you describe the area. Second, these were places of personal significance: this was their inheritance! We might think of the anticipation of hearing the reading of a will – the legal terminology might be dry, but we are listening attentively for details of what *we* are being given. Third, this is the land that God had promised his people centuries earlier and had been long in the waiting; a brief assertion that he gave it to Israel would have been feeble here. Rather as David Howard says, 'A deep sense of satisfaction would come if the reader could actually trace the fulfilment of these promises city by city, hill by hill, wadi by wadi, border by border.'[6] Again, teaching these passages will need to tap into these dynamics.

What we should do within these chapters is pay careful attention to any novel elements. That is, when we are told details of certain characters, hear their words relayed or their actions described, we should remember that they have been included for good reason. In this regard, what has been labelled the 'land grant narratives' are especially important. This term is coined by Richard Nelson who points out that in five episodes there is a specific request, usually based on a previous promise that is now claimed.[7]

We should also note the structure of the whole section, which can easily be lost. It is outlined below:

13:1–7: introduction to division of the land
13:8–33: division of the land east of the Jordan by Moses
14:1–5: introduction to division of the land west of the Jordan by Joshua
14:6–15: the example of Caleb possessing Hebron
15: the land allocated to Judah
16–17: the land allocated to Ephraim and Manasseh
18:1–10: introduction to dividing the remaining land
18:11–19:48: the land allocated to the remaining tribes
19:49–51: land allocated to Joshua, and summary

---

6 Howard, *Joshua*, 321.
7 These come in Joshua 14:6–14; 15:18–19; 17:3–6; 17:14–18; 21:1–3. Richard D. Nelson, *Joshua: A Commentary*, The Old Testament Library (Louisville: Westminster John Knox Press, 1997), 177–8.

JOSHUA

There are a variety of suggestions as to different structures that can be found here, but it is hard to argue for a single definitive outline.[8]

A few points are worthy of note:

- The section falls into two distinct phases. The process of possessing starts in chapter 14, but after the first three tribes it seems to halt and is then 'restarted' in chapter 18 with a challenge to take possession and a new survey of the land.
- Greater attention is given to the first three tribes, which each have significant description, whereas the remaining seven are covered much more briefly.
- The ordering starts with Caleb and ends with Joshua; these are the two spies who trusted that God would give them the land. Caleb's example is especially highlighted as he is given his own section in chapter 14 and then mentioned again within Judah in chapter 15.

We will discuss the relevance of these issues in more detail within the commentary below.

---

8 For one example, see Firth, *Joshua*, 242–4.

15

Inheriting the Land

Joshua 13

So far, we have seen Israel enter and conquer the Promised Land under Joshua's obedient leadership. There is a change of focus at this point in the book, from the 'taking' of the land to now 'inheriting' or 'possessing' the land.[1] As Trent Butler says, 'The passage turns the corner from conquest to settlement.'[2] Chapter 13 begins with general instructions for this phase of Israel's occupation and then summarises the land already possessed east of the Jordan. This serves as an introduction for the next chapters, which detail the land to be possessed west of the Jordan. More significantly, it pictures the land already granted east of the Jordan as of a piece with that to be granted on the west and points us to the significance of inheritance.

Land still to be taken

13 When Joshua had grown old, the Lord said to him, 'You are now very old, and there are still very large areas of land to be taken over.

2 'This is the land that remains: all the regions of the Philistines and Geshurites, **3** from the River Shihor on the east of Egypt to the territory of Ekron on the north, all of it counted as Canaanite though held by the five Philistine rulers in Gaza, Ashdod, Ashkelon, Gath and Ekron; the territory of the Avvites **4** on the south; all the land of the Canaanites, from Arah of the Sidonians as far as Aphek and the border of the Amorites; **5** the area of Byblos; and all Lebanon to the east, from Baal Gad below Mount Hermon to Lebo Hamath.

---

1 See the explanation of these terms in chapter 14, 'Introduction to Possessing the Land'.
2 Butler, *Joshua 1–12*, 7A:80.

6 'As for all the inhabitants of the mountain regions from Lebanon to Misrephoth Maim, that is, all the Sidonians, I myself will drive them out before the Israelites. Be sure to allocate this land to Israel for an inheritance, as I have instructed you, 7 and divide it as an inheritance among the nine tribes and half of the tribe of Manasseh.'

Division of the land east of the Jordan

8 The other half of Manasseh,[a] the Reubenites and the Gadites had received the inheritance that Moses had given them east of the Jordan, as he, the servant of the LORD, had assigned it to them.

9 It extended from Aroer on the rim of the Arnon Gorge, and from the town in the middle of the gorge, and included the whole plateau of Medeba as far as Dibon, 10 and all the towns of Sihon king of the Amorites, who ruled in Heshbon, out to the border of the Ammonites. 11 It also included Gilead, the territory of the people of Geshur and Maakah, all of Mount Hermon and all Bashan as far as Salekah – 12 that is, the whole kingdom of Og in Bashan, who had reigned in Ashtaroth and Edrei. (He was the last of the Rephaites.) Moses had defeated them and taken over their land. 13 But the Israelites did not drive out the people of Geshur and Maakah, so they continue to live among the Israelites to this day.

14 But to the tribe of Levi he gave no inheritance, since the food offerings presented to the LORD, the God of Israel, are their inheritance, as he promised them.

15 This is what Moses had given to the tribe of Reuben, according to its clans:

16 The territory from Aroer on the rim of the Arnon Gorge, and from the town in the middle of the gorge, and the whole plateau past Medeba 17 to Heshbon and all its towns on the plateau, including Dibon, Bamoth Baal, Beth Baal Meon, 18 Jahaz, Kedemoth, Mephaath, 19 Kiriathaim, Sibmah, Zereth Shahar on the hill in the valley, 20 Beth Peor, the slopes of Pisgah, and Beth Jeshimoth 21 – all the towns on the plateau and the entire realm of Sihon king of the Amorites, who ruled at Heshbon. Moses had defeated him and the Midianite chiefs, Evi, Rekem, Zur, Hur and Reba – princes allied with Sihon – who lived in that country. 22 In addition to those slain in battle, the Israelites had put to the sword Balaam son of Beor,

who practised divination. **23** The boundary of the Reubenites was the bank of the Jordan. These towns and their villages were the inheritance of the Reubenites, according to their clans.

24 This is what Moses had given to the tribe of Gad, according to its clans:

25 The territory of Jazer, all the towns of Gilead and half the Ammonite country as far as Aroer, near Rabbah; **26** and from Heshbon to Ramath Mizpah and Betonim, and from Mahanaim to the territory of Debir; **27** and in the valley, Beth Haram, Beth Nimrah, Sukkoth and Zaphon with the rest of the realm of Sihon king of Heshbon (the east side of the Jordan, the territory up to the end of the Sea of Galilee[b]). **28** These towns and their villages were the inheritance of the Gadites, according to their clans.

29 This is what Moses had given to the half-tribe of Manasseh, that is, to half the family of the descendants of Manasseh, according to its clans:

30 The territory extending from Mahanaim and including all of Bashan, the entire realm of Og king of Bashan – all the settlements of Jair in Bashan, sixty towns, **31** half of Gilead, and Ashtaroth and Edrei (the royal cities of Og in Bashan). This was for the descendants of Makir son of Manasseh – for half of the sons of Makir, according to their clans.

32 This is the inheritance Moses had given when he was in the plains of Moab across the Jordan east of Jericho. **33** But to the tribe of Levi, Moses had given no inheritance; the LORD, the God of Israel, is their inheritance, as he promised them.

---

a 8 Hebrew *With it* (that is, with the other half of Manasseh)
b 27 Hebrew *Kinnereth*

1. Instructions for possession of the land • Joshua 13:1–7

We move to a moment later in Joshua's life, but there is no way of knowing how much time has elapsed. Joshua's elderly age is emphasised by using two terms for it ('old' and 'advanced in age', amalgamated by the NIV), and then having them repeated by God to him. This echoes the start of chapter 1, with God repeating the fact of Moses's death. Back then, the 'fact' repeated indicated the start of Joshua's role; here the fact of his age encourages the completion of it. God's instruction is that there is still a great deal of land to be 'possessed' (NIV 'taken over'). In this way, the opening verses are programmatic for the second half of the book in a similar way that the opening verses of chapter 1 were for the first half.[3]

The land in question is specified in verses 2–6a, which broadly covers coastal plains in the north and south and mountains further north.[4] While the land is 'conquered' as a whole – and that was the emphasis at the end of chapter 11 and in chapter 12 – there are multiple pockets of resistance still outstanding. More than that, while the enemy may be defeated overall, Israel has not yet 'possessed' the land – occupying and living in it, such that it becomes their home.[5]

The NIV begins a new paragraph at verse 6 and seems to give a specific promise regarding the mountain regions mentioned. It is more likely that verse 6a continues the description of the land to be taken and that the promise refers to all the land mentioned. God promises to 'drive them out'. There is a connection in the words used here which is missed in English: the word 'possess' (verse 1) means 'to take possession of', but in a different form it means 'to seize or dispossess' (verse 6).[6] These two actions form two sides of one coin: it is in dispossessing the current inhabitants that Israel will take possession, or in failing to dispossess that they will not.[7] Hence in verse 6 God is promising to dispossess the inhabitants so that Israel can take possession.

Joshua is then commanded to allocate the land to the nine tribes and the half-tribe of Manasseh. There is a change in role for Joshua here: he is no longer the military commander but the land divider. The land has been conquered, now it is apportioned.[8] In instructing Joshua, the significant word 'inheritance' is used twice.[9] This was mentioned in

---

3 Firth, *Joshua*, 244.
4 Howard, *Joshua*, 295–6.
5 See discussion in chapter 14, 'Introduction to Possessing the Land'.
6 Creach, *Joshua*, 99.
7 This is seen frequently over the following chapters.
8 Johnson, *Teaching Joshua*, 294.
9 See 'The Promised Land: inheritance and resting place' in the Introduction.

chapter 1 as part of God's plan for his people (Joshua 1:6), but then is not used again until chapter 11:23 which looks forward to the second half of the book. From this point forward it is dominant, being used forty-eight times. It is the preeminent word describing what the land is to the Israelites: their inheritance from God.

2. Previous division east of the Jordan • Joshua 13:8–33

Outlining of land (13:8–13)

Having mentioned the nine and half tribes who are to receive their inheritance, we are now told of the two and a half tribes who have already received their inheritance. Verse 8 gives a general statement that these tribes received this from Moses, east of the Jordan river. Verses 9–13 then outline the whole territory for these two and a half tribes, mentioning once again the kings Sihon and Og whose territory it was (see map 2). This echoes chapter 12:2–5, but this time the focus is on receiving the land as an inheritance rather than conquering the kings.

Verse 13 strikes a negative note which we will see repeatedly in the following chapters. This is a failure to 'dispossess' and so a failure to 'take possession'. Later readers would also be aware of how these two towns appear in David's reign: Absolom's mother was the daughter of a king of Geshur and Absolom later took refuge there; the king of Maakah fought against David. These later references only add to the sense David Howard conveys 'that not all is entirely well at this juncture'.[10]

The special status of the tribe of Levi (13:14, 33)

Verse 14 tells us that Moses gave no inheritance to the tribe of Levi, and this is mentioned again in verse 33. This lack of land inheritance is expected because of previous instruction to that effect in Numbers and Deuteronomy.[11] The Levites stand as a unique tribe:

---
10 Howard, *Joshua*, 307.
11 See Numbers 18:20–24; Deuteronomy 10:9; 12:12; 14:27–9; 18:1; 26:12–13.

they symbolically stand for the whole nation in representing the firstborn of all the tribes and in serving all the tribes at the temple (see Numbers 8:5–26). Mention of the Levites is not expected here as they were not part of the two and a half tribes settling east of the Jordan. But referring to them signals their role across the whole nation, including the trans-Jordanian tribes; as Richard Hess comments, 'They are the tribe that links all the inheritances together.'[12] This reference also anticipates the Levitical towns which will be allocated in this region. In addition, it allows reference to their privileged status in relation to God early in the discussion of 'inheritance': having just read the description of the very first piece of land, we are reminded there is a different type of inheritance. This will be mentioned again in chapters 14 and 18 as a recurring note within the distribution.

The Levites' privileged status is given in verse 14 regarding the food contributions the people will bring them: they will be given pastureland but will receive food offerings from the people, and this is their inheritance. Later, in verse 33, it is God himself who is their inheritance. Doug Johnson calls this 'an infinitely richer inheritance' in which the 'totality of their needs is provided for in their relationship to, and service of, God himself'.[13] This is of great significance in our understanding of this rich theme (see further comments below).

Specifying the land for the separate tribes (13:15–32)

We then receive the details of each tribe's allocation of land. This is not simply at the level of the tribe but 'according to its clans' (verses 15, 24, 29). This phrase will be repeated throughout the land allocation.[14] Verses 15–23 describe the land allocated to Reuben, verses 24–8 that to Gad, and verses 29–31 that to the half-tribe of Manasseh. This detail is far greater than that given earlier in Deuteronomy 3:12–17. Within this, Sihon and Og are mentioned once again as the kings Moses defeated and whose land was occupied (verses 21, 27, 30). We are also reminded of Balaam, who had been employed to curse the

---

12 Hess, *Joshua*, 237.
13 Johnson, *Teaching Joshua*, 297.
14 Firth, *Joshua*, 250.

Israelites (see Numbers 22–25; 31:8). Verse 32 summarises that this was the land Moses had allocated as the inheritance.

KEY THEMES AND APPLICATION

Joshua and Moses aligned
We have previously seen the tight connection between Joshua and Moses: Joshua takes over and continues the work of Moses in bringing the people of God from slavery into the Promised Land. God is with Joshua just as he was with Moses; Joshua's great act in crossing the Jordan echoes that of Moses in crossing the Red Sea (see Joshua 4:14). In chapter 12 their military victories were set in parallel. Now they are aligned in their role of allotting the land to the tribes as their inheritance. That work started under Moses and will now be completed by Joshua.

The unity of God's people
The next chapters will focus on the division of the land for the tribes west of the Jordan. However, before that is described, we have this extensive recapitulation of the previous inheritance for the two and a half tribes. We noted this same point in the victory list in chapter 12: that list included the battles on the east side of the Jordan and aligned them with those on the west; this chapter aligns the process of inheritance in a similar way. The point is to portray the eastern and western tribes as united together. The eastern tribes were always in danger of being downgraded, and the detail of this chapter highlights them and places them alongside the main group of tribes in equal status. So we might speak of our shared and equal inheritance gained for each of us through Jesus (e.g., Ephesians 1:14). We are heirs together, no matter what other differences may separate us.

The inheritance of God's people
The theme of inheritance is very significant in Joshua, and this chapter is the first place it is properly encountered. As explained in the Introduction, this is best seen as a theme through the Bible which is now fulfilled in the inheritance promised to God's people.

That is seen in the new creation, which is the true Promised Land and inheritance for God's people.

We should also note the privileged position of the Levites. Their lack of physical inheritance in the land was a pointer to the greater inheritance they had in God himself. That can be seen as applying to the Old Testament believer generally, both because of the representative function of the Levites and the way inheritance or portion language is used elsewhere (see, for example, Psalm 73:26). As Oliver O'Donovan says of the Levites, 'They were an eschatological sign, an arrow into heaven, which pointed beyond the land to what it signified.'[15]

Christian believers today all have such an inheritance. Appropriate application can be made to New Testament passages such as these:

> The Father . . . has qualified you to share in the inheritance of his holy people in the kingdom of light. (Colossians 1:12)

> . . . the promised Holy Spirit, who is a deposit guaranteeing our inheritance . . . (Ephesians 1:13–14)

> . . . into an inheritance that can never perish, spoil or fade. This inheritance is kept in heaven for you . . . (1 Peter 1:4)

The seventeenth-century Bible commentator, Matthew Henry, said:

> Joshua must have the honour of dividing the land . . . that he might be herein a type of Christ, who has not only conquered for us the gates of hell but has opened to us the gates of heaven, and having purchased the eternal inheritance for all believers, will in due time put them all in possession of it.[16]

Believers should be left assured that their names are included in God's 'will', and so they will receive their promised inheritance. Such reassurance provokes humility, gratitude and hope.

---

15 O'Donovan, 'The Loss of a Sense of Place', 51.
16 Henry, *Commentary*, 2:560.

INHERITING THE LAND

Inheritance as a gift
The division of the land comes after the conquering of the land, where we saw the repeated emphasis that God has 'given' it to them. That same emphasis continues here. God reassures Joshua regarding the remaining inhabitants: 'I myself will drive them out' (verse 6). God will dispossess the inhabitants of the land so his people can possess and inherit it. All Joshua must do is divide it between the tribes. The previous inheritance of the eastern tribes acts as a reassurance in this as well with its emphasis on God's defeat of opposing kings and protection from Balaam.

The idea of 'gift' is contained within the concept of 'inheritance' as well. You do not do anything to inherit; it all turns on the will of the giver, not the actions of the recipient. Here, God has promised to gift his people the land. The same principle of grace runs through the New Testament promises of inheritance with attendant attitudes of amazement and praise (for example, Ephesians 1:11–14).

Inheritance not taken
We noted the failure of verse 13 where the Israelites did not dispossess the people of Geshur and Maakah, and so failed to possess it for themselves. In this passage, that is one sour note within an overall sweet account. However, it is a note that will be repeated and, while it will not become dominant, it will cast a shadow over the inheritance account as a whole. At this stage, it should be noted to alert the reader to what is to come.

16

The Model of Inheritance

Joshua 14

We have had the division of the land introduced and a reminder of the land that was divided on the east side of the Jordan. We turn now to the division of the land on the west side of the Jordan. The passage starts with an introduction and reiteration of the situation: Moses allocated land on the east; now the tribes are allotted their inheritance on the west. But we are then told of the example of Caleb, who approaches Joshua to ask for the land he has been promised. This involves reflection on the failure to take the land forty years earlier because of people's disbelief. In contrast to this, Caleb stands as a preeminent example of the believing Israelite. Placing him at the start of the allocation highlights him as a model of how the Israelites should take their inheritance.

Division of the land west of the Jordan

14 Now these are the areas the Israelites received as an inheritance in the land of Canaan, which Eleazar the priest, Joshua son of Nun and the heads of the tribal clans of Israel allotted to them. ²Their inheritances were assigned by lot to the nine-and-a-half tribes, as the LORD had commanded through Moses. ³Moses had granted the two-and-a-half tribes their inheritance east of the Jordan but had not granted the Levites an inheritance among the rest, ⁴for Joseph's descendants had become two tribes – Manasseh and Ephraim. The Levites received no share of the land but only towns to live in, with pasture-lands for their flocks and herds. ⁵So the Israelites divided the land, just as the LORD had commanded Moses.

Land allotted to Caleb

⁶Now the people of Judah approached Joshua at Gilgal, and Caleb son of Jephunneh the Kenizzite said to him, 'You know what the LORD said to Moses the man of God

at Kadesh Barnea about you and me. ⁷I was forty years old when Moses the servant of the LORD sent me from Kadesh Barnea to explore the land. And I brought him back a report according to my convictions, ⁸but my fellow Israelites who went up with me made the hearts of the people sink.ᵃ I, however, followed the LORD my God wholeheartedly. ⁹So on that day Moses swore to me, "The land on which your feet have walked will be your inheritance and that of your children for ever, because you have followed the LORD my God wholeheartedly."ᵇ

¹⁰'Now then, just as the LORD promised, he has kept me alive for forty-five years since the time he said this to Moses, while Israel moved about in the wilderness. So here I am today, eighty-five years old! ¹¹I am still as strong today as the day Moses sent me out; I'm just as vigorous to go out to battle now as I was then. ¹²Now give me this hill country that the LORD promised me that day. You yourself heard then that the Anakites were there and their cities were large and fortified, but, the LORD helping me, I will drive them out just as he said.'

¹³Then Joshua blessed Caleb son of Jephunneh and gave him Hebron as his inheritance. ¹⁴So Hebron has belonged to Caleb son of Jephunneh the Kenizzite ever since, because he followed the LORD, the God of Israel, wholeheartedly. ¹⁵(Hebron used to be called Kiriath Arba after Arba, who was the greatest man among the Anakites.)

Then the land had rest from war.

---

a 8 Hebrew *melt*
b 9 Deut. 1:36

1. Introduction to division of the land • Joshua 14:1–5

The opening verses are dominated by the word 'inheritance', which comes in different forms five times in the first three verses (not always translated by the NIV). Verse 1 acts as an introduction to the following sections which will detail the inheritances within the land of Canaan. It is clarified how this process takes place: it is performed not only by Joshua but also by Eleazar the priest and the heads of the tribes.[1] This is the first mention of Eleazar in Joshua, but he will be significant in the distribution of the land,

---

[1] See also Joshua 17:4; 19:51; 21:1.

and his death is recorded alongside that of Joshua at the end of the book (Joshua 24:33).

It is also said that the process of allocation is by casting lots, although how this is done is not made clear. This whole process of allocation by this group of leaders is referred to again in Joshua 19:51, which forms a bookend to this passage. The process is said to be in obedience to the LORD via Moses.[2] Verses 3 begins with 'For' and acts as an explanation of the number (nine and a half) in verse 2. The Levites not receiving a portion of land is included to aid the explanation of numbers: two and a half plus nine and a half. For the background to the tribe of Joseph becoming two tribes, see Genesis 48. It is repeated that the Levites had no 'portion' or allotment, but only had towns to live in and pasture for their animals, which anticipates the Levitical towns in chapter 21. The section ends with an emphasis on obedience by the whole nation: the land was allotted as the LORD had commanded Moses.

2. The commendable example of Caleb • Joshua 14:6–15

Caleb's background (14:6–9)

The site of Gilgal is assumed to be where the allocation process occurs. But before we are told of any allocations, we hear from Caleb. His words form the longest section of recorded speech within the land allocation, along with being placed at the start, and so due attention must be paid to them. We note that Caleb's ethnicity is described as Kenizzite both here and again in closing this section (verse 14). The Kenizzites were one of the tribes listed in Genesis 15:19–21 as those whose land would be given to the Israelites. Caleb is also listed in Numbers 13:6 as from the tribe of Judah. It seems most likely that his family was from this non-Jewish nation and was absorbed into Judah at some earlier point.[3] This fits the ongoing theme of

---

2 For the background to this, see Numbers 26:52–6; 33:54; 34:13–29.
3 See discussion by Woudstra, *Joshua*, 227. The contrast of being considered a 'foreigner' and yet in reality being a true Israelite is increased by Caleb's name meaning 'dog'; see McConville and Williams, *Joshua*, 65–6.

the inclusion of pagan nations into Israel and, more than that, such people acting as model believers.

Caleb, along with Joshua, was part of the group that spied out the land under Moses, and he rehearses the history of that event here. The background to this can be read in Numbers 13–14 and this section can only be understood with reference to that passage. Caleb focuses on the difference between the disbelieving report of the majority of the spies and his own conviction. We read in Numbers 13 of his belief that they could defeat the inhabitants because God had promised them the land. Only he and Joshua expressed this; the report of the other spies caused the people's hearts to sink (paralleling the later response of the inhabitants of the land).[4] His example is expressed in verse 8 in terms of following the LORD wholeheartedly. This phrase captures the sense of the original (more literally it is 'went after God fully'). The same language of following God is used later to refer to covenant loyalty.[5] In describing himself this way, Caleb is repeating the description of him given by God in Numbers 14:24.

In Numbers, God promised to reward Caleb's trusting loyalty, saying that he (and Joshua) would enter the land. That promise was elaborated later when God said of Caleb, 'He will see it, and I will give him and his descendants the land he set his feet on, because he followed the LORD wholeheartedly' (Deuteronomy 1:36). That is what Caleb now quotes in verse 9. The actual land Caleb walked on is not specified but it becomes clear it centres on Hebron.

Caleb's recap of history begins and ends with his main point: what God promised him through Moses. That is what he is now raising with Joshua as he comes to make his claim on that promise.

Caleb's current claim (14:10–12)

'Now' in verse 10 sees Caleb moving to apply the history he has reiterated (again in verse 12). He begins by referring to God's faithfulness in keeping him alive during the wilderness wanderings as he had

---

[4] See Joshua 2:9, 11, 24 and 5:1, although a different word is used here.
[5] Joshua 22:16, 18, 23, 29 (although it is translated differently by the NIV). Hess, *Joshua*, 240.

promised – i.e., he has preserved me and brought me to enter the land. His reference to his age and God keeping him alive for forty-five years gives us some perspective on periods of time: the wilderness wanderings lasted for thirty-eight years following the spying of the land. As Caleb is now eighty-five, there have been approximately seven years since the entry to the land to this moment in the book.[6] Caleb's point, though, is that he is as strong now as he was then. While this is a comment on physical strength, it also seems connected to his confidence in God: his physical vigour for battle comes from his spiritual vitality. So he asks Joshua to now be given what he was promised (verse 12).

Caleb reminds Joshua that the Anakites lived there. The Anakites formed a key part of the disbelieving report of the majority of spies because of their famous size and because their cities were large and fortified (see Deuteronomy 1:28; Joshua 11:21). So it was and presumably still is a daunting task, but Caleb believes in what God promised, and so expects to drive them out with God's help, 'just as he said'.[7]

Joshua's response (14:13–15)

Joshua's blessing may be to bring the gift of land that follows or to aid Caleb in his undertaking of taking it. Hebron is then given as his inheritance and the reasoning is spelled out for us in verse 14: it was 'because he followed the LORD, the God of Israel, wholeheartedly'. This is the third time that description is used in this section (previously in verses 8 and 9). Caleb is given his full family title here, forming a bracket with verse 6, emphasising that it is someone of non-Israelite heritage who acts as an exemplar for the possessing of the land. Firth suggests, 'Caleb thus becomes a parallel to Rahab, the foreigner who is a paradigmatic figure for the first twelve chapters.'[8]

Verse 15 gives an aside about the naming of Hebron after the greatest of the Anakites, which reinforces the impression from verse

---

6 Firth, *Joshua*, 258.
7 Some translations include the word 'perhaps' or 'it may be' with reference to God's help in verse 12; no doubt is meant to be conveyed, only that Caleb does not presume he can dictate to God. See Harstad, *Joshua*, 519.
8 Firth, *Joshua*, 257. There is a further parallel in their both referring to the people's hearts 'sinking' or 'melting'.

12 about the presence of this formidable group. The section ends with the land having rest from war. As with Joshua 11:23, this is a reference to cessation of fighting; it is not yet the 'rest' promised and entered into later.[9]

KEY THEMES AND APPLICATION

Caleb's example of wholeheartedness
The background in Numbers 13–14 speaks of Caleb and Joshua standing apart from the rest of the spies in their trust in God. Caleb is highlighted in this and spoken of as following God wholeheartedly, which is then emphasised in this passage. We should see that this exemplary following of God is not only being referred to as a historic attitude in Numbers. Rather, Caleb is exhibiting the same spirit now. When his wholeheartedness is referred to in verse 14, it could be referring to the incident in Numbers, or his attitude towards Hebron now, or both. Caleb exudes confidence in God's promise and so wants to lead the charge in taking his inheritance.

Caleb thus stands as a challenge and inspiration in living for God today. He paints a portrait of someone taking God's word seriously and so living in dependent but vigorous activity. Here is the model Israelite living in the light of God's promises. The challenge to later readers to follow such an example is emphasised by Caleb's non-Israelite background as he shows up the pure-blood Israelites.

Such a portrayal of wholeheartedness can challenge us today. That might be because of the inactivity that comes from love of ease and comfort in Western culture. Alternatively, David Oginde points to a tendency in Africa to complain and blame others rather than taking any initiative.[10] Whatever our cultural situation, Caleb calls us to a determined pursuit of realising God's promises. There might be a particular application to those who are older in years who, in some cultures, will be tempted to 'slow down' and 'take it easy'. While physical stamina may well decline, spiritual vigour should not. As

---

9 The word for 'rest' used here and in Joshua 11:23 means cessation of war and is different from the holistic rest referred to in Joshua 1:15; 21:44; 22:4; 23:1.
10 Oginde, 'Joshua', 286.

THE MODEL OF INHERITANCE

the nineteenth-century Lutheran George Stoeckhardt said, 'Those who remain firm when they are tempted, and faithfully follow God, increase in the strength of the Lord, remaining alert and faithful even though they have grown old, and inherit the blessing.'[11]

How wholeheartedness works

We also gain insight into how Caleb came to be someone following God wholeheartedly. This heart attitude comes from deep confidence in God's promises. Caleb's difference from the other spies was that he believed God's promise that they could defeat the inhabitants of the land, fearsome as they may have been. He displays that same attitude to God's word in the present. He says, 'just as the LORD promised' (verse 10), 'give me this hill country that the LORD promised me' (verse 12), and 'I will drive them just as he said' (verse 12). Hence, Caleb's confidence and commitment come from knowing what God has said to him.

This is of great help to us if we feel we are not like Caleb. We do not look to summon up wholeheartedness from within us; rather, we look to God and what he has said. Confidence and commitment like Caleb's do not grow in a vacuum; they grow in the soil of knowledge of God and are nurtured by his promises. As Paul said, 'Faith comes from hearing' (Romans 10:17). In teaching this material we should remember that great examples can crush as well as inspire. Being aware of that will mean we sympathise with our hearers and aid them in how they can be more like Caleb, rather than only telling them to be.

Our need for a faithful Israelite

This example starts the whole section on inheriting the land under Joshua. As a result, Caleb is presented as the 'model Israelite' who trusts God and gains his inheritance. The hope would be that the rest of nation follows suit. At this stage the reader might not know what will subsequently happen, but any later Israelite does know: Israel fails to take the land in this way. This is where the structure

---

11 George Stoeckhardt, 'The Biblical History of the Old Testament', in Nichols, *ESV Church History Study Bible*, 324.

of this section becomes important: it starts here with Caleb and finishes in chapter 19 with Joshua. Framing it between these two 'faithful' Israelites shows that they exemplify what is needed, but also what Israel fails to be. Hence it looks forward to the coming of the faithful Israelite, Jesus, who will trust God completely and win the inheritance for his people. We will return to this same point later in this section.

What should be recognised in teaching this material is that, although this section should inspire God's people to greater wholeheartedness themselves, that must be set within the larger pattern. Left to our ourselves, we fail; Caleb and Joshua were the exceptions, not the norm. We should let them point us to the one we all need, who has not only been an example, but has also won the land for us.

The casting of lots
Passages like this that mention the casting of lots sometimes raise the issue of decision making and seeking guidance from God, and specifically whether casting lots is still to be done. We should recognise that here this process was specifically commanded by God; the reason being that he would thereby sovereignly allot territory to each tribe (see Proverbs 16:33). Not to have used this process would have been to disobey and take the decision out of God's hands. The Christian today is in a very different situation where such use is never commanded, but rather a process of discernment is normative (see Romans 12:1–2). The only New Testament example of casting lots is in Acts 1 to choose a replacement apostle. A key issue there is that there were two men who had already been identified as meeting the required criteria and so this was a way of giving the final decision over to God.

The issue of casting lots has reappeared at various times through church history, sometimes with very unfortunate results and even claiming divine sanction for foolish or ungodly behaviour.

Land ownership and justice today
In some areas of the world, discussion of dividing the land will raise contemporary issues because of the history of land ownership and

related issues of justice.[12] These will usually be in areas where land ownership is much more significant for families and wealth creation than it often is in western nations. We must realise that God's command to divide this land is a unique moment in the history of his people. In that sense we should not move from this passage to contemporary land disputes. Having said that, it would be wise to be aware that for some people that will be the immediate issue that comes to mind, and this may mean that we address it in some way. What we can say is that God divides his land fairly among his people, and that he is a God who stands for justice.[13]

---

12 Jesurathnam, 'Joshua', 285–6.
13 For further thought on this topic, see Jerome F. D. Creach, 'Joshua 13–21 and the Politics of Land Division', *Interpretation: A Journal of Bible and Theology* 66, no. 2 (2012): 153–63.

17

Judah: Examples and Priority

Joshua 15

With Israel having conquered the land, we are now seeing the division of the land among the tribes. They are receiving their promised inheritance from God. That began with the individual example of Caleb who prompted the division process by asking for his allotment. He modelled exemplary confidence in God, believing that he would give him his inheritance just as he promised. We now move to the division of the land to the tribes proper. The process of allocation was described in Joshua 14:1–5: it is by lot, and it starts with the tribe of Judah. The bulk of the chapter is a description of the boundaries of its territory along with a list of the towns within it. Within this we read more specifically of Caleb again and his family. As we discussed in Introduction to Possessing the Land (chapter 14), we will say little about the location of the boundaries and the towns but rather focus on the dialogue around Caleb, which gives us further examples to follow.

Land allotted to Judah

15 The land allotted to the tribe of Judah, according to its clans, extended down to the territory of Edom, to the Desert of Zin in the extreme south.

² Their southern boundary started from the bay at the southern end of the Dead Sea, ³ crossed south of Scorpion Pass, continued on to Zin and went over to the south of Kadesh Barnea. Then it ran past Hezron up to Addar and curved around to Karka. ⁴ It then passed along to Azmon and joined the Wadi of Egypt, ending at the Mediterranean Sea. This is their[a] southern boundary.

⁵ The eastern boundary is the Dead Sea as far as the mouth of the Jordan.

The northern boundary started from the bay of the sea at the mouth of the Jordan, **6** went up to Beth Hoglah and continued north of Beth Arabah to the Stone of Bohan son of Reuben. **7** The boundary then went up to Debir from the Valley of Achor and turned north to Gilgal, which faces the Pass of Adummim south of the gorge. It continued along to the waters of En Shemesh and came out at En Rogel. **8** Then it ran up the Valley of Ben Hinnom along the southern slope of the Jebusite city (that is, Jerusalem). From there it climbed to the top of the hill west of the Hinnom Valley at the northern end of the Valley of Rephaim. **9** From the hilltop the boundary headed towards the spring of the waters of Nephtoah, came out at the towns of Mount Ephron and went down towards Baalah (that is, Kiriath Jearim). **10** Then it curved westward from Baalah to Mount Seir, ran along the northern slope of Mount Jearim (that is, Kesalon), continued down to Beth Shemesh and crossed to Timnah. **11** It went to the northern slope of Ekron, turned toward Shikkeron, passed along to Mount Baalah and reached Jabneel. The boundary ended at the sea.

12 The western boundary is the coastline of the Mediterranean Sea. These are the boundaries around the people of Judah by their clans.

13 In accordance with the LORD's command to him, Joshua gave to Caleb son of Jephunneh a portion in Judah – Kiriath Arba, that is, Hebron. (Arba was the forefather of Anak.) **14** From Hebron Caleb drove out the three Anakites – Sheshai, Ahiman and Talmai, the sons of Anak. **15** From there he marched against the people living in Debir (formerly called Kiriath Sepher). **16** And Caleb said, 'I will give my daughter Aksah in marriage to the man who attacks and captures Kiriath Sepher.' **17** Othniel son of Kenaz, Caleb's brother, took it; so Caleb gave his daughter Aksah to him in marriage.

18 One day when she came to Othniel, she urged him[b] to ask her father for a field. When she got off her donkey, Caleb asked her, 'What can I do for you?'

19 She replied, 'Do me a special favour. Since you have given me land in the Negev, give me also springs of water.' So Caleb gave her the upper and lower springs.

20 This is the inheritance of the tribe of Judah, according to its clans:

JUDAH: EXAMPLES AND PRIORITY

21 The southernmost towns of the tribe of Judah in the Negev towards the boundary of Edom were:

Kabzeel, Eder, Jagur, **22** Kinah, Dimonah, Adadah, **23** Kedesh, Hazor, Ithnan, **24** Ziph, Telem, Bealoth, **25** Hazor Hadattah, Kerioth Hezron (that is, Hazor), **26** Amam, Shema, Moladah, **27** Hazar Gaddah, Heshmon, Beth Pelet, **28** Hazar Shual, Beersheba, Biziothiah, **29** Baalah, Iyim, Ezem, **30** Eltolad, Kesil, Hormah, **31** Ziklag, Madmannah, Sansannah, **32** Lebaoth, Shilhim, Ain and Rimmon - a total of twenty-nine towns and their villages.

33 In the western foothills:

Eshtaol, Zorah, Ashnah, **34** Zanoah, En Gannim, Tappuah, Enam, **35** Jarmuth, Adullam, Sokoh, Azekah, **36** Shaaraim, Adithaim and Gederah (or Gederothaim)[c] - fourteen towns and their villages.

37 Zenan, Hadashah, Migdal Gad, **38** Dilean, Mizpah, Joktheel, **39** Lachish, Bozkath, Eglon, **40** Kabbon, Lahmas, Kitlish, **41** Gederoth, Beth Dagon, Naamah and Makkedah - sixteen towns and their villages.

42 Libnah, Ether, Ashan, **43** Iphtah, Ashnah, Nezib, **44** Keilah, Akzib and Mareshah - nine towns and their villages.

45 Ekron, with its surrounding settlements and villages; **46** west of Ekron, all that were in the vicinity of Ashdod, together with their villages; **47** Ashdod, its surrounding settlements and villages; and Gaza, its settlements and villages, as far as the Wadi of Egypt and the coastline of the Mediterranean Sea.

48 In the hill country:

Shamir, Jattir, Sokoh, **49** Dannah, Kiriath Sannah (that is, Debir), **50** Anab, Eshtemoh, Anim, **51** Goshen, Holon and Giloh - eleven towns and their villages.

52 Arab, Dumah, Eshan, **53** Janim, Beth Tappuah, Aphekah, **54** Humtah, Kiriath Arba (that is, Hebron) and Zior - nine towns and their villages.

55 Maon, Carmel, Ziph, Juttah, **56** Jezreel, Jokdeam, Zanoah, **57** Kain, Gibeah and Timnah - ten towns and their villages.

58 Halhul, Beth Zur, Gedor, **59** Maarath, Beth Anoth and Eltekon - six towns and their villages.[d]

60 Kiriath Baal (that is, Kiriath Jearim) and Rabbah - two towns and their villages.

61 In the wilderness:

Beth Arabah, Middin, Sekakah, **62** Nibshan, the City of Salt and En Gedi – six towns and their villages.

63 Judah could not dislodge the Jebusites, who were living in Jerusalem; to this day the Jebusites live there with the people of Judah.

<hr>

a 4 Septuagint; Hebrew *your*
b 18 Hebrew and some Septuagint manuscripts; other Septuagint manuscripts (see also note at Judges 1:14) *Othniel, he urged her*
c 36 Or *Gederah and Gederothaim*
d 59 The Septuagint adds another district of eleven towns, including Tekoa and Ephrathah (Bethlehem).

1. The boundaries of the land • Joshua 15:1–12

The section starts with what becomes a standardised formula (see Joshua 16:1; 17:1) and moves straight into a description of the boundaries of Judah's territory (see map 2). It begins by tracing the southern boundary from the southern tip of Dead Sea westward across to the Mediterranean coast (verses 2–4). The eastern boundary is formed by the Dead Sea itself (verse 5a). The northern boundary runs from the northern tip of the Dead Sea almost directly west across the country to the coast again (verses 5b–11). The western boundary is the coastline of the Mediterranean Sea (verse 12).

The description allows someone familiar with the geography to trace a line in their mind's eye across the landscape. David Howard draws attention to the vivid way the boundary is described using a variety of verbs ('crossed', 'continued', 'ran', 'passed', etc). He suggests that for the original readers this would be the ancient equivalent of 'virtual reality' today, 'watching a borderline being drawn in "real time" with a computer-generated line, moving up and down, in and out, twisting and turning'.[1]

<hr>

1 Howard, *Joshua*, 334.

2. The example of Caleb, Othniel and Aksah • Joshua 15:13–19

Before we move to the listing of towns, we are given details of Caleb and his family. We have already been told of the assigning of Hebron to Caleb in the previous chapter. The repetition here has resulted in some authors hypothesising over an original account that contained both sections (and sometimes the account in Judges 1:11–15 as well). That is not necessary, as there are good reasons for both accounts, and our concern here is with the compilation of the book as we have been given it. Caleb's inclusion here is appropriate as it forms part of Judah's inheritance; it also advances the story by telling us what happened, whereas chapter 14 only stated the gift of Hebron. Placing Caleb's request before the division of the land proper highlighted his exemplary attitude; here we see that attitude in action.

Having been reminded that the gift of Hebron was in accordance with God's command (verse 13), we are told of Caleb's actions in taking the town and surrounding area. In particular, he drove out the three named Anakites, mentioned in the scouting of the land in Numbers 13:22 and probably the Anakites whom the other spies feared so greatly (Numbers 13:31–33). Thus, Caleb's original confidence in Numbers 13, repeated in Joshua 14, is now vindicated.[2] The mention of different names for the town may point to occupancy by different tribal groups and to the strategic significance of the town.[3]

Caleb also marched against Debir (about 10 miles south of Hebron), but rather than taking it himself he offers his daughter to whoever will do so. This is done by Othniel, Caleb's nephew. The challenge to take this town can be seen as a test of character, and Othniel is portrayed as being in Caleb's image in his successful endeavour. Othniel appears later as the first of the judges (Judges 3:7–11).

---

2 Firth, *Joshua*, 271.
3 Hess, *Joshua*, 244–5.

There is then a portrayal of Aksah herself. The narrative is sparse, shining the spotlight on her action and boldness.[4] The start of verse 18 is unclear in who is doing what, but it is most likely that Aksah urges Othniel to ask her father for a field (as the NIV renders it). The narrative is focused on Aksah so we do not see Othniel making the request. Instead, we move to Aksah asking Caleb directly for water; this seems to follow on from the previous request because she says, 'Since you have given me land . . .' Carolyn Pressler points out that while Caleb was a non-Israelite, Aksah is a non-Israelite woman, but she is 'hardly a passive or submissive character; her initiative is rewarded'.[5]

Aksah's request is for a 'blessing' (NIV, 'special favour') in the form of springs of water. Adolf Harstad points out that blessing is passed from Joshua to Caleb (Joshua 14:13), and now from Caleb to Aksah. So God's blessing of his people is being received as they respond in faith:

> By phrasing her petition with the term 'blessing', she acknowledges that the entire land is a gift from God that Israel has received solely by God's grace . . . In faith she seeks a portion of this blessing of grace for herself, her husband, and her future children.[6]

Joshua responds by giving two springs. Presumably the land that has been granted does not have access to water and this request is either to extend the land further to include these water sources or to have access to them. In this request, Aksah shows boldness and confidence.

3. The towns allotted to Judah • Joshua 15:20–63

The last section is introduced as the 'inheritance of the tribe of Judah' (verse 20). However, there is debate as to whether verse 20 is introducing what follows (as in the NIV) or summarising what has come

---

4 L. Daniel Hawk, *Joshua, Berit Olam: Studies in Hebrew Narrative and Poetry* (Collegeville: Liturgical Press, 2022), 201.
5 Pressler, *Joshua, Judges and Ruth*, 95.
6 Harstad, *Joshua*, 544.

JUDAH: EXAMPLES AND PRIORITY

before.[7] If it is what follows, then the towns are seen as constituting the 'inheritance' specifically. The towns listed are grouped into those in the south (verses 21–32), the west (verses 33–47), the hill country (verses 48–60) and the wilderness near the Dead Sea (verses 61–2). The listing ends with another of the sour notes we saw in chapter 13, that Judah could not drive out the Jebusites who lived in Jerusalem. As in chapter 13, the word used here ('dislodge', NIV) implies that the failure to 'dispossess' means a failure for them to 'possess'. Jerusalem is on the border of what will become Benjamite territory and we will later read of their inability to take the city as well (Judges 1:21).

The towns are placed in groups, the totals of which are listed (verses 32, 36, 41, 44, 51, 54, 56, 59, 60, 62). This is unlikely to be the actual number of towns as some appear to not be counted in verses 45–7; in addition, some of the figures given are clearly not the total of the towns listed (e.g., in verses 21–32). Numbers in the Bible are often listed for their symbolism as much as their historicity. Here the total number is that of 112. That does not seem a meaningful number in itself, but it is exactly the total of all the towns allotted to the other tribes in the following chapters added together. That cannot be a coincidence and points towards Judah being a semi-independent entity or at least pre-eminent among the tribes.[8]

KEY THEMES AND APPLICATION

The reality of living in the land
This is the first moment that Israel is allocated sections of the land for people to live in as their home. As David Firth says:

> Up to this point, Israel has been capturing the land (or portions of it), but they had not yet begun to dwell in it. Only by doing so could they truly 'possess the city gates of their enemies' as they had been promised (Gen 22:17).[9]

---

7 Woudstra, *Joshua*, 242.
8 Elie Assis, "'How Long Are You Slack to Go to Possess the Land" (Jos. XVIII 3): Ideal and Reality in the Distribution Descriptions in Joshua XIII-XIX', *Vetus Testamentum* 53, no. 1 (2003): 22.
9 Firth, *Joshua*, 283.

In that sense, what could be a rather dry chapter to read is actually momentous. God's promise to Abraham to give the land to his descendants is being realised (Genesis 12:7). That brings a significance and even an excitement to the boundary lines and city lists – this is theirs. As we said in the Introduction to Possessing the Land (chapter 14), we need to help people grasp this today. Even describing the boundaries of an area that can be visualised, say in your locality, will help people see that the description here is meaningful. But more than that, to realise this is describing their inheritance which they are now living in. It's like walking round the rooms of a new house and saying to yourselves, 'This is ours.'

We should then move to think again of the inheritance of Christian believers today: the new creation which we are promised. We can remind people that this is a reality that we will live in and share together. The 'real estate' nature of this chapter should impress upon us the embodied, physical nature of the new creation. There is often a tendency to 'spiritualise' the future so that it seems less substantial than this world. But, in C. S. Lewis's words, compared to this creation, the new world is 'more like the real thing'.[10]

Positive and negative examples
We have already seen how Caleb functions as an exemplary figure in chapter 14:6–15: he sets the pattern of how the land should be taken. Marten Woudstra says Caleb is paradigmatic: 'With like faith, but exercised at the successive stages of redemption history, all of God's promises would be fulfilled equally.'[11]

The example of Othniel and Aksah function in a similar way. Here are Israelites who believe God's promise of inheritance and so step forward and take the land. Even when granted land, Aksah is positively forward in asking for the blessing of water, reflecting a belief that God wants his people to be blessed in the land – which he does! Hence the attitude displayed here is to be emulated. This contrasts with the end of the chapter and the inability to dispossess the Jebusites and so possess Jerusalem. Given God's promises, this

---

10 C. S. Lewis, *The Last Battle* (London: Lion, 1989), 158.
11 Woudstra, *Joshua*, 241.

must be read as a failure by the Israelites concerned. The contrast is magnified by Caleb's driving out the Anakite leaders from Hebron: if he can do that, then why can the Jebusites not be removed?

This combination has two effects. First, it encourages positive belief and action and warns against the opposite. Second, it raises the question: how successful will Israel be in taking the land? That is a theme worth pointing out at this stage, but the answer will not come until later in the book.

The status of women

The description of Aksah has caused reflection on the status of women in the Bible. That the Old Testament portrays a society that is overall led by men is clear, but the rights of women are respected and guarded in many ways (see comments on inheritance in the next chapter). This episode has been read different ways. The offer of Aksah as a 'prize' is seen by some to show the wrong 'ownership' of women by men. But others have assumed that Aksah was in agreement with this arrangement, and that, rather than being degrading, it honoured her in setting a high standard for her husband-to-be. Further, her request is seen as a positive example that she sets for others, and the granting of it shows respect for her and her rights over the land.[12]

The significance of Judah

Several features point to the significance of Judah among the tribes: being listed first, receiving a larger portion of land which is described in greater detail and, most significantly, its towns numbering the total of those given to the other tribes. The idea of Judah as an entity in her own right, equal with the remaining tribes, starts to anticipate the future of the country and its division into two: Judah in the south and the rest of Israel in the north. In addition, those familiar with the previous biblical books will know of Jacob's blessing on the tribes in Genesis 49. Within this the blessing on Judah is noteworthy:

---

12 See these examples and discussion in Taylor and DeGroot, *Women of War, Women of Woe*, 55–6.

> Judah, your brothers will praise you;
>   your hand will be on the neck of your enemies;
>   your father's sons will bow down to you.
> You are a lion's cub, Judah;
>   you return from the prey, my son.
> Like a lion he crouches and lies down,
>   like a lioness – who dares to rouse him?
> The sceptre will not depart from Judah,
>   nor the ruler's staff from between his feet,
> until he to whom it belongs shall come
>   and the obedience of the nations shall be his.
> He will tether his donkey to a vine,
>   his colt to the choicest branch;
> he will wash his garments in wine,
>   his robes in the blood of grapes.
> His eyes will be darker than wine,
>   his teeth whiter than milk.
>
> (Genesis 49:8–12)

This points to the other tribes acknowledging Judah's strength and power, but particularly its role in ruling or kingship. This ruling includes the prediction of one to whom the ruler's staff belongs and that 'the obedience of the nations shall be his'. This is a messianic prediction, fulfilled in Jesus. This sort of background means we are not surprised to see Judah being highlighted as it is in Joshua. The reformer John Calvin says of Judah's pre-eminence here, 'Who does not see that it is raised to the highest rank, in order that the prophecy of Jacob may be fulfilled.'[13] Some commentators see the theme of unity in Joshua as being so strong they cannot countenance the idea that Judah is being highlighted.[14] But the two themes are not mutually exclusive – an exalted role leading to the Messiah need not override the unity of the nation. Indeed, it is in and through him that everything will be united (Ephesians 1:10).

---

13 Calvin, *Joshua*, 4:201.
14 For example, see Firth, *Joshua*, 266–7.

18

Joseph: Examples and Warnings

Joshua 16–17

We are in the section dividing the land among the tribes as described in Joshua 14:1–5. The whole section started with the exemplary attitude of Caleb, and we have seen his example repeated and then echoed in his family. We now move to the land allotted to the next tribe, which is Joseph. As we have already been told in Joshua, Joseph's tribe had become two, Ephraim and Manasseh (Joshua 14:4; see Genesis 48). In this section they are treated as one tribe at the start and at the end, but as separate entities receiving their own inheritance in the middle. They are also paralleled in their failures in driving out some of the inhabitants. Within the broad descriptions, we are given two more request stories where groups come to Joshua to ask for something. As with earlier accounts, these provide models to follow or warnings to avoid.

Land allotted to Ephraim and Manasseh

16 The land allotted to Joseph began at the Jordan, east of the springs of Jericho, and went up from there through the desert into the hill country of Bethel. **2** It went on from Bethel (that is, Luz),[a] crossed over to the territory of the Arkites in Ataroth, **3** descended westward to the territory of the Japhletites as far as the region of Lower Beth Horon and on to Gezer, ending at the Mediterranean Sea. **4** So Manasseh and Ephraim, the descendants of Joseph, received their inheritance.

5 This was the territory of Ephraim, according to its clans:

The boundary of their inheritance went from Ataroth Addar in the east to Upper Beth Horon **6** and continued to the Mediterranean Sea. From Mikmethath on

215

the north it curved eastward to Taanath Shiloh, passing by it to Janoah on the east. **7** Then it went down from Janoah to Ataroth and Naarah, touched Jericho and came out at the Jordan. **8** From Tappuah the border went west to the Kanah Ravine and ended at the Mediterranean Sea. This was the inheritance of the tribe of the Ephraimites, according to its clans. **9** It also included all the towns and their villages that were set aside for the Ephraimites within the inheritance of the Manassites.

10 They did not dislodge the Canaanites living in Gezer; to this day the Canaanites live among the people of Ephraim but are required to do forced labour.

17

This was the land allotted to the tribe of Manasseh as Joseph's firstborn, that is, for Makir, Manasseh's firstborn. Makir was the ancestor of the Gileadites, who had received Gilead and Bashan because the Makirites were great soldiers. **2** So this land was allotted to the rest of the people of Manasseh – the clans of Abiezer, Helek, Asriel, Shechem, Hepher and Shemida. These are the other male descendants of Manasseh son of Joseph by their clans.

3 Now Zelophehad son of Hepher, the son of Gilead, the son of Makir, the son of Manasseh, had no sons but only daughters, whose names were Mahlah, Noah, Hoglah, Milkah and Tirzah. **4** They went to Eleazar the priest, Joshua son of Nun, and the leaders and said, 'The LORD commanded Moses to give us an inheritance among our relatives.' So Joshua gave them an inheritance along with the brothers of their father, according to the LORD's command. **5** Manasseh's share consisted of ten tracts of land besides Gilead and Bashan east of the Jordan, **6** because the daughters of the tribe of Manasseh received an inheritance among the sons. The land of Gilead belonged to the rest of the descendants of Manasseh.

7 The territory of Manasseh extended from Asher to Mikmethath east of Shechem. The boundary ran southward from there to include the people living at En Tappuah. **8** (Manasseh had the land of Tappuah, but Tappuah itself, on the boundary of Manasseh, belonged to the Ephraimites.) **9** Then the boundary continued south to the Kanah Ravine. There were towns belonging to Ephraim lying among the towns of Manasseh, but the boundary of Manasseh was the northern side of the ravine and ended at the Mediterranean Sea. **10** On the south the land belonged to Ephraim, on the north to Manasseh. The territory of Manasseh reached the Mediterranean Sea and bordered Asher on the north and Issachar on the east.

11 Within Issachar and Asher, Manasseh also had Beth Shan, Ibleam and the people of Dor, Endor, Taanach and Megiddo, together with their surrounding settlements (the third in the list is Naphoth[a]).

12 Yet the Manassites were not able to occupy these towns, for the Canaanites were determined to live in that region. 13 However, when the Israelites grew stronger, they subjected the Canaanites to forced labour but did not drive them out completely.

14 The people of Joseph said to Joshua, 'Why have you allotted us only one portion of land and one share for an inheritance? We are a numerous people, and the LORD has blessed us abundantly.'

15 'If you are so numerous,' Joshua answered, 'and if the hill country of Ephraim is too small for you, go up into the forest and clear land for yourselves there in the land of the Perizzites and Rephaites.'

16 The people of Joseph replied, 'The hill country is not enough for us, and all the Canaanites who live in the plain have chariots fitted with iron, both those in Beth Shan and its settlements and those in the Valley of Jezreel.'

17 But Joshua said to the tribes of Joseph – to Ephraim and Manasseh – 'You are numerous and very powerful. You will have not only one portion of land allotted to you 18 but the forested hill country as well. Clear it, and its farthest limits will be yours; though the Canaanites have chariots fitted with iron and though they are strong, you can drive them out.'

---

a 2 Septuagint; Hebrew *Bethel to Luz*
a 11 That is, Naphoth Dor

1. The allotment to Joseph • Joshua 16:1–17:13

The land for the whole tribe (16:1–4)

The territory for the combined tribe is described first starting at its south-east corner near Jericho and moving westward, eventually arriving at the Mediterranean Sea (see map 2). This only describes the southern boundary and so the reader is invited to picture it containing the land to the north of this line. Verse 4, stating that the two tribes received their inheritance, acts as a bridge from the initial boundary line to the more detailed outline of territory that follows. While their birth order is given in verse 4, Manasseh and then Ephraim, this is switched in describing their territory, which may recognise the priority of Ephraim in Jacob's blessing (see Genesis 48:17–20).[1]

The territory for Ephraim (16:5–10)

There is debate about the boundaries described here. The territory is described by its southern and northern boundary lines, and then its eastern boundary moving south to Jericho, followed by the western boundary, although some sections remain vague. Verse 8b summarises by repeating the phrasing of verse 5, so emphasising this was the 'inheritance' of Ephraim (NIV 'territory'). Verse 9 is unusual in indicating that some of the towns allotted to Ephraim were within Manasseh's territory (see further in 17:7–11).[2] While the towns are not listed, they clearly include Gezer, mentioned in verse 3 and whose king was defeated when he came to the aid of Lachish (Joshua 10:33).[3] As with Jerusalem, they do not 'dispossess' (NIV 'dislodge') the inhabitants, who are called Canaanites. The anomaly of their presence is reinforced by repetition of the word 'Canaanites' and saying they live among them, even though they are reduced to a servant status.

The territory for Manasseh (17:1–2)

The territory for the tribe of Manasseh is introduced differently, focusing on the firstborn sons, Manasseh and then Makir. Makir is given Gilead and Bashan, which are east of the Jordan and were allocated by Moses (see Joshua 13:29–31). The explanation given may reflect the fighting in taking those areas by his descendants.[4]

---

[1] So argued by Davis, *Joshua*, 130–31.
[2] This occurs elsewhere as well, although it is not highlighted in the text. Howard, *Joshua*, 353.
[3] Gezer appears to have a Canaanite population until it is defeated by Pharaoh; see 1 Kings 9:16–17.
[4] See Numbers 32:39–42. The text says that 'he was a man of war' but this appears to be applied to his descendants.

Having explained this initial allotment, the remaining clans in line for inheritance are listed in verse 2; they are the grandchildren of Manasseh through his only son Makir and Makir's only son Gilead (see Numbers 26:29–33). They are referred to here as the 'other male descendants' of Manasseh, which leads into the next section addressing female descendants.[5]

The request from the daughters of Zelophehad (17:3–6)

Before the territory for the sons mentioned can be listed, the flow is interrupted by the request of verses 3–4, which explains why the number of portions of land changes from what might have been expected (verse 5). The background to this request can be read in Numbers 27:1–7. In that passage, these daughters came to Moses and Eleazar and asked that they be allotted land. The usual process was for land to be inherited through the male line, but they pointed out that their father 'left no sons' (Numbers 27:3). As a result, there was a danger their father's name would disappear from their clan. Moses consulted with God and was told, 'What Zelophehad's daughters are saying is right. You must certainly give them property as an inheritance among their father's relatives and give their father's inheritance to them' (Numbers 27:7). In Numbers 27, this leads into a more general statement of the rules of inheritance that will allow for this type of circumstance.

Verse 3 of Joshua 17 reiterates the key elements of this background, and the daughters come to Eleazar and Joshua to remind them of God's command and to claim their inheritance. Joshua immediately complies with this, and they receive an inheritance alongside their father's brothers. Zelophehad was the son of Hepher, mentioned in verses 2 and 3; the five daughters now take his place along with the five other brothers. The daughters are allocated a portion of land each rather than sharing one between them, as might have been expected; they have effectively been upgraded in the line of descent to each become equivalent to Hepher's sons. This means that the number of portions of land involved becomes ten (verse 5–6).

---

5 Firth, *Joshua*, 293.

The boundaries of Manasseh's territory (17:7–13)

The boundaries of Manasseh's land, to the north of that for Ephraim, are now given. The description starts with the northern boundary line; its eastern edge is the Jordan river, and on the west lies the Mediterranean Sea. There is debate about the placing of many descriptions in these verses.[6]

It is clarified that some of the towns belong to Ephraimites, particularly the town of Tappuah, which perhaps was contested (verses 8–9; compare 16:9). We are then also told of the bordering tribes of Asher and Issachar, anticipating their allocation in the next chapter, and that Manasseh owns some of the towns in their territory. But the last note is a negative one: they are not able to 'take possession' (NIV 'occupy') of these towns because of the resistance of the Canaanites. There is a rare glance to the future to when they will be able to subject this group to forced labour, but they are not able to 'dispossess' them (NIV 'drive them out').[7] As with Joshua 16:10, there is repeated use of the word 'Canaanite' to emphasise the peculiarity of their ongoing presence.

2. *The request from the tribe of Joseph* • *Joshua 17:14–18*

The 'people of Joseph', now as a combined group, make a request to Joshua. However, it is not so much a request as a complaint. They say they have been given one 'portion' and one 'share'. The first of these terms refers to the allotment given by the casting of lots; the second to the land apportioned to them. They seem to be complaining that they have been treated as one tribe and so only received one allocation from the lot system. Their reasoning is that they are numerous because God has blessed them, and so they ought to be allotted more. The figures given in the census in Numbers 26 support their contention for their size, but their land

---

6 See, for example, Woudstra, *Joshua*, 264–6.
7 This repeats the key word for 'possess'/'dispossess'. Here it uses a combination of words to emphasise totality; hence they were not driven out 'completely'.

allocation is correspondingly larger.[8] We should remember that they are contesting what has been allocated by lot and therefore by God; they are showing themselves discontent with what he has considered appropriate. Indeed, if God has blessed them in their numbers, would he now be mean with land? There is therefore a negative slant to this episode from the start.

Joshua's reply is to encourage them to clear more land. This is apparently land within their allocated territory but is currently occupied by the Perizzites and Rephaites. The people reply and add to their complaint: the Canaanites on the 'plain' have chariots 'fitted with iron'. They clearly think these reinforced or armoured chariots mean this territory is off limits.

There is some debate about which territories are being specified here, and whether Joshua is telling the tribe to expand within their current allotment or to extend outside it.[9] Whichever it is, the Josephites are both unhappy with their allotment and hesitant to go to battle with the local Canaanites, thinking they are better armed. They have clearly forgotten the lessons of Joshua 11:6: larger armies with better hardware are no obstacle to Israelites with faith in God.

Joshua gives them an encouragement that returns to their opening claim: he says they will have more than one portion because they will have the forests he has spoken of. The Canaanites are also no issue, despite their iron-clad chariots. This is an encouragement to the Josephites to take this land, but is also an unanswered challenge: will they?

KEY THEMES AND APPLICATION

Confidence in claiming God's promise
The daughters of Zelophehad provide another positive example of those who believe and so claim God's promise. The promise was made specifically to them many years earlier; one might imagine their repeating it to themselves and reminding each other of it in the intervening years. Now, finally, the day has arrived, and they

---
8 Firth, *Joshua*, 297–8.
9 Howard, *Joshua*, 356–7.

boldly step forward to ask for what God said. In doing so, they show their belief that God's promise stands and that they desire to claim what is theirs. They stand in the line of Caleb and themselves model an exemplary stance. Adolph Harstad says of them (and of other examples in these chapters):

> They are not being greedy or selfish. Instead, they act in bold faith to lay claim to their inheritance from the LORD. They trust his Word and are confident that the LORD will enable them to receive what he has promised.[10]

An appropriate cross-reference in the New Testament would be material from Hebrews which encourages an ongoing confidence in God's promise and warns against the opposite. For example:

> So do not throw away your confidence; it will be richly rewarded.

> You need to persevere so that when you have done the will of God, you will receive what he has promised . . . But we do not belong to those who shrink back and are destroyed, but to those who have faith and are saved. (Hebrews 10:35–6, 39)

This passage in Hebrews leads into the examples of faith in chapter 11 who trusted God for what they could not yet see and endured suffering because of their confidence in the future. That is the example these women provide us with here.

Hesitancy in claiming God's promise
The interaction at the end of the section provides a counter-example to the daughters of Zelophehad. The tribe is complaining and reluctant to trust God's help in taking the land. In speaking of the Canaanites and their iron chariots, they should have thought of the examples earlier in Joshua (11:6), and also remembered God's commands in general. For example:

---
10 Harstad, *Joshua*, 565.

> When you go to war against your enemies and see horses and chariots and an army greater than yours, do not be afraid of them, because the LORD your God, who brought you up out of Egypt, will be with you. (Deuteronomy 20:1)

Rather than boldly claiming the inheritance promised, they shy away and balk at the prospect. As we saw above, Joshua gives them an encouraging challenge, telling them that the land can be theirs. It is left unknown how they respond. That would work for the reader as an implicit challenge: am I hesitant or confident of God's promises? In terms of Hebrews 10 cited above: are we of those who shrink back or who have faith?

Failure in claiming God's promise
We also saw the failure to drive out the original inhabitants for both Ephraim in 16:10 and Manasseh in 17:12–13. We saw the emphasis in both examples of the anomaly of Canaanites remaining in the land. In this we see a failure to take God at his word as he allotted these cities to them. We should remember both the previous warnings given of the danger of allowing the inhabitants to remain in the land (Deuteronomy 20:16–18) and the promises of victory that God has given (Joshua 1:3–6; 10:25). So, while stated as observational facts, these observations are really reprimands.[11]
The sixteenth-century reformer John Calvin says:

> And yet their not gaining possession of those cities is attributed to their fault, because the lots assigning it to them was an indubitable pledge of victory. The reason therefore, why they could not expel the inhabitants was, because they were not fully persuaded in their minds that God is true, and stifled his agency by their own sluggishness.[12]

This failure to 'dispossess' them, and so not to 'possess' the land fully, adds to the trend that started in 13:13 and was seen again in 15:63.

---

11 Harstad, *Joshua*, 558.
12 Calvin, *Joshua*, 4:217.

In teaching this passage, that growing trend might be pointed out. We will discuss it more fully towards the end of the land allocation.

Some commentators take these failures, and the results we read later, as a warning for the Christian life now. For example, the Lutheran commentator Paul Kretzmann said:

> This foolish indulgence later proved disastrous to the Israelites, for the heathen seduced the people of God to idolatry. Christians who love the world and enter into friendships with unbelievers are in danger of accepting the wrong views of God to the detriment of their souls.[13]

We would want to be careful with the understanding of 'friendship' here: having non-Christian friends is normal and expected; what is being warned of is adopting non-Christians' views and being shaped by them.

The inclusion and status of women
Israelite society was clearly patriarchal in that inheritance was through the male line. The case of Zelophehad's daughters pushes this system and we see God's concern both for those women in question and for the ongoing inheritance of their family. The response is to affirm their right to inherit, and their test case results in more generalised laws that specify women inheriting in the absence of any brothers (Numbers 27:8–11). We see in this an example of concern for the status and position of women in Israelite society and an affirmation of their dignity. It is true, as some commentators point out, that the concern is more over the inheritance of the family line than the status of women; however, that they can inherit in this way still points to their recognition. That is made all the more pointed by their positive example in responding to God's promise, especially when compared to the tribe as a whole at the end of the chapter. As Daniel Hawk comments:

---

13 Paul Kretzmann, 'Popular Commentary of the Bible: Old Testament', in Nichols, *ESV Church History Study Bible*, 326.

JOSEPH: EXAMPLES AND WARNINGS

Women who claim and own land demonstrate essential participation in the life promised by YHWH and thus in the community that occupies it. The daughters thus personify what Achsah anticipates, that 'Israel' cannot be identified fundamentally in male terms only.[14]

Application of this will vary depending on the cultural setting into which it is being applied. In some cultures, the biblical system focusing on the male line will be seen as oppressive and unjust, and we might need to appropriately defend that. We can explain that it was a mechanism for providing inheritance and care for the whole family and clan and we can point out here God's concern for and commendation of these women. In other cultures, where women are less highly regarded, it will be appropriate to highlight the dignity accorded to women here and encourage the church to recognise this.[15]

---

14 Hawk, *Berit Olam*, 209.
15 Jesurathnam, 'Joshua', 287–8.

19

Being Slow to Inherit

Joshua 18–19

Chapters 13–17 have focused on the division of the land. The division east of the Jordan was summarised and then the process of dividing the inheritance for those settling west of the Jordan was started. Within this we have seen key features of the attitude of God's people in claiming their inheritance. We move now to a second stage in the division of land. This section has raised many questions in how it relates to the previous chapters. As we will see, it is very significant in the presentation of Israel and how they possess the land, and so for the picture painted by the book as a whole. What we see is the failure of the remaining tribes to take hold of their inheritances, and so a second round of allotment is needed. The small negative elements we have noted so far gain momentum and end in the worst example of Dan losing their inheritance altogether.

Division of the rest of the land

18 The whole assembly of the Israelites gathered at Shiloh and set up the tent of meeting there. The country was brought under their control, **2** but there were still seven Israelite tribes who had not yet received their inheritance.

3 So Joshua said to the Israelites: 'How long will you wait before you begin to take possession of the land that the LORD, the God of your ancestors, has given you? **4** Appoint three men from each tribe. I will send them out to make a survey of the land and to write a description of it, according to the inheritance of each. Then they will return to me. **5** You are to divide the land into seven parts. Judah is to remain in its territory on the south and the tribes of Joseph in their territory on the north. **6** After you have written descriptions of the seven parts of the land, bring them here to me and I will cast lots for you in the presence of the LORD our God. ⁷ The Levites, however, do not get a portion among you, because the priestly service of the LORD is their inheritance. And Gad, Reuben and the half-tribe of Manasseh have already received their inheritance on the east side of the Jordan. Moses the servant of the LORD gave it to them.'

⁸ As the men started on their way to map out the land, Joshua instructed them, 'Go and make a survey of the land and write a description of it. Then return to me, and I will cast lots for you here at Shiloh in the presence of the LORD.' ⁹ So the men left and went through the land. They wrote its description on a scroll, town by town, in seven parts, and returned to Joshua in the camp at Shiloh. ¹⁰ Joshua then cast lots for them in Shiloh in the presence of the LORD, and there he distributed the land to the Israelites according to their tribal divisions.

Land allotted to Benjamin

¹¹ The first lot came up for the tribe of Benjamin according to its clans. Their allotted territory lay between the tribes of Judah and Joseph:

¹² On the north side their boundary began at the Jordan, passed the northern slope of Jericho and headed west into the hill country, coming out at the wilderness of Beth Aven. ¹³ From there it crossed to the south slope of Luz (that is, Bethel) and went down to Ataroth Addar on the hill south of Lower Beth Horon.

¹⁴ From the hill facing Beth Horon on the south the boundary turned south along the western side and came out at Kiriath Baal (that is, Kiriath Jearim), a town of the people of Judah. This was the western side.

¹⁵ The southern side began at the outskirts of Kiriath Jearim on the west, and the boundary came out at the spring of the waters of Nephtoah. ¹⁶ The boundary went down to the foot of the hill facing the Valley of Ben Hinnom, north of the Valley of Rephaim. It continued down the Hinnom Valley along the southern slope of the Jebusite city and so to En Rogel. ¹⁷ It then curved north, went to En Shemesh, continued to Geliloth, which faces the Pass of Adummim, and ran down to the Stone of Bohan son of Reuben. ¹⁸ It continued to the northern slope of Beth Arabah[a] and on down into the Arabah. ¹⁹ It then went to the northern slope of Beth Hoglah and came out at the northern bay of the Dead Sea, at the mouth of the Jordan in the south. This was the southern boundary.

20 The Jordan formed the boundary on the eastern side.

These were the boundaries that marked out the inheritance of the clans of Benjamin on all sides.

21 The tribe of Benjamin, according to its clans, had the following cities:

Jericho, Beth Hoglah, Emek Keziz, **22** Beth Arabah, Zemaraim, Bethel, **23** Avvim, Parah, Ophrah, **24** Kephar Ammoni, Ophni and Geba – twelve towns and their villages.

25 Gibeon, Ramah, Beeroth, **26** Mizpah, Kephirah, Mozah, **27** Rekem, Irpeel, Taralah, **28** Zelah, Haeleph, the Jebusite city (that is, Jerusalem), Gibeah and Kiriath – fourteen towns and their villages.

This was the inheritance of Benjamin for its clans.

Land allotted to Simeon

19 The second lot came out for the tribe of Simeon according to its clans. Their inheritance lay within the territory of Judah. **2** It included:

Beersheba (or Sheba),[a] Moladah, **3** Hazar Shual, Balah, Ezem, **4** Eltolad, Bethul, Hormah, **5** Ziklag, Beth Markaboth, Hazar Susah, **6** Beth Lebaoth and Sharuhen – thirteen towns and their villages;

7 Ain, Rimmon, Ether and Ashan – four towns and their villages – **8** and all the villages around these towns as far as Baalath Beer (Ramah in the Negev).

This was the inheritance of the tribe of the Simeonites, according to its clans. **9** The inheritance of the Simeonites was taken from the share of Judah, because Judah's portion was more than they needed. So the Simeonites received their inheritance within the territory of Judah.

Land allotted to Zebulun

10 The third lot came up for Zebulun according to its clans:

The boundary of their inheritance went as far as Sarid. **11** Going west it ran to Maralah, touched Dabbesheth, and extended to the ravine near Jokneam. **12** It turned east from Sarid towards the sunrise to the territory of Kisloth Tabor and went on to Daberath and up to Japhia. **13** Then it continued eastward to Gath Hepher and Eth Kazin; it came out at Rimmon and turned towards Neah. **14** There the boundary went round on the north to Hannathon and ended at the Valley of Iphtah El. **15** Included were Kattath, Nahalal, Shimron, Idalah and Bethlehem. There were twelve towns and their villages.

16 These towns and their villages

were the inheritance of Zebulun, according to its clans.

Land allotted to Issachar

17 The fourth lot came out for Issachar according to its clans. **18** Their territory included:

Jezreel, Kesulloth, Shunem, **19** Hapharaim, Shion, Anaharath, **20** Rabbith, Kishion, Ebez, **21** Remeth, En Gannim, En Haddah and Beth Pazzez. **22** The boundary touched Tabor, Shahazumah and Beth Shemesh, and ended at the Jordan. There were sixteen towns and their villages.
23 These towns and their villages were the inheritance of the tribe of Issachar, according to its clans.

Land allotted to Asher

24 The fifth lot came out for the tribe of Asher according to its clans. **25** Their territory included:

Helkath, Hali, Beten, Akshaph, **26** Allammelek, Amad and Mishal. On the west the boundary touched Carmel and Shihor Libnath. **27** It then turned east towards Beth Dagon, touched Zebulun and the Valley of Iphtah El, and went north to Beth Emek and Neiel, passing Kabul on the left. **28** It went to Abdon,[b] Rehob, Hammon and Kanah, as far as Greater Sidon. **29** The boundary then turned back towards Ramah and went to the fortified city of Tyre, turned towards Hosah and came out at the Mediterranean Sea in the region of Akzib, **30** Ummah, Aphek and Rehob. There were twenty-two towns and their villages.
31 These towns and their villages were the inheritance of the tribe of Asher, according to its clans.

Land allotted to Naphtali

32 The sixth lot came out for Naphtali according to its clans:

33 Their boundary went from Heleph and the large tree in Zaanannim, passing Adami Nekeb and Jabneel to Lakkum and ending at the Jordan. **34** The boundary ran west through Aznoth Tabor and came out at Hukkok. It touched Zebulun on the south, Asher on the west and the Jordan[c] on the east. **35** The fortified cities were Ziddim, Zer, Hammath, Rakkath, Kinnereth, **36** Adamah, Ramah, Hazor, **37** Kedesh, Edrei, En Hazor, **38** Iron, Migdal El, Horem, Beth Anath and Beth Shemesh. There were nineteen towns and their villages.
39 These towns and their villages were the inheritance of the tribe of Naphtali, according to its clans.

Land allotted to Dan

40 The seventh lot came out for the tribe of Dan according to its clans. **41** The territory of their inheritance included:

Zorah, Eshtaol, Ir Shemesh, **42** Shaalabbin, Aijalon, Ithlah, **43** Elon, Timnah, Ekron, **44** Eltekeh, Gibbethon, Baalath, **45** Jehud, Bene Berak, Gath Rimmon, **46** Me Jarkon and Rakkon, with the area facing Joppa.

47 (When the territory of the Danites was lost to them, they went up and attacked Leshem, took it, put it to the sword and occupied it. They settled in Leshem and named it Dan after their ancestor.)

48 These towns and their villages were the inheritance of the tribe of Dan, according to its clans.

Land allotted to Joshua

49 When they had finished dividing the land into its allotted portions, the Israelites gave Joshua son of Nun an inheritance among them, **50** as the LORD had commanded. They gave him the town he asked for – Timnath Serah[d] in the hill country of Ephraim. And he built up the town and settled there.

51 These are the territories that Eleazar the priest, Joshua son of Nun and the heads of the tribal clans of Israel assigned by lot at Shiloh in the presence of the LORD at the entrance to the tent of meeting. And so they finished dividing the land.

---

a 18 Septuagint; Hebrew *slope facing the Arabah*
a 2 Or *Beersheba, Sheba*; 1 Chron. 4:28 does not have *Sheba*.
b 28 Some Hebrew manuscripts (see also 21:30); most Hebrew manuscripts *Ebron*
c 34 Septuagint; Hebrew *west, and Judah, the Jordan,*
d 50 Also known as *Timnath Heres* (see Judges 2:9)

1. Joshua's challenge and the second division • Joshua 18:1–10

The second round of land division raises significant questions: (a) Why is it needed? (b) Were the remaining seven tribes not given an allocation earlier? (c) Why are the territories allocated significantly smaller than those for Judah and Joseph? (d) Have the original boundaries of the land changed? Interpretation of this passage turns on whether we regard this second division as needed because these tribes have not yet been allocated land or see it as a remedy for a failure to take land already allocated. The second position is adopted here, and appropriate explanation will be given below.[1]

Joshua's challenge (18:1–3)

This episode occurs an indefinite length of time after the previous allocations. There is a change in location from Gilgal to Shiloh.[2] There is another difference in that they set up the Tent of Meeting.[3] This means that the casting of lots that follows is done 'in the presence of the LORD' (verse 6, 8, 10). This is the first reference to the Tent of Meeting in the book; we do not know if it was previously operational at Gilgal. All of Israel 'gathered' for this event (verse 1): the word used here often refers to more formal gatherings of God's people to meet with him.[4]

The introductory description is very significant here. First, the land 'was brought under their control' (verse 1). This is not an activity they performed but the situation as it stands: the land lies 'subdued before them'. This contrasts with verse 2: 'but there were still seven Israelite tribes who had not yet received their inheritance'. This is presented as a wrong state of affairs: the land is open to them, but they have not taken it.

That is why Joshua expresses an accusing question in verse 3, 'How long will you wait . . .?' More literally it is, 'How long will you be slack?' While the question asks, 'How long', the sense is more, 'Why haven't you done it?' The force of the question is added to by reference to the land as that which 'the LORD, the God of your ancestors, has given you'. This points them to the long history of promise regarding this land plus the certainty that it is theirs already, and so emphasises the incongruity of their not having taken it.[5]

---

1 For an introduction and general overview of positions, see Assis, 'How Long Are You Slack', 1–7.
2 No location was specified in Joshua 14:1–5, but it is commonly taken to be Gilgal (see 14:6).
3 This is also called the Tabernacle and was prescribed by God as his dwelling place among his people. For more details on its content and arrangement, see Exodus 40.
4 For example, in Exodus 35:1; Leviticus 8:3; Numbers 1:18; Deuteronomy 31:12. This is its only use in that way in Joshua.
5 Firth, *Joshua*, 309.

Daniel Hawk says this continues the theme from the end of chapter 17: 'the lack of Israelite determination and the presence of land yet to be occupied'.[6] It is damning of the remaining tribes that they are being slack with what they ought to have been grasping.

Against this 'negative' reading it is sometimes argued that these tribes could not have taken possession of their land because it has not yet been allocated to them: verse 2 could be read as saying that their allocation had not happened. But that does not fit with Joshua's words in verse 3. There is also no reason to think that the allocation process started in Joshua 14:1–5 would have ended after the first two tribes; indeed, the command was for it to be distributed among all the tribes that remained (Joshua 13:7).[7] Another argument to counter this negative reading is that the drawing of lots to divide the land that follows shows that it has not happened earlier. However, there is good reason to think that this is a new, smaller allocation, as discussed below.

Joshua's proposal and dividing of the land (18:4–10)

Joshua proposes a survey of the land by three men from each tribe. They will write out a description of it, divide it into seven appropriate sections, and return. Joshua will then divide this land between the remaining seven tribes by casting lots for them (verse 6). Within this, there is reference to the allocation already made: Judah and Joseph stay in the territory they have, the Levites are not allocated land because their inheritance is in the service at the tabernacle (see Joshua 13:14, 33), and the trans-Jordanian tribes have already received their inheritance through Moses. This acts to summarise the situation so far and to make it clear that the whole allocation process is not starting again for every tribe. Rather, the issue is dividing the remaining land among the seven tribes who have not yet taken possession.

Joshua's proposal is repeated in verse 8 to the men appointed: a survey, a description and casting lots. It is then repeated in terms

---

6 Hawk, *Berit Olam*, 214.
7 Assis, 'How Long Are You Slack', 7–8.

of being enacted (verses 9–10). So we have a threefold repetition of the same actions to emphasise their significance. This points us to the idea that this is a new land allocation. No survey or description was needed in Joshua 14:1–5, but now it is required; division by lot seems to have happened already in Joshua 14:1–5, and now it happens again.

To anticipate comments below, what is happening is that the boundaries of the land are changed in this second division; specifically, they are reduced. While the boundaries in the first allotment are not given, there is good reason to read these allotments as a watered-down version of what was originally proposed. Elie Assis proposes that this is Joshua's compromise given the people's reluctance to possess the full extent of the land. The boundaries seen in chapters 18–19 are smaller than the remaining land listed in Joshua 13:1–6. This is a division of land previous conquered and so more easily occupied.[8]

2. The land allotted to the remaining seven tribes • Joshua 18:11–19:48

The land allotted to each tribe is introduced in the same way: the lot 'comes up' according to that tribes' clans. Also, each tribal allocation has a similar summary statement following the boundary description. For the usual understanding of these territories see map 2.

Benjamin (18:11–28)

Benjamin receives a slot of land between Judah and Joseph on the eastern side of the country. The boundary is described moving from the northern, to the western, to the southern and then the eastern boundary line, and the town are listed. This borders Judah's territory as Jerusalem was spoken of as being part of Judah but now as part of Benjamin (see 15:63 and 18:16, 28).

---

[8] Assis, 'How Long Are You Slack', 8–12.

Simeon (19:1–9)

The unusual feature of Simeon's inheritance is that it comes from within the land already allocated to Judah. This is stated in verse 1 and is then repeated twice more in verse 9, so stressing its oddity. Verse 9 also contains the explanation that Judah has more land than they require. Even though this means there is space for Simeon, the impression is given that this was not the original plan. Nine cities that were originally listed as belonging to Judah are now allocated to Simeon.[9] The boundary line is not described, and indeed there might not be a clear one; rather, there is a group of towns in a distinct area. Many commentators see here a fulfilment of the prophecy that Simeon would be dispersed through Israel (Genesis 49:5–7); the same prediction is made of Levi whose cities are spread through the land.[10]

Zebulun (19:10–16)

Zebulun receives a portion just north of Manasseh. The description describes the southern boundary line moving west and then east, then moving north along its eastern edge. Its western boundary remains unclear but may include the list of towns in verse 15 (in which Bethlehem is not the famous town in Judah).[11]

Issachar (19:17–23)

Issachar receives a portion adjacent to Zebulun, placed to their south-east. No overall boundary is given, but rather a list of towns and a partial boundary line in verse 22.

Asher (19:24–31)

Asher's allotment is in the northwest corner of the country, running along the coastline. Its interior boundary line is unclear.

---

9 Howard, *Joshua*, 366.
10 Howard, *Joshua*, 366–7.
11 Firth, *Joshua*, 319.

Naphtali (19:32–9)

Naphtali is also in the north of the country, running parallel to Asher but inland. Again, its boundary line is uncertain; its city list is specifically 'fortified cities'.

Dan (19:40–48)

The last of the tribes to be listed is Dan. Their land is placed between Judah and Ephraim and west of Benjamin; there is no boundary given but a list of towns grouped together. Given the previous ordering of tribes, Dan is out of place here both in birth order of the brothers and in the geographical movement across the country (we were moving north but now jump back south). This is to draws attention to Dan and its unique feature – that they lose their territory (verse 47). This looks ahead to the events in Judges 18 where they move north and settle in Leshem (or Laish). While this is given to explain why the Danites moved location, the idea of losing the inheritance allocated by God is horrendous. The wording here gives it added poignancy: the lot 'came out' for the tribe of Dan (verse 40) and then their territory 'came out' from them (verse 47). What was allocated slipped from their hands; what was given to them was given away.

3. *Land allotted to Joshua • Joshua 19:49–51*

Joshua is part of the tribe of Ephraim but was not mentioned in their allocation. Rather, his allocation is reserved for when the allotment process has finished. It is described as the Israelites giving Joshua an inheritance, and that this is in obedience to the command of the LORD.[12] He is given the town of Timnath-Serah and lives there.

This forms a 'bookend' with the story of Caleb, which started the land allocation process in Joshua 14:6–15. The two passages are parallels in being allocations to individuals rather than to tribes, they are each

---

12 There is no record of this command elsewhere in Scripture. Howard, *Joshua*, 378.

given a named city, and the allocation is said to be in obedience to a command of God. Joshua and Caleb are also the two spies who believed God's word that they would be able to enter the land and defeat the inhabitants. They therefore stand as examples of those who trust God's promises and live by them; they are model faithful Israelites. Starting and ending this section with them is deliberate. They form a faithful frame around a story of increasing failure. We will comment on the significance of this below.

Verse 51 draws this section to a close with connections back to Joshua 18:1–10: the location of Shiloh, the presence of the LORD and the Tent of Meeting. But it also draws a conclusion to the larger section that started in Joshua 14:1–5. From that earlier passage it repeats the process of assigning by lot, and mentions the leaders involved and the key theme of 'inheritance' (NIV 'territory'). The overall process was described as 'dividing' or 'allotting' the land (Joshua 14:5), and that is now said to be complete (verse 51).

We can outline the structure of this section as follows:

A: Dividing the land (14:1–5)
    B: Caleb's inheritance (14:6–15)
        C: Judah's and Joseph's inheritances (15:1–17:18)
            D: Joshua's charge and reallocation (18:1–10)
        C: Seven tribes' inheritances (18:11–19:48)
    B: Joshua's inheritance (19:49–50)
A: End of dividing the land (19:51)

Some outlines of this section see the middle passage in 18:1–10 as a high point; rather here, we see it as a low point.[13]

---

[13] There is a wider structure running from chapter 13 to 21 that utilises this 'high point' view. This stems from an original work by H. J. Koorevaar, *De Opbouw van Het Boek Jozua* (Heverlee: Centrum voor Bijbelse Vorming België, 1990). It is summarised by Howard, *Joshua*, 294. This structure is also followed by Johnson, *Teaching Joshua*, 67–71.

KEY THEMES AND APPLICATION

The failure to take the land as commanded
Joshua's questioning of the seven remaining tribes and the subsequent need for the reallocation of land is condemning of this group. God has given them the land and they are now to possess it, trusting him for the victories he will give and grateful for his gift. Instead, they hang back and seem reluctant. We are not told why – Joshua's question remains unanswered. It might be feeling unable to possess the land, in which case their faith in God's promise is lacking. It might be not valuing what they have been promised, in which case their priorities are appalling. Whatever the reason, it stands as a rebuke to them and so a challenge to later readers: what is their attitude to the land? More broadly we can ask, what is our attitude to God's words of promise? Do we enter into what he has already given us? Charles Simeon draws a parallel with the Christian today reading the Scriptures:

> The Scriptures contain, not only the will which makes over to us the grant of this inheritance, but the title-deeds themselves, yea, a map also of the whole estate, a description of everything that is valuable in it, and clear directions for securing to ourselves the everlasting possession of it . . . Do we search that blessed book with half the interest that we ought? Do we mark everything in it that can assist us either in discovering our title to heaven, or in securing the attainment of it? Let us ask ourselves, whether we do not often find less interest in it than in a common newspaper? . . . Does not this then shew how justly the reproof of 'slackness' may be applied to us?[14]

More broadly, Dale Ralph Davis says that God's promises 'are intended not as sedatives but as stimulants'; they are to spur us on to live for

---

14 Simeon, *Horae Homileticae*, 2:604.

God, not make us lazy.[15] We might think of New Testament passages where God's provision and promise are emphasised and are then to lead to activity. For example:

> His divine power has given us everything we need for a godly life through our knowledge of him who called us by his own glory and goodness. Through these he has given us his very great and precious promises, so that through them you may participate in the divine nature, having escaped the corruption in the world caused by evil desires.
>
> For this very reason, make every effort to add to your faith . . . (2 Peter 1:3–5)

Failure described and anticipated
We have seen a progressive failure to take the land as commanded. This is seen in the cities not possessed, in the unwillingness of the Josephites to occupy their land, in the reluctance of the seven tribes to possess the land allocated to them, in the reduction of the land and, finally, in Dan losing their inheritance. The entry into the land was triumphant; the possession of it far less so.

Some of that failure was present in Joshua's day; some follows later. John Goldingay writes that the book of Joshua 'invites its readers to imagine facing facts ahead of time.' This applies specifically to Dan's loss of their inheritance. He goes on, 'This is only the beginning of the disappointment. Gradually but inexorably, the endowments of every clan without exception will be compromised.'[16] Such reading should be sobering, and ideally would prompt repentance and lead to reliance on future grace. God's people should know they even fail to receive his gracious gift as they should and can only throw themselves on his mercy.

Faithfulness and failure contrasted
The failure to take the land is bracketed by the examples of Caleb and Joshua. Caleb stands as the model example of trusting obedience,

---

15 Davis, *Joshua*, 142.
16 Goldingay, *Joshua*, 356.

which means he drives out the feared Anakites and takes possession of what God has promised. Joshua's inheritance is related much more briefly, but mention of him brings his faithful following of God to mind. Beginning and ending with these two men deliberately draws a contrast between their faithfulness and the failures of the nation.

Along with the rebuke to the seven tribes above, this should be seen as a challenge to people's faith – will they be like Caleb and Joshua? However, we should also see it as a reminder of our inability to live for God as we should, and so our inability to claim our inheritance. What we all need is a faithful Israelite who will trust and obey on our behalf and so win entry into God's kingdom for us; one who invites us to join him in his inheritance. In this way, Caleb and Joshua picture the Lord Jesus, and this whole section teaches us the gospel. While the book of Joshua inspires us to trust and live for God ourselves, it also humbles us because we fail, like the Israelites did. However, it then encourages and comforts us, because its big lesson is that we need a new Joshua to get us into God's land. Wonderfully, God has sent him.

20

God's Concern for Justice

Joshua 20

Chapters 13–19 described the division of the land so that each tribe received their inheritance, and that process is now over. The main action of the book of Joshua is therefore complete: the land has been conquered and then divided. However, there are still some outstanding issues before life in the land is fully set up as God specified. In this chapter and the following one, arrangements are made in accordance with previous instructions given in Numbers and Deuteronomy. In the first case, this is to allocate some cities as 'cities of refuge'. This will show us God's concern for justice and protection within his land.

Cities of refuge

20 Then the LORD said to Joshua: **2** 'Tell the Israelites to designate the cities of refuge, as I instructed you through Moses, **3** so that anyone who kills a person accidentally and unintentionally may flee there and find protection from the avenger of blood. **4** When they flee to one of these cities, they are to stand in the entrance of the city gate and state their case before the elders of that city. Then the elders are to admit the fugitive into their city and provide a place to live among them. **5** If the avenger of blood comes in pursuit, the elders must not surrender the fugitive, because the fugitive killed their neighbour unintentionally and without malice aforethought. **6** They are to stay in that city until they have stood trial before the assembly and until the death of the high priest who is serving at that time. Then they may go back to their own home in the town from which they fled.'

7 So they set apart Kedesh in Galilee in the hill country of Naphtali, Shechem in the hill country of Ephraim, and Kiriath Arba (that is, Hebron) in the hill country of

Judah. **8** East of the Jordan (on the other side from Jericho) they designated Bezer in the wilderness on the plateau in the tribe of Reuben, Ramoth in Gilead in the tribe of Gad, and Golan in Bashan in the tribe of Manasseh. **9** Any of the Israelites or any foreigner residing among them who killed someone accidentally could flee to these designated cities and not be killed by the avenger of blood prior to standing trial before the assembly.

1. The background to the cities of refuge

The idea of protection for causing accidental death is first introduced in Exodus 21:12–14. In that passage a person may flee to a place God will designate. That provision is then specified more fully in Numbers 35, which introduces both the idea of towns for the Levites and the cities of refuge; there is overlap between the two, with six of the Levitical towns also being designated as cities of refuge. The principle behind the cities of refuge is explained in Numbers 35:9–15: they will be a place that someone can flee following an accidental death. In such an instance, the perpetrator would be in danger from 'the avenger' (Numbers 35:12). This might be a family member or someone in a more official position. They might seek appropriate retribution and not be expected to distinguish between an intentional and accidental death.[1] Protection from such an avenger would be found in one of these cities so that a trial could be conducted to determine their guilt or innocence.

Numbers 35 then distinguishes between acts of murder and accidental manslaughter (Numbers 35:16–24). In the case of manslaughter, the person in question will be protected from revenge by staying in the city of refuge; if they stray outside, then they become legally liable for retribution. They are to stay in the city of refuge until the high priest dies (Numbers 35:25–34) – which we will return to below.

In Deuteronomy we are told that Moses allocated three cities of refuge in the territory east of the Jordan: Bezer, Ramoth and Golan (Deuteronomy 4:41–3). There is then instruction in Deuteronomy

---

[1] Woudstra, *Joshua*, 299.

19 that three more cities are to be allocated in the land west of the Jordan, with appropriate spacing between them, with a repetition of the function of these cities (Deuteronomy 19:1–13).

2. The commands to Joshua • Joshua 20:1–6

The background above is what lies behind God's words to Joshua here, and the comment, 'as I instructed you through Moses' (verse 2). God speaks to Joshua, telling him it is now time for the Israelites to put these commands into practice. They should designate these cities 'for themselves' (not translated by the NIV), indicating that these are for their own benefit.[2] The concept and explanation of how they are to work is then repeated, with some elaboration. These cities are so that a person responsible for an accidental death may flee from someone seeking revenge. They are to state their case before the elders of city, who are then to admit them and provide protection; it is repeated that they are offered such protection because of the accidental nature of the death in question. Incidentally, we see here both the norm of a group of elders overseeing the affairs of a city and the city gate as the place of such city business being conducted.

This protection is to allow due process in the form of trial: the person stands before an assembly for 'judgment' (NIV 'trial'). We should presume that if they are found guilty of intentional murder then the appropriate sentence will be carried out (see Numbers 35:16–21), but here it is assumed that they are found innocent. Even then, they must remain in the city of refuge until the death of the high priest, and only then may they return to their home town.[3] There is some speculation as to why this last element is commanded. First, why may they not be at liberty immediately, given that they are innocent of murder? This may be because a death has taken place, accidental or not, and this hangs over the

---

[2] Howard, *Joshua*, 381–2.
[3] There is some debate over the restrictions, but this seems the most likely understanding. Woudstra, *Joshua*, 300–301.

perpetrator: 'bloodshed pollutes the land' (Numbers 35:33). This might be parallel to where the Levitical instruction sees guilt and the need for atonement even when sin is accidental (see Leviticus 4–5).[4] Second, why does the death of the high priest act as the marker for their full freedom? This is most likely because the death of the high priest in some way makes atonement for the death. We will return to this below.

3. The designation of the towns • Joshua 20:7–9

Obedience to God's command through Joshua follows and three more cities are designated as cities of refuge: Kedesh, Shechem and Kiriath Arber (or Hebron). The term 'set apart' shows they are designated for a special purpose.[5] We have noted the allocation of Hebron to Caleb in chapter 14. The designation as a city of refuge need not mean it has been removed from him as his inheritance; only that it will serve this purpose as well. Verse 8 says that they also designate the three cities already listed in Deuteronomy 4 which were allocated by Moses. This acts to group them together with the new cities west of the Jordan. Looking at the placement of these cities on a map shows they are appropriately spaced across the country so that no one would be too far from one of them (see map 3).

The final verse reiterates the purpose of the cities just listed and so emphasises their importance. It makes the additional comment that they are for any Israelite or 'foreigner' who is living in Israel; hence we have an example of the equity of God's Law for those who might be more vulnerable because of their ethnic background.

---

4 Howard, *Joshua*, 382–3.
5 The word used is 'to make holy', illustrating that the idea of 'holiness' is fundamentally that of being 'set apart' or 'separate' rather than 'morally pure', although it can go on to have that meaning.

KEY THEMES AND APPLICATION

God's concern for justice
We see in the cities of refuge an example of God's concern for justice in his land. God's justice means he is against the guilty going unpunished but also against the innocent being wrongly punished. This passage gives a preventative measure for the latter. It revolves around the instance of accidental death but reflects the reality that injustice can occur in such circumstances. God is against such injustice and so makes provision for protection and the conducting of a proper trial with appropriate sentencing. This should be so whatever the ethnic identity of the individual involved.

As the allocation of such towns is now not relevant to us, in teaching this passage we might wish to emphasise God's concern for justice generally. In some cultures that is required because the church has not appropriately realised such concern, and/or the wider society perceives the church to be a place of injustice. In some cases, there may be instances of the church itself having committed unjust acts and even perpetuating them. This would be an appropriate moment for comment on such cases and repentance if needed.

We may also wish to point to God's instituting of systems of justice through governments in the New Testament. In Romans 13:1–5, the government is seen as God's instrument of justice. This recognises that God's people no longer live as a religious state governed directly by God, but rather are dispersed among the nations. As a result, we do not conduct trials over legal affairs within the church but rather submit to the governing authorities. This call to submit to our rulers and their role follows the call in Romans 12:17–21 not to take revenge ourselves but to leave vengeance to God. Hence, we are to trust God to bring justice himself rather than to take it into our own hands, and we see that one way he may bring it is through human rulers.

Given that God's commands here are for how his people are to live in his kingdom, we might also make application to the church. The church should be a place of justice. That might challenge practices that show preference or favouritism; we might especially identify anything that works against the care of the more vulnerable (see James 2:1–4).

The sanctity of life

The broader biblical theme behind this passage is the sanctity of life. The unauthorised taking of life is prohibited and is punishable by death precisely because life is sacred. This is connected to humanity's creation in God's image – this is what bestows such value and why such a severe punishment is due (Genesis 9:6). This results in the sixth commandment 'You shall not murder' (Exodus 20:13), and then the more detailed laws in Numbers 35 and other passages. All of this lies behind Joshua 20.[6] While this may not be the focus of teaching this passage, appropriate reference might be made to it depending on the context.

The need for and provision of atonement

We saw the role of the high priest within the cities of refuge and that their death signals the full freedom of the person concerned. The background to this may lie in the explanation in Numbers 35. A key verse in this regard is as follows:

> Do not pollute the land where you are. Bloodshed pollutes the land, and atonement cannot be made for the land on which blood has been shed, except by the blood of the one who shed it. (Numbers 35:33)

'Bloodshed' here is simply 'blood', and does not necessarily refer to deliberate murder but to all death, including accidental ones. Such spilling of blood pollutes the land, and cleansing only comes from the atoning effect of another's death. That is usually the death of the one who caused the blood to be spilt – i.e., the murderer. In the case of accidental death, the perpetrator could be killed outside the city of refuge, and this would not be considered murder (Numbers 35:27); in other words, they are in some sense considered guilty and a 'death' is owed. This connects with the fact that no

---

6 See Harstad, *Joshua*, 643–4.

ransom is possible for killing someone else, only a death (Numbers 35:32). Hence, the perpetrator must wait for a death – that of the high priest – before atonement has been made. Timothy Ashley summarises, 'Both murder and inadvertent killing pollute the land. Murder is atoned for by the death of the murderer, inadvertent killing by the death of the high priest on behalf of the killer.'[7]

The fact that it is the high priest whose death marks the person's freedom is highly significant. The high priest is the one who makes representation before God and offers sacrifices for a person's atonement. Now the death of the high priest sets them free. As Moshe Greenburg says, 'The sole personage whose religious-cultic importance might endow his death with expiatory value for the people at large is the high priest.'[8] We therefore have an instance of a 'representative death' where one dies on behalf of another. This is an example of where institutional patterns in the Old Testament look forward to the New: the death of the great high priest, Jesus, who sets us free (see Hebrews 9:11–15). A seventeenth-century commentary wrote:

> We are to understand that the death of the high priest was herein a type of our High Priest, Jesus Christ, who, by his previous death, has wrought a perfect reconciliation between God and us, and has procured the full pardon of all our sins, and perfect liberty from the pursuing wrath of God, and all the enemies of our salvation.[9]

---

[7] Timothy R. Ashley, *The Book of Numbers: The New International Commentary on the Old Testament* (Grand Rapids: Eerdmans, 1993), 656.

[8] Moshe Greenberg, 'The Biblical Conception of Asylum', *Journal of Biblical Literature* 78, no. 2 (1959): 130.

[9] 'English Annotations, Annotations on Joshua 20:6', in Nichols, *ESV Church History Study Bible*, 173.

21

God's Concern for Relationship

Joshua 21

Having overseen the allotment of inheritances for each tribe, Joshua is now dealing with the outstanding issues in organising the ongoing life of Israel in the land. We have seen the designation of cities of refuge. The remaining issue is the designation of towns for the Levites to live in. As with the cities of refuge, this is expected because of previous instruction through Moses. It has also been anticipated in Joshua because of comments in previous chapters that the Levites have not received land in the same way as the other tribes but will receive towns (Joshua 14:4). This provision for the Levites highlights the significance of their role in mediating the people's relationship with God. Once this task is done, a major section of the book ends, and this is marked by a climatic summary statement with its affirmation that God has fulfilled all his promises.

Towns for the Levites

21 Now the family heads of the Levites approached Eleazar the priest, Joshua son of Nun, and the heads of the other tribal families of Israel **2** at Shiloh in Canaan and said to them, 'The LORD commanded through Moses that you give us towns to live in, with pasture-lands for our livestock.' **3** So, as the LORD had commanded, the Israelites gave the Levites the following towns and pasture-lands out of their own inheritance:

4 The first lot came out for the Kohathites, according to their clans. The Levites who were descendants of Aaron the priest were allotted thirteen towns from the tribes of Judah, Simeon and Benjamin. **5** The rest of Kohath's descendants were allotted ten towns from the clans of the tribes of Ephraim, Dan and half of Manasseh.

6 The descendants of Gershon were allotted thirteen towns from the clans of the tribes of Issachar, Asher, Naphtali and the half-tribe of Manasseh in Bashan.

7 The descendants of Merari, according to their clans, received twelve towns from the tribes of Reuben, Gad and Zebulun.

8 So the Israelites allotted to the Levites these towns and their pasture-lands, as the LORD had commanded through Moses.

9 From the tribes of Judah and Simeon they allotted the following towns by name **10** (these towns were assigned to the descendants of Aaron who were from the Kohathite clans of the Levites, because the first lot fell to them):

11 They gave them Kiriath Arba (that is, Hebron), with its surrounding pasture-land, in the hill country of Judah. (Arba was the forefather of Anak.) **12** But the fields and villages around the city they had given to Caleb son of Jephunneh as his possession.

13 So to the descendants of Aaron the priest they gave Hebron (a city of refuge for one accused of murder), Libnah, **14** Jattir, Eshtemoa, **15** Holon, Debir, **16** Ain, Juttah and Beth Shemesh, together with their pasture-lands – nine towns from these two tribes.

17 And from the tribe of Benjamin they gave them Gibeon, Geba, **18** Anathoth and Almon, together with their pasture-lands – four towns.

19 The total number of towns for the priests, the descendants of Aaron, came to thirteen, together with their pasture-lands.

20 The rest of the Kohathite clans of the Levites were allotted towns from the tribe of Ephraim:

21 In the hill country of Ephraim they were given Shechem (a city of refuge for one accused of murder) and Gezer, **22** Kibzaim and Beth Horon, together with their pasture-lands – four towns.

23 Also from the tribe of Dan they received Eltekeh, Gibbethon, **24** Aijalon and Gath Rimmon, together with their pasture-lands – four towns.

25 From half the tribe of Manasseh they received Taanach and Gath Rimmon, together with their pasture-lands – two towns.

26 All these ten towns and their pasturelands were given to the rest of the Kohathite clans.

27 The Levite clans of the Gershonites were given:

from the half-tribe of Manasseh, Golan in Bashan (a city of refuge for one accused of murder) and Be Eshterah, together with their pasture-lands – two towns;

28 from the tribe of Issachar, Kishion, Daberath, **29** Jarmuth and En Gannim, together with

GOD'S CONCERN FOR RELATIONSHIP

their pasture-lands – four towns; 30 from the tribe of Asher, Mishal, Abdon, 31 Helkath and Rehob, together with their pasture-lands – four towns; 32 from the tribe of Naphtali, Kedesh in Galilee (a city of refuge for one accused of murder), Hammoth Dor and Kartan, together with their pasture-lands – three towns.

33 The total number of towns of the Gershonite clans came to thirteen, together with their pasture-lands.

34 The Merarite clans (the rest of the Levites) were given: from the tribe of Zebulun, Jokneam, Kartah, 35 Dimnah and Nahalal, together with their pasture-lands – four towns; 36 from the tribe of Reuben, Bezer, Jahaz, 37 Kedemoth and Mephaath, together with their pasture-lands – four towns; 38 from the tribe of Gad, Ramoth in Gilead (a city of refuge for one accused of murder), Mahanaim, 39 Heshbon and Jazer, together with their pasture-lands – four towns in all.

40 The total number of towns allotted to the Merarite clans, who were the rest of the Levites, came to twelve.

41 The towns of the Levites in the territory held by the Israelites were forty-eight in all, together with their pasture-lands. 42 Each of these towns had pasture-lands surrounding it; this was true for all these towns.

43 So the LORD gave Israel all the land he had sworn to give their ancestors, and they took possession of it and settled there. 44 The LORD gave them rest on every side, just as he had sworn to their ancestors. Not one of their enemies withstood them; the LORD gave all their enemies into their hands. 45 Not one of all the LORD's good promises to Israel failed; every one was fulfilled.

1. *The background in Numbers*

The concept of towns for the Levites is mentioned in Leviticus 25:32–4, but the instructions proper come in Numbers 35:1–8, where the Israelites are commanded to give towns from within their inheritance for the Levites to live in, along with pastureland around those towns for their livestock. There were to be forty-eight towns in all, and their selection from the tribes was to be proportional to the number any one tribe owned. This is the background to the Levites' request in our passage.

2. The request and allotment in Joshua • Joshua 21:1–42

The request of the Levites (21:1–3)

The leaders of the Levites come to Eleazar, Joshua and the other tribal leaders at Shiloh with their request. Mention of this group and location places this allocation with the previous land division – see Joshua 19:51. They remind them of God's command in Numbers 35, and their response is described immediately (verse 3). It is said that the 'Israelites' gave in accordance with the LORD's command. This focuses on the start and the end of the chain of command (God and the nation) while assuming the role of the leaders as intermediaries. It is also said that that they gave 'out of their own inheritance', showing both that this is a giving up of what is already theirs and that the Levites do not own these towns in the way the other tribes own theirs. We see this later in verse 41, where their towns are said to be within the territory (or possession) of the Israelites. Adolph Harstad says:

> The Levitical cities are never called the 'inheritance' or 'possession' of the Levites themselves. The Levites could live in these cities and make use of them, but they were not attached to or rooted in these cities as their permanent residences in the same way that the other tribes were grounded in their own territories.[1]

This connects to what we have seen previously about the Levites' inheritance being in their food provision, in God himself and in their service (13:14; 13:33; 18:7). This provision of cities and pastureland is to provide for their physical needs, not their inheritance.

---

[1] Harstad, *Joshua*, 661.

The allotment of towns (21:4–42)

The allotment is given first in broad brush strokes and then in finer detail.[2] The tribe of Levi can be divided into three groups under Levi's three sons (Genesis 46:11). Hence, in verses 4–8 we are told of the allotment to the Kohathites, the Gershonites and the Merarites and the number of towns they each receive from which tribes. For the Kohathites there is specification of the towns for the descendants of Aaron, but otherwise they are treated as one group. As expected from Numbers 35, the number of towns allocated totals forty-eight. The allocation is by 'lot', as it was with the tribal lands.

The allotment is then given in greater detail, naming the towns in question. The order is kept the same and the descendants of Aaron are again singled out. The focus on Aaron's descendants is because they form the priesthood. All the priests were Levites, but not all Levites were priests; only those in the line of Aaron (see verse 19). Referring to map 4 shows a key feature of the allocation: that the Levites are evenly distributed throughout the land. While the Aaronic clan lies with proximity to Jerusalem, perhaps anticipating their future role in the Temple, the tribe as a whole is spread across Israel. This connects to their representative and mediatorial role that we will discuss below.

There are some explanatory comments along the way, most notably involving Hebron. This is because of the previous allocation of Hebron to Caleb which this designation as a Levitical town now draws into question. It is now clarified that Caleb received the villages and fields around the town (verse 12). With the listing of the towns, the cities of refuge are listed, all of which are also Levitical towns (verses 13, 21, 27, 32, 38; compare Numbers 35:6–8). This only lists five of the six cities of refuge; Bezer is not identified, although it is listed in verse 36. It is unclear why it is not labelled as a city of refuge along with the others. Verses 41–2 close the listing and emphasise that the towns were given with their pasturelands. Marten Woudstra

---

[2] There is a similar list in 1 Chronicles 6. See the comparison and discussion in Harstad, 664–5.

says that this emphasises the function of these towns: 'The Levites were not to possess them . . . but to be users of them.'[3]

3. The fulfilment of God's promises • Joshua 21:43–5

These verses are significant in both marking the end of a major section in the book and indicating its key themes. It formally brings to a close the distribution of the land from chapters 13–21, but also looks back to chapter 1 and further back to God's promises to Abraham. More than that, it is a celebration and exultation in all that God has achieved, and that he has done it all in faithfulness to his promises. God's promises or oaths are referred to repeatedly.[4] Dale Ralph Davis calls this 'sledgehammer theology', which pounds home the point about God's faithfulness.[5]

The verbs in verse 43 cover all that God has done and enabled Israel to do. First, the Lord 'gave' Israel all the land he promised. This looks back to Joshua 1:2–3 which encapsulates God's promise. This giving of the land was previously sworn to their ancestors (verse 43), and so it also looks back to the initial promise in Genesis 12:7 and subsequent repetition. The land God promised has now been given.

Second, Israel 'possessed' it. This has been a key word through Joshua, especially in the second half of the book. It was how Joshua described in 1:11 what would happen. This too looks back to promises to Abraham in Genesis 15:7 and has been repeated many times subsequently.

Third, the 'giving' of the land to 'possess' results in Israel 'settling' in the land. This refers to their dwelling in it as their home. This does not have the same prominence in earlier promises as the first two terms but can been seen as the expected result and is sometimes referred to when picturing life in the land in the future (e.g., Leviticus 25:18; Deuteronomy 12:10).

What God has given Israel is then summed up in the word 'rest'

---

3 Woudstra, *Joshua*, 313.
4 There is no word for 'promise' in Hebrew and so verse 45 refers to God's 'words', but they function as promises.
5 Davis, *Joshua*, 158.

(verse 44). This is again said to be in accordance with what he swore to their ancestors. The giving of such rest requires the totality of victory over their enemies that is emphasised here. Rest pictures the harmonious and peaceful experience God promised his people. This word was last used in Joshua in the opening chapter to describe the rest that God had already given the trans-Jordanian tribes and would give the remaining tribes (Joshua 1:13, 15).[6] It ties into the rich biblical theme of rest as part of God's salvation purposes (see, for example, Exodus 20:11; 33:14; Deuteronomy 12:10).[7]

This leads to the final comment in verse 45 that not one of God's promises has failed. This picks up the two previous references to what God has sworn to their ancestors: those promises have now come to fulfilment. This is stressed by stating it negatively (not one failed) and then positively (every one was fulfilled). In addition, these are 'good' promises: God has good intent towards his people; he promised them good things and has now delivered.

A repeated word through the section is 'all'; it comes six times, stressing totality each time. It refers to:

- Giving 'all' the land.
- Giving rest according to 'all' he had sworn.
- None of 'all' of their enemies withstanding them.
- Giving 'all' their enemies into their hands.
- None of 'all' of God's promises failing.
- 'All' of God's promises being fulfilled.

Having read the previous chapters, we know that these words are both true and idealistic. They are true in that God has indeed given them victory and the land just as he promised; they are idealistic in that we have already noted Israel's failures in taking the land.[8] The failures are, of course, entirely the fault of Israel; God has been completely true to his promises. David Firth speaks of these words operating on two levels:

---

[6] It is used elsewhere in Joshua with other meanings. Note that the word for 'rest' in Joshua 11:23 and 14:15 is different and refers to the cessation of fighting.
[7] See 'The Promised Land: inheritance and resting place' in the Introduction.
[8] McConville and Williams, *Joshua*, 83.

At every point where Israel had claimed God's promise, they had received it. So it could be said that he had given them rest. But there are also points where Israel made no such claim on the promise, most notably in Dan's failure to keep the land allotted to them (19:47). Therefore, at a second level, these verses also function as an exhortation to faithfulness which claims God's promises.[9]

KEY THEMES AND APPLICATION

God's desire for relationship
The allocation of Levitical towns is to provide places for the Levites to live. We have previously noted the Levites' special position: they receive no physical inheritance in the land because the Lord is their inheritance (Joshua 13:33). They will also receive food offerings from the people (Joshua 13:14). While not all the Levites are priests, they all stand in a special position in relation to God and they all aid the nation's relationship with God in some way. For example, the Levites are responsible for the Tabernacle and will be later for the Temple (Numbers 1:47–53; 3:21–37). Within the Levites are the priests who mediate the nation's relationship with God in making offerings (Numbers 18:1–7). They are also responsible for teaching and instruction (e.g., Malachi 2:7). Moses's blessing said of the Levites:

> He teaches your precepts to Jacob
>   and your law to Israel.
> He offers incense before you
>   and whole burnt offerings on your altar.
> (Deuteronomy 33:10)

This is one reason why the Levitical towns are distributed throughout the country. As John Mayer explained:

> Thus the Levites did not have cities all together in one allotment of land, as did the other tribes, but in every part of the land that there might be some in every tribe to teach the laws of

---

9 Firth, *Joshua*, 346.

GOD'S CONCERN FOR RELATIONSHIP

God, and to judge righteously; and that it might not be thought that the worship of God and the maintenance of his ministers pertained to one place only, but to them all.[10]

Therefore, this allocation of towns does not simply provide necessary accommodation but also provides the means for relationship. God wants his people to know him, to be able to approach him and to receive forgiveness from him. God's plan was to dwell with his people: 'Then I will dwell among the Israelites and be their God' (Exodus 29:45). The Levites make that dwelling and relationship possible. As Carolyn Pressler says, through this chapter we 'envision the Levites spread throughout Israelite territory, a visible emblem of the invisible presence of God'.[11]

For the believer today, of course, things have changed, as there is no tribe like this and no specific priesthood. Instead, these themes are fulfilled in Jesus who is the great high priest; he destroys the old Temple and establishes a new way of relating God through his own body (Hebrews 10:19–22). All believers now have access to God through the one mediator, Jesus (1 Timothy 2:5–6). And all believers then become priests in the new Temple built on Jesus (Ephesians 2:20–22; 1 Peter 2:4–5). In Joshua 21 we see God's desire for a relationship with his people, and therefore the provision of the towns for the Levites; what we now celebrate is the fulfilment of that theme in our identity in the church, and we look forward to its final fulfilment in the new creation (Revelation 21:22; 22:4).

Support of Christian ministers

The pattern seen in Joshua is that the Levites are supported by the other tribes. They are granted towns out of those tribes' inheritance. They are given pastureland, which implies they are to be partially self-supporting, but this too is a gift. They will also receive food through the offering system. In the New Testament this is taken as a pattern that those who serve God's people on God's behalf

---

10 John Mayer, 'Commentary on Joshua 21:1', in Amos, *Reformation Commentary*, 173.
11 Pressler, *Joshua, Judges and Ruth*, 103.

should be provided for by God's people. We must remember the point above, that the priesthood does not exist in the same form today, but serving God's people in different ways does still exist. Whether leaders of congregations, missionaries or other church positions, God's people should provide support (see 1 Corinthians 9:3–14; 1 Timothy 5:17–18). The Lutheran commentator Paul Kretzmann says:

> Thus the men in charge of the worship in the Jewish church were provided for with all that they needed to support their body and life, even as it is the will of the Lord today that they who preach the gospel should live off the gospel.[12]

The faithfulness of God
The last verses of the chapter are key in the message of Joshua and in its portrayal of God. God keeps his promises. These verses would take an Israelite's mind back through the generations to their ultimate ancestor, Abraham, and then forward again through the patriarchs and their preservation in Egypt, the growth of the nation in slavery, the redemption through Moses, the covenant at Sinai, the wilderness wanderings and the eventual entry into the land, triumph over their enemies and the dividing of the land. God's promises of giving the land and of giving rest in the land stand as a banner over this history, giving it meaning, purpose and certainty. Now is the moment to pause, look back and realise what God has done. This should result in wonder and gratitude for what has been given, and reassurance and confidence for whatever the future holds. The seventeenth-century minister John Owen wrote of this:

> God has done all according 'as he promised' (Josh 22:4; 2 Sam 7:21). He brought out his people of old with a mighty hand, with temptations, signs, and wonders, and a stretched-out arm; and all because he would keep the oath that he had sworn and the engagement that he had made to their fathers (Deut

---

12 Paul Kretzmann, 'Popular Commentary of the Bible: Old Testament', in Nichols, *ESV Church History Study Bible*, 332.

7:8). Whatsoever obstacles may lie in the way, he has done it, he will do it.[13]

So the reader of Joshua would be encouraged by God's actions and reassured by God's character. As Adolph Harstad says:

> Since the Lord has fulfilled his promise to give the land of Canaan to his covenant people Israel as their inheritance, his people can trust all of his promises and live in covenant faithfulness as his grateful heirs until the second Joshua, the greater Rest-giver, comes to this land.[14]

The New Testament believer can look backwards and forwards with regard to God's promises in a similar way. These promises stretch back to Genesis 3 to the one who would crush the serpent and undo his evil work. They stretch forward to the new creation when all God's salvation plans come to fulfilment, and he grants rest to his people. They centre on Jesus, through whom they are all fulfilled: 'For no matter how many promises God has made, they are "Yes" in Christ' (2 Corinthians 1:20).

God's plan for rest and need for victory
These last verses also point us to God's plan for his people. His desire is for his people to be at rest in his land. God is rescuing his people so they can be with him in his kingdom. The Exodus was to release them from slavery, but that was so they could be his people and be at home with him. This is the moment at which that is realised. This theme is fulfilled in Jesus and his offer of rest in him (Matthew 11:28–30). It fits in the biblical theological scheme of God rescuing his people so that they can live under his blessing in his place, and one way of describing that harmony and perfection is to be given 'rest'.

Within this we see the need for victory over enemies; as Marten

---

13 John Owen, *Works of John Owen*, ed. W. H. Goold (London: The Banner of Truth Trust, 1991), 8:113.
14 Harstad, *Joshua*, 670.

Woudstra says, 'The rest obtained for Israel had as its necessary corollary the defeat of Israel's *enemies*.'[15] Hence, God's purpose, even in the violence of destruction, is ultimately for peace for his people, and there can be no peace until victory is won. We see the same need for victory in the New Testament: the final arrival of rest and peace with God only takes place after the defeat of God's enemies (1 Corinthians 15:25–8; Revelation 19:11–16). Then we can, and will, finally be at rest.

---

15 Woudstra, *Joshua*, 315 (emphasis original).

PART THREE

JOSHUA 22–4

22

Unity and Its Preservation

Joshua 22

We have now seen the two main sections of the book of Joshua. Chapters 1–12 outlined the conquest of the land, and then chapters 13–21 the division of the land. That section ended with the high point of the book, in detailing God's faithfulness to all his promises and the granting of rest. The book now moves to its closing stages. The last three chapters focus on the future of Israel: how will they live in the land they have now been given? As Dale Ralph Davis expresses it, while the end of chapter 21 'emphatically underscores Yahweh's fidelity to his promise', these chapters are now 'preoccupied with the theme of Israel's fidelity to Yahweh'.[1]

The first activity is the return of the eastern tribes to their land. The focus, though, is not so much on their return as on the dangers that immediately arise from their building an altar. The prospect of apostasy by them, with the response of war from the rest of the nation, suddenly looms large. Wonderfully, it is revealed to be a misunderstanding and the crisis is resolved. Within the book this makes links back to Joshua's instructions to the eastern tribes in chapter 1 and to the theme of the unity of the nation in the distribution of the land. However, it also functions to raise the spectre of apostasy as a possibility and so prepares the way for Joshua's following speeches.

Eastern tribes return home

22 Then Joshua summoned the Reubenites, the Gadites and the half-tribe of Manasseh **2** and said to them, 'You have done all that Moses the servant of the Lord commanded, and you have obeyed me in everything I commanded. **3** For a long time now - to this very day - you have not deserted your fellow

---
[1] Davis, *Joshua*, 165.

Israelites but have carried out the mission the LORD your God gave you. **4** Now that the LORD your God has given them rest as he promised, return to your homes in the land that Moses the servant of the LORD gave you on the other side of the Jordan. **5** But be very careful to keep the commandment and the law that Moses the servant of the LORD gave you: to love the LORD your God, to walk in obedience to him, to keep his commands, to hold fast to him and to serve him with all your heart and with all your soul.'

6 Then Joshua blessed them and sent them away, and they went to their homes. **7** (To the half-tribe of Manasseh Moses had given land in Bashan, and to the other half of the tribe Joshua gave land on the west side of the Jordan along with their fellow Israelites.) When Joshua sent them home, he blessed them, **8** saying, 'Return to your homes with your great wealth – with large herds of livestock, with silver, gold, bronze and iron, and a great quantity of clothing – and divide the plunder from your enemies with your fellow Israelites.'

9 So the Reubenites, the Gadites and the half-tribe of Manasseh left the Israelites at Shiloh in Canaan to return to Gilead, their own land, which they had acquired in accordance with the command of the LORD through Moses.

10 When they came to Geliloth near the Jordan in the land of Canaan, the Reubenites, the Gadites and the half-tribe of Manasseh built an imposing altar there by the Jordan. **11** And when the Israelites heard that they had built the altar on the border of Canaan at Geliloth near the Jordan on the Israelite side, **12** the whole assembly of Israel gathered at Shiloh to go to war against them.

13 So the Israelites sent Phinehas son of Eleazar, the priest, to the land of Gilead – to Reuben, Gad and the half-tribe of Manasseh. **14** With him they sent ten of the chief men, one from each of the tribes of Israel, each the head of a family division among the Israelite clans.

15 When they went to Gilead – to Reuben, Gad and the half-tribe of Manasseh – they said to them: **16** 'The whole assembly of the LORD says: "How could you break faith with the God of Israel like this? How could you turn away from the LORD and build yourselves an altar in rebellion against him now? **17** Was not the sin of Peor enough for us? Up to this very day we have not cleansed ourselves from that sin, even though a plague fell on the community of the LORD! **18** And are you now turning away from the LORD?

' "If you rebel against the LORD today, tomorrow he will be angry with the whole community of Israel. **19** If the land you possess is defiled, come over to the LORD's land, where the LORD's tabernacle stands, and share the land with us. But do not rebel against the LORD or against us by building an altar for yourselves, other than the altar of the LORD our God. **20** When Achan son of Zerah was unfaithful in regard to the devoted things,[a] did not wrath come on the whole community of Israel? He was not the only one who died for his sin."'

21 Then Reuben, Gad and the half-tribe of Manasseh replied to the heads of the clans of Israel: **22** 'The Mighty One, God, the LORD! The Mighty One, God, the LORD! He knows! And let Israel know! If this has been in rebellion or disobedience to the LORD, do not spare us this day. **23** If we have built our own altar to turn away from the LORD and to offer burnt offerings and grain offerings, or to sacrifice fellowship offerings on it, may the LORD himself call us to account.

24 'No! We did it for fear that some day your descendants might say to ours, "What do you have to do with the LORD, the God of Israel? **25** The LORD has made the Jordan a boundary between us and you – you Reubenites and Gadites! You have no share in the LORD." So your descendants might cause ours to stop fearing the LORD.

26 'That is why we said, "Let us get ready and build an altar – but not for burnt offerings or sacrifices." **27** On the contrary, it is to be a witness between us and you and the generations that follow, that we will worship the LORD at his sanctuary with our burnt offerings, sacrifices and fellowship offerings. Then in the future your descendants will not be able to say to ours, "You have no share in the LORD."

28 'And we said, "If they ever say this to us, or to our descendants, we will answer: look at the replica of the LORD's altar, which our ancestors built, not for burnt offerings and sacrifices, but as a witness between us and you."

29 'Far be it from us to rebel against the LORD and turn away from him today by building an altar for burnt offerings, grain offerings and sacrifices, other than the altar of the LORD our God that stands before his tabernacle.'

30 When Phinehas the priest and the leaders of the community – the heads of the clans of the Israelites – heard what Reuben, Gad and Manasseh had to say, they were pleased. **31** And Phinehas son of Eleazar, the priest, said to Reuben, Gad and Manasseh, 'Today we know that the LORD is with us, because you have not been unfaithful to the LORD in this matter. Now you have rescued the Israelites from the LORD's hand.'

32 Then Phinehas son of Eleazar, the priest, and the leaders returned to Canaan from their meeting with the Reubenites and Gadites in Gilead and reported to the Israelites. 33 They were glad to hear the report and praised God. And they talked no more about going to war against them to devastate the country where the Reubenites and the Gadites lived.

34 And the Reubenites and the Gadites gave the altar this name: A Witness Between Us – that the LORD is God.

---

a 20 The Hebrew term refers to the irrevocable giving over of things or persons to the LORD, often by totally destroying them.

1. Joshua's speech sending the eastern tribes home • Joshua 22:1–9

This section connects with Joshua 1:12–15, both in theme and in key words. In chapter 1, Joshua told these tribes they were to cross over with their fellow Israelites to help them in conquering the land until God would grant rest. Then they would be able to return home to their land east of the Jordan. As Joshua says in verse 4, that moment has now come (Joshua 21:44).

Joshua comments on their aiding the other tribes: that was in obedience to Moses's command (see Numbers 32:20–42), to Joshua's own command, which was a reinforcement of that from Moses (Joshua 1:13–15), and so they have obeyed God himself (verses 2–3). This is a lovely example of commendation of obedience and service. While this is only what these tribes previously committed to do, their dutiful completion of it over a long time is spoken of with honour. The seventeenth-century Bible commentator, Matthew Henry, expressed this well:

> Though their service was a due debt, and the performance of a promise, and they had done no more than was their duty to do, yet he highly commends them; not only gives them up their bonds, as it were, now that they had fulfilled the condition, but applauds their good services. Though it was by the favour of God and his power that Israel got possession of this land, and he must have all the glory, yet Joshua thought there was a thankful acknowledgment due to their brethren who assisted

them, and whose sword and bow were employed for them. God must be chiefly eyed in our praises, yet instruments must not be altogether overlooked.[2]

Joshua's overriding concern as they leave is to encourage covenant loyalty to God as their highest priority: they are to be 'very careful' to do this (verse 5). Joshua's words here highlight key previous instruction from Moses (see, for example, Deuteronomy 6:4–9; 10:12–13). The content of this covenant loyalty is unpacked in rich terms. It centres on 'love' for the LORD their God. That love will be shown as they 'walk' in his ways, 'keep' his commands, 'hold fast' to him and 'serve' him with all their heart and soul. This collection of terms describes a heartfelt devotion and allegiance which is lived out in obedience and service. The reformer John Calvin speaks of the inward nature of this command (compare Matthew 22:37–40):

> He touches also on the end and sum of the Law, love to God, and adherence to him, because outward worship would otherwise be of little value. He confirms the same thing by other words, by which sincerity is denoted, namely serving the Lord with their whole heart and soul.[3]

This call for devotion and allegiance, in both heart and life, introduces the theme of covenant loyalty which dominates the last chapters of the book. It is addressed here to the eastern tribes but will soon be enforced on the rest of the nations (Joshua 23:8, 11; 24:21).

Joshua blesses them and sends them home (verse 6). There is then an explanatory comment about the allocation of land to the two halves of the tribe of Manasseh east and west of the Jordan. Richard Hess suggests this is mentioned to raise the issue of a divided tribe and so potential disunity.[4] Alternatively, it explains why, in the following narrative, occasional reference is made to Gad and Reuben as a pair, suggesting Manasseh was not seen as an entirely trans-Jordanian tribe

---

[2] Henry, *Commentary*, 2:576.
[3] Calvin, *Joshua*, 4:251.
[4] Hess, *Joshua*, 290.

JOSHUA

(Joshua 22:25, 32–4). The narrative that follows raises the question of who is part of Israel, and the greatest doubt falls on these two tribes.[5] Joshua sends them with great wealth from their various campaigns in Canaan (verse 8). This is to be shared with those who remained in the eastern land, as only those of fighting age crossed over with Joshua.[6] An alternative reading sees this as referring to division of plunder among the tribes now, in which case it is a picture of their current unity.[7] So we are told that they return to Gilead, and it is again made clear that this is in accordance with God's command (verse 9).

2. *The threat to unity and resolution* • *Joshua 22:10–34*

The structure of the passage

John Goldingay has helpfully shown the structure of this passage as follows:[8]

> Easterners build the altar (verse 10)
>   Westerns prepare for war (verses 11–12)
>   Westerners send a delegation (verses 13–14)
>   Westerners accuse the easterners (verses 15–20)
>   Easterners deny the accusation (verses 21–3)
>   Easterners explain the altar (verses 24–8)
>   Easterners deny the accusation (verse 29)
>   Westerners accept the explanation (verses 30–31)
>   Western delegation returns (verse 32)
>   Westerners call off war (verse 33)
> Easterners name the altar (verse 34)

This structure helpfully focuses attention on the explanation at the centre of the passage. It also shows the movement involved from the altars' building to its naming and what changes over that process.

---

5 Howard, *Joshua*, 413.
6 See a previous example in Numbers 31:27.
7 Howard, *Joshua*, 404–5.
8 Goldingay, *Joshua*, 382. Repeated here with minor modification.

The building of an altar and the threat of war (22:10–20)

We are immediately told of the eastern tribes building an altar: it seems to be on the border of the Jordan, and it is huge in scale. It is either 'on' the Israelite side or 'across' from it; it would make more sense that it was on the eastern bank but either location could work.[9] At this stage, the purpose of the altar is left unstated and instead the consequences described. The western tribes hear of it and immediately gather for war against the eastern tribes. This is on the supposition that the altar demonstrates abandonment of God for worship of a false god. The response of war is to be expected from Deuteronomy 13, which is clear in the eradication of false worship from Israel; in fact, such worship makes people liable to be 'devoted' and so destroyed completely, as the inhabitants of the land were (Deuteronomy 13:15).[10] An alternative is that the new altar is for worship of the true God; but if so, this contravenes Deuteronomy 12 which specifies that such an altar must only be at the site God chooses. They are told specifically, 'Be careful not to sacrifice your burnt offerings anywhere you please. Offer them only at the place the lord will choose in one of your tribes, and there observe everything I command you' (Deuteronomy 12:13–14). Whichever understanding, the eastern tribes appear to be flouting God's commands.

Rather than simply attacking, the western tribes send a delegation headed by Phinehas, son of Eleazar the priest. The selection of Phinehas is significant because he was known for his actions when Israel turned away from the Lord in Numbers 25; he showed his concern for covenant loyalty then, and so he is the right man for the role now. This delegation speaks to the eastern tribes and relays a message from the 'whole assembly of the lord' (verse 16). The use of the phrase 'whole assembly' here, and earlier in verse 12 ('the whole assembly of Israel'), implies that the ten tribes now form 'Israel' and

---

9 The location of Geliloth is mentioned as part of the allotment to Benjamin in Joshua 18:17. However, there is still some debate over the exact location of this altar; McConville and Williams, *Joshua*, 84–5.
10 See Excursus: Devoting to the LORD.

assume the apostasy of the eastern tribes; that the language changes by the end of the chapter is significant.[11]

The accusation from the delegation is that the eastern tribes have broken faith with God (verse 16). This is a strong term, meaning an unfaithful or treacherous act; we last saw it in Joshua with regard to Achan (Joshua 7:1). Their action is also described as 'turn[ing] away' from the Lord and 'rebellion' against him. The word for rebellion used here is rare and may echo Joshua's warning to Israel not to rebel against the Lord in Numbers 14:9.[12] Such acts are paralleled with the 'sin of Peor' (verse 17): this is the event in Numbers 25 where the Israelites turned away from God and yoked themselves to 'Baal of Peor' – i.e., they committed apostasy and pledged loyalty to a false god. God responded by killing twenty-four thousand in a plague (this is where Phinehas showed his zeal for loyalty to God). Peor became known as the archetypal moment of covenant disloyalty, the cloud of which still hung over Israel. The charge here is that the eastern tribes have not learnt from this past incident, but rather are repeating it.

The potential consequences of such apostasy are spelt out in verses 18b–20. Rebellion today will result in God's anger tomorrow; and that anger will be on all Israel, not just on them, as was seen in the sin of Achan. The offer is made to cross over and share the land west of the Jordan, if they regard their land as 'defiled'. It is unclear why they would regard the land as unclean in this way and what connection this has with the altar; possibly they think an altar has to be built in the Promised Land itself because of the impurity of the eastern lands. Whatever the connection, the western tribes are desperate to persuade them not to rebel against God, or against them. It is worth noting the vertical and horizontal aspects of disloyalty here: it is against God and so against their fellow Israelites.[13]

---

11 See Polzin's argument, which is repeated in other commentaries, Robert Polzin, *Moses and the Deuteronomist: Deuteronomy, Joshua, Judges* (New York: Seabury Press, 1980), 135–7.
12 Firth, *Joshua*, 359.
13 Some translations change the verb in verse 19 to become causative, so meaning that they make the Israelites rebels as well. See Woudstra, *Joshua*, 325.

The response of the eastern tribes (22:21–9)

We now hear the reply from the eastern tribes. They begin with a declaration of God's sovereign authority: he is the Mighty One, God, their covenant Lord.[14] He knows the truth of what has happened, and they want Israel to know. If what they have done is indeed an act of rebellion or turning away from God, then Israel should not spare them, and God will call them to account. The effect of this opening is to assert that this is not what has happened and to place them alongside the western tribes. As Marten Woudstra says, 'Both the accusers and the accused stand together in their outright condemnation of anything remotely resembling a form of worship practice other than that of the Lord alone.'[15]

The explanation then comes in verses 24–8. The altar was built out of concern that later generations of the western tribes would consider the eastern tribes separate from them and deny their covenant relationship with the Lord. The boundary of the Jordan river might lead to this separation and the attitude of the western tribes might lead to neglect of God from the eastern tribes (verse 25). Hence, the altar is not to offer sacrifices but to act as a 'witness'. It is meant as a preventative measure in bearing testimony that the two groups of tribes are united and will worship God at his sanctuary. If the western tribes were ever to cast aspersions on the eastern tribes and question their 'share in the Lord', then they would respond by pointing to this altar. It is mentioned at this stage that the altar in question is a 'replica' of the Lord's altar and so points to it. Finally, they assert their loyalty: they will not rebel or turn away from the Lord and will only offer sacrifices at the appointed altar (verse 29).

---

14 There is a series of alternative translations such as, 'The LORD, God of gods', Howard, *Joshua*, 411–12.
15 Woudstra, *Joshua*, 327.

The delight of the western tribes (22:30–34)

The delegation from the western tribes is 'pleased' when they hear this (more literally, it is 'good in their eyes'). They assert that God is with them because an act of disloyalty has not happened, and the eastern tribes have 'rescued' them from God's hand. This last comment must mean there was a threat of doing something that would incur God's anger, and that has been averted (compare verses 18, 20).[16] The delegation returns home and reports to the wider community: the response is identical, it is 'good in their eyes' (NIV 'glad'), and the thought of going to war evaporates.

The section ends with the naming of the altar. This could be rendered 'A Witness' which is then explained, or the whole title may be longer, as in the NIV translation. The point is the same: it stands as a testimony between the two groups of tribes that the Lord is God, that they share in that confession and are bound together in it.

KEY THEMES AND APPLICATION

The enforcement of covenant loyalty
We need to ask why so much time is spent on a misunderstanding. In particular, why do we hear the lengthy accusation and warning from Phinehas and then the equally lengthy explanation and protestations of covenant loyalty in reply? The issue might have been resolved in a few verses. The reason must be to allow the airing of both accusation and protestation in detail. That allows the reader to enter into the idea of such breaking faith with God and its consequences, to entertain that idea as a reality and then to be reassured and rejoice in the reply. The hiding of the motivation for building the altar and hearing the accusation and reply means that the reader feels the full force of the 'what if' and emotionally engages with the possibility. The overall rhetorical effect is to act as warning against

---

[16] The same word is used in Joshua 2:13 for the rescue of Rahab, and in Joshua 9:26 of the Gibeonites.

such disloyalty by enforcing on the reader how appalling it would have been.[17]

Within this, we should see that the reaction of the western tribes in being ready to fight is the correct one. It is what God has previously commanded (Deuteronomy 13) and it shows their right concern over apostasy. Many commentators today condemn their over-eagerness to go to war, but not to do so would have been an over-laxity towards covenant loyalty. This raises the question as to whether we have such concern for loyalty to God in our churches, and so willingness to act in appropriate ways when needed. This would be seen in enquiry, encouragement, warning and, finally, the hard decisions of church discipline when required.

The theme of covenant loyalty begins with Joshua's call to the eastern tribes in verse 5. He calls for such loyalty, and then the horrific prospect of its absence is immediately raised and rhetorically explored. For later readers this would have a poignant edge to it. They would know of the splitting of the nation in two and the building of alternative altars in the north of the country (1 Kings 12). While this split is along different lines, the theme is very similar. They would have the sadness of knowing that what was here only raised as a possibility later became a reality.

The unity of the nation
The misunderstanding here acts to raise the issue of the unity of Israel as one group and the concern that no section of God's people might exclude another. Relationship with God, on the basis of the same covenant, means there is both equality and unity among his people. No one can claim superiority; no one can be pushed out. The unity of God's people is a key theme throughout Scripture, both in being celebrated as a beautiful thing when present (e.g., Psalm 133) and in being condemned when it is not (e.g., Malachi 2:10).

These themes are seen even more fully in the new covenant,

---

[17] Some approach this passage as an example of how to resolve disputes, making points such as not jumping to conclusions and the need for good communication. While these are fair points, they do not really appreciate how the chapter works: the ignorance of the western tribes is required for the threat of apostasy and division to loom so large and so to be entered into by the reader.

which explicitly unites those of every ethnicity, class in society and both genders. For example:

> There is neither Jew nor Gentile, neither slave nor free, nor is there male and female, for you are all one in Christ Jesus. If you belong to Christ, then you are Abraham's seed, and heirs according to the promise. (Galatians 3:28–9)

In particular, in Ephesians Paul is concerned to affirm that Gentile believers are equally part of God's people and should not be made to feel like 'second-class citizens':

> Consequently, you are no longer foreigners and strangers, but fellow citizens with God's people and also members of his household, built on the foundation of the apostles and prophets, with Christ Jesus himself as the chief cornerstone. In him the whole building is joined together and rises to become a holy temple in the Lord. And in him you too are being built together to become a dwelling in which God lives by his Spirit. (Ephesians 2:19–22)

In Joshua 22, the altar serves as a 'witness' to remind the tribes of their unity in God. In the New Testament we can see the Lord's Supper having the same function. It asserts the unity of all those who take part: 'Because there is one loaf, we, who are many, are one body, for we all share the one loaf' (1 Corinthians 10:17). Any exclusion of members of the congregation is seen to be a denial of what the Supper symbolises (1 Corinthians 11:17–34). Similarly, Paul rebukes any who would say that others are not a necessary part of the body of Christ (1 Corinthians 12:21–6). If anything is said or done that would make a true believer feel they had no 'share in the LORD' (Joshua 22:27), that would be a travesty.

The need for appropriate worship
While the key issue at hand is the covenant loyalty of the eastern tribes, the way this is brought to the surface is through an altar. As we said above, such an altar could have been to a pagan god and

so an act of blatant apostasy, or it may have been to the true God and so an act of disobedience in how God was to be worshipped (Deuteronomy 12). Behind this is a key principle: God is the one who determines what acceptable worship comprises. This is seen in the second commandment where we must not create a representation of God in order to worship him; it is also seen in specific incidents such as Abihu and Nadab offering 'unauthorised fire before the LORD' (Leviticus 10:1–3).

This has often been summarised in the so-called 'regulative principle', which says that whatever God has not commanded in his worship is forbidden; i.e., we are not free to create new worship practices ourselves. Such a principle was particularly significant in the Puritan movement in England in the sixteenth and seventeenth centuries. One expression by the Independent Puritan Jeremiah Burroughs (1599–1646) says this:

> Hence I say that all things in God's worship must have a warrant out of God's word, must be commanded. It is not enough that it is not forbidden . . . Now when a man shall put a religious respect upon a thing by virtue of his own institution, when he hath not a warrant from God: here is superstition. We must all be willing worshippers but not will-worshippers: we must come freely to worship God but we must not worship God according to our own wills.[18]

While this is not what the eastern tribes were doing, the prospect that they were was raised and entertained, and so the warning still stands.

---

18 Jeremiah Burroughs, *Gospel-Worship, or, The Right Manner of Sanctifying the Name of God in General* (London: Peter Cole, 1653), 9–10.

23

Joshua's Call to Loyalty

Joshua 23

The major sections of the book are passed; the land is conquered and divided. The focus at the end is on the covenant loyalty of God's people as they now live in the land. The previous chapter focused on the trans-Jordanian tribes, their loyalty and so the unity of the nation. In the final two chapters we come to Joshua's farewell to Israel and his calling them to loyalty. This comes in two parts: in this chapter the focus is on the leaders of the nation; in the next, it is on the people as a whole. The themes are similar in both: Joshua is calling them to wholehearted covenant loyalty to God and warning them what will happen if they turn away from God. As a result, these chapters are setting Israel up for ongoing life in the land. While the two speeches are overlapping in theme, there are differences between them which we will identify on the way through. The tone and style of these speeches are very similar to those of Moses in Deuteronomy. This is one of many parallels between the two men, showing Joshua to be the true successor to Moses.[1]

Joshua's farewell to the leaders

23 After a long time had passed and the LORD had given Israel rest from all their enemies around them, Joshua, by then a very old man, ²summoned all Israel – their elders, leaders, judges and officials – and said to them: 'I am very old. ³You yourselves have seen everything the LORD your God has done to all these nations for your sake; it was the LORD your God who fought for you. ⁴Remember how I have allotted as an inheritance for your tribes all the land of the nations that remain – the nations

---

1 Howard, *Joshua*, 416.

I conquered – between the Jordan and the Mediterranean Sea in the west. ⁵The Lord your God himself will push them out for your sake. He will drive them out before you, and you will take possession of their land, as the Lord your God promised you.

⁶'Be very strong; be careful to obey all that is written in the Book of the Law of Moses, without turning aside to the right or to the left. ⁷Do not associate with these nations that remain among you; do not invoke the names of their gods or swear by them. You must not serve them or bow down to them. ⁸But you are to hold fast to the Lord your God, as you have until now.

⁹'The Lord has driven out before you great and powerful nations; to this day no one has been able to withstand you. ¹⁰One of you routs a thousand, because the Lord your God fights for you, just as he promised. ¹¹So be very careful to love the Lord your God.

¹²'But if you turn away and ally yourselves with the survivors of these nations that remain among you and if you intermarry with them and associate with them, ¹³then you may be sure that the Lord your God will no longer drive out these nations before you. Instead, they will become snares and traps for you, whips on your backs and thorns in your eyes, until you perish from this good land, which the Lord your God has given you.

¹⁴'Now I am about to go the way of all the earth. You know with all your heart and soul that not one of all the good promises the Lord your God gave you has failed. Every promise has been fulfilled; not one has failed. ¹⁵But just as all the good things the Lord your God has promised you have come to you, so he will bring on you all the evil things he has threatened, until the Lord your God has destroyed you from this good land he has given you. ¹⁶If you violate the covenant of the Lord your God, which he commanded you, and go and serve other gods and bow down to them, the Lord's anger will burn against you, and you will quickly perish from the good land he has given you.'

1. Introduction: their current position • Joshua 23:1–5

The timing given for these speeches is indefinite but is a 'long time' after the previous events. God has given 'rest' to Israel from her enemies and so the promises with regard to the land are fulfilled (compare Joshua 21:44; 22:4). It is also when Joshua is now a 'very old man' (the expression used is the same as in Joshua 13:1); while we do not know how long the intervening years have been, he is now near death (see verse 14).[2] Joshua begins his speech in verse 2, referring to his advanced age, and so indicates this is preparing them for life in his absence.

There is some debate over who this speech is to: verse 2 refers to 'all Israel' but then specifies a series of leadership groups. Probably it is all Israel as represented by these leaders.[3] That would explain why it is followed by the speech and covenant renewal in the next chapter, which is explicitly with all the tribes and all the people (Joshua 24:1–2).

The opening of the speech reminds the leaders of God's past actions and rehearses their current position. He says that they have 'seen' all that God has done for them and how he fought for them (compare Joshua 10:14, 42). He then calls them to 'see' (NIV 'remember') that they have been allotted their inheritance in the land. This is land from the nations that have been defeated and those that remain (verse 4).[4] Hence, although the inheritance is granted, the work of possession is only partially complete, which is why he reassures them in verse 5 that the LORD will drive out the remaining peoples and they will possess the land as promised.

This is a summary of their current position. This helps us understand that the division process of chapters 14–21, while containing some future snapshots within them, was primarily allotment not achievement. The ongoing process of possessing the land is what will occupy the following book of Judges. What Joshua is doing here is setting the leaders up for that task which lies ahead of them. In particular, this involves their relationship with the 'nations' that remain around them. This word has only occurred previously in

---

2 We know that Joshua was 110 when he died; Howard suggests that if he was a similar age to Caleb then these speeches were around twenty-five years after the first distribution of the land (see Joshua 14:10). Howard, 419–20.

3 Hence the NIV's section heading, 'Joshua's farewell to the leaders'.

4 The NIV makes this one referent: the remaining nations are the ones Joshua conquered. It is better read as referring to two groups: the remaining nations, including those that have been conquered.

Joshua with reference to Israel as a nation; now it is used seven times in this chapter, primarily of those nations that 'remain', highlighting this key theme.[5]

2. Joshua's charge and warning • Joshua 23:6–16

The charge to loyalty (23:6–11)

Joshua now calls them to be strong, not physically, but in their obedience to God's Law: they must be careful to 'keep so as to do' all the Law, and not turn from it. Joshua's call directly echoes what God said to him in Joshua 1:7. Hence the responsibility for obedience to God is being transferred from Joshua to this group.

The implications of such obedience are then spelt out. The primary concern is framed negatively: not to 'associate' with the nations; that is, to mix with them wrongly so that their identity is blurred and their obedience is compromised. Such association would be seen in what follows: turning to the gods of those nations, using their names or worshipping them. Rather, framed positively, they are to 'hold fast' to the LORD. This term is used for 'cleaving together' in marriage in Genesis 2:24 and denotes faithfulness and loyalty in relationship.[6] It is later used in commendation of Hezekiah's loyalty to God (2 Kings 18:6). Joshua can say that this is what they have done so far: clearly this has not been perfect, but it is true to say that, overall, this generation has 'held fast' to God.

This echoes what had been commanded previously through Moses (see Deuteronomy 10:20; 11:22; 13:4). The need for such loyalty is reinforced by a reminder of how God has driven out 'great and powerful nations' before them (verse 9). The assertion that no one has withstood them takes God's promise to Joshua in 1:5 and applies it to the whole nation; one man routing a thousand echoes Moses from Deuteronomy 32:30. These references assert that God is with them as he promised, but also that loyalty only to him makes sense.

---

5 Joshua 23:3, 4(x2), 7, 9, 12, 13.
6 Interestingly, in modern Hebrew this word means 'glue', indicating the sense of sticking closely. Howard, *Joshua*, 422.

JOSHUA'S CALL TO LOYALTY

The logic runs: he is on your side, so stay on his side. The call to loyalty is repeated, framed in terms of the greatest commandment: 'be very careful to love the LORD your God' (compare Deuteronomy 6:5; 10:12; 11:1, 13, 22). The American biblical scholar George Bush (1796–1859) wrote:

> Let not the assurance of the divine favour, presence, and protection tend to relax your diligence, or weaken the sense of obligation to love and serve him; on the contrary, let it operate as an additional motive to the most intense affection and devotedness toward your heavenly benefactor.[7]

The opening and closing calls of this section parallel each other: they are to be 'very strong' and to be 'very careful' (verses 6, 11). These commands will not be their default setting or easy to do; they will need to be resolute and alert to fulfil this charge.

The warning not to turn away (23:12–13)

Having called them to loyalty to the Lord, Joshua now warns them as to what will happen if they do the opposite – i.e., if they 'turn' from God and 'ally' themselves with the remaining nations around them (verse 12). The word for 'ally' here is the same as that used for relationship with God in verse 8: it pictures them 'holding fast' to the people around them instead of to God. That will be seen by intermarriage and 'association' (the opposite of verse 7).

Such disloyalty from God's people means that he will no longer give them success in driving out the nations; rather they will become a source of danger to lead them astray ('snares and traps') and a hostile and malign presence ('whips' and 'thorns'). This will start a downward trend, resulting in Israel perishing from the good land God has given (verse 13). Again, this echoes previous warnings from Moses (Numbers 33:55–6; Deuteronomy 4:26; 7:16; 8:19–20), particularly the curses for disobedience in Deuteronomy 28 which

---

[7] George Bush, 'Notes, Critical and Practical, on the Book of Joshua', in Nichols, *ESV Church History Study Bible*, 336.

have previously been recounted on Mount Ebal (Joshua 8:30–35). Joshua will return to this theme more explicitly below.

The double-edged nature of God's faithfulness (23:14–16)

Joshua concludes by referring to his imminent death and so repeating the sense of transfer of leadership. In doing so, he is exhorting these leaders to loyalty to God by reminding them of God's faithfulness to his promises. Such faithfulness is double-edged. There is the fulfilment of all the good promises God has made and the assertion that the Israelites know this to be true ('heart and soul'). This echoes Joshua 21:45 and emphasises it by stating it negatively ('not one . . . has failed'), then positively ('every promise has been fulfilled') and again negatively ('not one has failed'). But there will also be the fulfilment of all the evil things God has threatened, the end result of which is being 'destroyed' (verse 15). This warning is then summarised in verse 16: 'violation' or 'transgression' of the covenant by turning to other gods will result in God's anger burning against them and they will quickly perish from the good land (as in verse 13).

God's anger burned against Israel once before in Joshua (see Joshua 7:1). It is commonly referred to in Deuteronomy as part of Moses's warnings (e.g., Deuteronomy 6:15; 7:4; 11:17). More broadly, the language of these verses draws again from Deuteronomy 28.[8] The point is clear: God will keep both kinds of promises towards his people. This is very clear in Deuteronomy, most notably in a summary of the blessings and curses: 'Just as it pleased the LORD to make you prosper and increase in number, so it will please him to ruin and destroy you' (Deuteronomy 28:63). Marten Woudstra points out that while the word 'covenant' is used infrequently in Joshua, 'its idea is present everywhere'.[9] That is certainly the case here; this is the covenant rehearsed on Mount Ebal spelt out in its blessings and curses.

While double-edged, there is also an asymmetry here. The emphasis

---

[8] The final end of being 'destroyed' comes seven times in Deuteronomy 28 (verses 20, 24, 45, 48, 51, 61, 63).
[9] Woudstra, *Joshua*, 339.

JOSHUA'S CALL TO LOYALTY

is on God's goodness to Israel: the word 'good' comes five times in these verses, referring to the good land (three times) given to them and God's good promises/things (twice).[10] God is a good God doing them good; that is the normal experience of the covenant. But they need to know that the reverse side of covenant curses, while not equally reflective of God, are equally real.

KEY THEMES AND APPLICATION

Understanding the blessings and curses
This passage sets up expectations for the future life of Israel. This has already been done in Deuteronomy but, as we have seen, Joshua draws on that material and applies it to this setting. The covenant background means that Israel's experience of God is determined by her obedience to God, resulting in blessing or cursing. We should be careful in understanding this in at least two ways. First, it is not that all disobedience resulted in curses; rather the sacrificial system provided the means for forgiveness for sin. Curses came if God's people rebelled against him and followed other gods. In other words, God was looking for loyalty, not perfection, and that is reflected in the terminology employed here about holding fast (verse 8), loving (verse 11) and not turning away (verse 12). Second, new covenant believers today do not live under this schema. It is not that our obedience is meaningless in our experience of God; indeed, Jesus promises to bless it (see for example, Mark 10:29–30; John 14:21–3). But what is very clear is that 'curses' such as material poverty or poor health or tragedy are not necessarily a result of disobedience – nor their opposites a result of obedience. Indeed, Jesus can say that we are 'blessed' when we suffer (Matthew 5:11–12).

These points are of great importance in applying this passage today. We must not give the false impression that the Old Testament believers needed to be perfect; nor give any support to the 'prosperity gospel' teaching that says material blessings will come if we obey God, or that their absence indicates disobedience.[11]

---

10 The word used can refer to God's words or things he brings about.
11 See similar points made in the comments on Joshua 1.

Loyalty and our picture of God
Joshua is calling the leaders to ongoing loyalty to God. Key to that loyalty is their picture of God. We will see in the next chapter that a significant part of this is in knowing what God has done for them in the past – i.e., knowing his goodness. In this passage, the focus is more on knowing his character: he is faithful to what he has said, both positive and negative. For many, the greatest shock of this passage will be God's faithfulness in bringing his promise of 'evil things' to bear on his people (verse 15). As David Firth says, 'These are not promises that anyone wants to claim.'[12] If we are shocked by this, the challenge is ultimately to our picture of God; he is not a genial figure who only gives presents; he is an awesome God who is a 'consuming fire' (Deuteronomy 4:24; Hebrews 12:29).

The Israelite leaders are being warned that, while God is a God to be confident of, he is not a God to take casually. While he is a good God who has given them good things, he is not a God to take lightly. Casual and light views of God lead to a disregard for his commands and an ignoring of his warnings. Joshua is calling them to take God seriously.

We should be aware that applying this will depend on what picture of God is predominant in our context. It may be that people are inappropriately frightened of God and need to be reassured, while not losing their awe of him. But in some contexts, such awe is precisely what is lacking, and an emphasis on God's care and compassion results in an easy-going complacency. We might want to consider New Testament passages such as these:

> But I will show you whom you should fear: fear him who, after your body has been killed, has authority to throw you into hell. Yes, I tell you, fear him. (Luke 12:5)

> Therefore, my dear friends, as you have always obeyed – not only in my presence, but now much more in my absence – continue to work out your salvation with fear and trembling, for it is God who works in you to will and to act in order to fulfil his good purpose. (Philippians 2:12–13)

---

12 Firth, *Joshua*, 380.

Since you call on a Father who judges each person's work impartially, live out your time as foreigners here in reverent fear. (1 Peter 1:17)

The obedience of leaders
In the opening chapter we saw the crucial nature of Joshua's obedience. He needed to obey so that he would be successful in the task God had given him. Here, that same dynamic is transferred to the leaders of Israel. The future success of driving out the remaining inhabitants, and indeed the success of their future life in the land, turns on these leaders and those after them staying loyal to God. This sees the leaders as having both a representative function – they stand for the nation – and an influential role – they lead the nation in its life. Hence, loyal and faithful leaders will result in the nation experiencing God's good promises; disloyal and unfaithful leaders will result in their experiencing God's curses.

We can apply this to the need for godly and faithful leaders in churches today, and even in handing over leadership in calling new leaders to loyalty. However, in Joshua there is a shadow hanging over this transfer. Any later reader would know of the failure of leadership that followed; the nation did indeed experience the curses mentioned and did eventually perish from the land. This, then, points us to the need for a faithful leader who will never turn away from God, who will always love him and hold fast to him and who will walk in obedience to him. It points us to our need for Jesus.

Being in the world but not of the world
We noted the focus on the 'nations' around Israel. Israel is called not to 'associate' with the peoples of the nations around them. This does not mean there was no relationship or communication between them. We have seen that some of these nations became their servants, and so there would have been dialogue of some form (e.g., Joshua 16:10; 17:13). Rather, this term refers to an inappropriate 'mixing', where the distinctiveness of being God's people is lost and they take on the values and practices of the nations around. This points to the idea of being 'in the world' as our place of living, but not 'of the world' in terms of our identity and values.

Jesus speaks about the identity of his followers in this way:

> I have given them your word and the world has hated them, for they are not of the world any more than I am of the world. My prayer is not that you take them out of the world but that you protect them from the evil one. They are not of the world, even as I am not of it. Sanctify them by the truth; your word is truth. (John 17:14–17)

Also very relevant is the call from the apostle John:

> Do not love the world or anything in the world. If anyone loves the world, love for the Father is not in them. For everything in the world – the lust of the flesh, the lust of the eyes, and the pride of life – comes not from the Father but from the world. The world and its desires pass away, but whoever does the will of God lives forever. (1 John 2:15–17)

And that of Paul:

> Do not be yoked together with unbelievers. For what do righteousness and wickedness have in common? Or what fellowship can light have with darkness? What harmony is there between Christ and Belial? Or what does a believer have in common with an unbeliever? What agreement is there between the temple of God and idols? For we are the temple of the living God. As God has said:
>
> > 'I will live with them
> > and walk among them,
> > and I will be their God,
> > and they will be my people.'
> > (2 Corinthians 6:14–16)

Avoidance of idolatry

The loyalty of God's people is seen most pointedly in the idea of idolatry: Israel was not to invoke the names of the pagan gods, swear by them, serve them or bow down to them (Joshua 23:7). One might imagine an Israelite farmer, concerned for his crop, considering a brief prayer to a Canaanite god of harvests. To utter such a prayer would be to call on the gods of the surrounding nations.

An equivalent today is seen in some cultures where prayers might be made to ancestors, or rituals might be conducted to ward off evil spirits. In some contexts, this is embedded in the culture and so is done by virtually everyone in society and there is great pressure to take part. In such places the Christian believer's distinctiveness will be obvious by their refusal to do so. In other cultures, taking on the idolatry of those around will be much more subtle but no less real. There will be no clear 'gods' identified and no set religious practices to avoid. However, that culture will orientate its life in accordance with what it worships, whether money, success or personal freedom. The believer here must also stand apart and be distinctive.

Marriage outside the covenant community

A specific prohibited aspect of mixing with the remaining nations is 'intermarrying with them' (verse 12). This was forbidden earlier by Moses in Deuteronomy 7:3–4. The reasoning given there is that they will 'turn your children away from following me to serve other gods' – i.e., it is an extreme form of influence. The prohibition on marrying outside the covenant community is because it is also seen to be wrong in itself, not just dangerous in its influence. God's people were holy and so to be separate from the nations around; the bond of marriage, which involves becoming 'one flesh' (Genesis 2:24), is seen to go against this. In Ezra, this intermarriage is described as having 'mingled the holy race with the peoples around them' and is described as 'unfaithfulness' (Ezra 9:2).

In the New Testament, we might refer to 2 Corinthians 6, quoted above, which refers to not being 'yoked' with unbelievers. This is more general than marriage but surely includes it. In 1 Corinthians 7:39 Paul says that those who are free to marry must do so to someone who belongs 'to the Lord'. Hence, we may use this passage to warn people against joining in marriage with a non-Christian. We should note that this passage and command has been used inappropriately to prohibit interracial marriages, and more broadly to support segregation. Such 'association' between races is not God's concern here; in fact, we have seen the inclusion of other racial groups within Israel in Joshua itself. Unity between different ethnic groups is exactly what *should* be seen in the church. As Jerome Creach says, 'The problem in the book of Joshua is not ethnic purity but spiritual purity.'[13]

In addressing this, we must make reference to anyone who is already married to an unbeliever and reassure them that they are to stay in that marriage. In the Old Testament, such marriages were renounced (see Ezra 10), but Paul tells believers in such a situation to stay married. Rather than the presence of the non-Christian partner making the marriage unclean, the presence of the Christian makes it 'holy' (1 Corinthians 7:10–14).

---

13 Creach, *Joshua*, 118.

24

Joshua's Call to Serve the Lord

Joshua 24:1–28

Following the conquering and division of the land, Joshua finishes with a focus on covenant loyalty. In the previous chapter we saw Joshua's speech to the next generation of leaders; in this chapter we move to Joshua's second speech, this time given to the whole nation. The themes of the two speeches overlap but have different targets. Both are aimed at loyalty to their covenant God, but chapter 23 was concerned with loyalty as opposed to mixing with the world, while chapter 24 is concerned with loyalty as opposed to following other gods. Richard Nelson helpfully expresses this as the difference between *how* God is to be served, as opposed to *who* is to be served.[1] This speech also has a more formal tone: the history of the nation is reviewed, covenant loyalty is called for, and the people respond. There is the setting up of a stone as a witness to the oaths made. This is described as the making of a covenant (Joshua 24:25), whereas chapter 23 was an exhortation. Apart from a brief appendix, this speech and ceremony conclude the book, and do so on the note of the people's promise of ongoing loyalty. As we will see, while this note is the right one, it leaves the reader unsure of the future.

The covenant renewed at Shechem

24 Then Joshua assembled all the tribes of Israel at Shechem. He summoned the elders, leaders, judges and officials of Israel, and they presented themselves before God.

2 Joshua said to all the people, 'This is what the LORD, the God of Israel, says: "Long ago your ancestors, including Terah the father of Abraham and Nahor, lived beyond the River Euphrates and worshipped other gods. **3** But I took your father

---

1 Nelson, *Joshua*, 268.

JOSHUA

Abraham from the land beyond the Euphrates and led him throughout Canaan and gave him many descendants. I gave him Isaac, **4** and to Isaac I gave Jacob and Esau. I assigned the hill country of Seir to Esau, but Jacob and his family went down to Egypt.

5 ' "Then I sent Moses and Aaron, and I afflicted the Egyptians by what I did there, and I brought you out. **6** When I brought your people out of Egypt, you came to the sea, and the Egyptians pursued them with chariots and horsemen[a] as far as the Red Sea.[b] **7** But they cried to the LORD for help, and he put darkness between you and the Egyptians; he brought the sea over them and covered them. You saw with your own eyes what I did to the Egyptians. Then you lived in the wilderness for a long time.

8 ' "I brought you to the land of the Amorites who lived east of the Jordan. They fought against you, but I gave them into your hands. I destroyed them from before you, and you took possession of their land. **9** When Balak son of Zippor, the king of Moab, prepared to fight against Israel, he sent for Balaam son of Beor to put a curse on you. **10** But I would not listen to Balaam, so he blessed you again and again, and I delivered you out of his hand.

11 ' "Then you crossed the Jordan and came to Jericho. The citizens of Jericho fought against you, as did also the Amorites, Perizzites, Canaanites, Hittites, Girgashites, Hivites and Jebusites, but I gave them into your hands. **12** I sent the hornet ahead of you, which drove them out before you – also the two Amorite kings. You did not do it with your own sword and bow. **13** So I gave you a land on which you did not toil and cities you did not build; and you live in them and eat from vineyards and olive groves that you did not plant."

14 'Now fear the LORD and serve him with all faithfulness. Throw away the gods your ancestors worshipped beyond the River Euphrates and in Egypt, and serve the LORD. **15** But if serving the LORD seems undesirable to you, then choose for yourselves this day whom you will serve, whether the gods your ancestors served beyond the Euphrates, or the gods of the Amorites, in whose land you are living. But as for me and my household, we will serve the LORD.'

16 Then the people answered, 'Far be it from us to forsake the LORD to serve other gods! **17** It was the LORD our God himself who brought us and our parents up out of Egypt, from that land of slavery, and performed those great signs before our eyes. He protected us on our entire journey and among all the nations through which we travelled. **18** And the LORD drove out before us all the nations, including the Amorites, who lived in the land. We too will serve the LORD, because he is our God.'

19 Joshua said to the people, 'You are not able to serve the LORD. He is a holy God; he is a jealous God. He will not forgive your rebellion and your sins. **20** If you forsake the LORD and serve foreign gods, he will turn and bring disaster on you and make an end of you, after he has been good to you.'

21 But the people said to Joshua, 'No! We will serve the LORD.'

22 Then Joshua said, 'You are witnesses against yourselves that you have chosen to serve the LORD.'

'Yes, we are witnesses,' they replied.

23 'Now then,' said Joshua, 'throw away the foreign gods that are among you and yield your hearts to the LORD, the God of Israel.'

24 And the people said to Joshua, 'We will serve the LORD our God and obey him.'

25 On that day Joshua made a covenant for the people, and there at Shechem he reaffirmed for them decrees and laws. **26** And Joshua recorded these things in the Book of the Law of God. Then he took a large stone and set it up there under the oak near the holy place of the LORD.

27 'See!' he said to all the people. 'This stone will be a witness against us. It has heard all the words the LORD has said to us. It will be a witness against you if you are untrue to your God.'

28 Then Joshua dismissed the people, each to their own inheritance.

---

a 6 Or *charioteers*
b 6 Or *the Sea of Reeds*

1. A rehearsal of God's goodness to Israel • Joshua 24:1–13

Joshua calls 'all the tribes' along with their leaders to gather at Shechem (the location in chapter 23 was unspecified). This was where Abraham was first promised the land and where he first built an altar upon entering the land (Genesis 12:7); Jacob bought land and built an altar there (Genesis 33:18–20) and it was where he buried foreign gods in his household (Genesis 35:1–5). This background leads C. J. Goslinga to say:

> At Shechem the voice of history spoke of God's faithfulness in fulfilling his promise to Abraham and of Israel's solemn calling to make a radical break with all idolatry. These were the two main

lessons that Joshua wanted to drive home to the Israelites; so Shechem was admirably suited to the purpose of the assembly. Its own history could only increase the gravity of his words and stamp them indelibly on the people's memory.[2]

The people 'presented' themselves before God (verse 1), giving this a more formal ceremonial tone that is reminiscent of the Sinai covenant.[3] Joshua then speaks to 'all the people' (verse 2), relaying God's word to them. This begins by rehearsing the history of the nation from Abraham to the present day in chronological order.

It has been noted that what follows parallels the content and structure of ancient treaties, especially those that would govern the relationship between a king and a subordinate group.[4] While this is true, Joshua 24 does not fit the standard outline in various ways. At least part of the explanation is, as David Howard explains, 'that Joshua 24 does not claim to be the *text* of a treaty or covenant but rather a *report* of a covenant-renewal ceremony'.[5] In addition, while comparison with such ancient treaties is illuminating, we must not think that God was tied to such forms; his relationship with his people was different because he is different.

Abraham and the patriarchs (24:2–4)

Joshua specifies both where Abraham's family lived, 'beyond the River' (the Euphrates), and that they worshipped 'other gods' (Abraham's life there is described in Genesis 11:27–32). These 'other gods' are one of the key points of contrast through the passage: they are referred to again in verses 15 and 16 and are the same as the 'foreign gods' of verses 20 and 23. God took Abraham from there to the land of Canaan (Genesis 12:1–7) and gave him descendants, specifically Isaac, Jacob and Esau. Esau's territory is mentioned, but we immediately

---

[2] C. J. Goslinga, *Joshua, Judges, Ruth*, trans. Ray Togtman, Bible Student's Commentary (Grand Rapids, Mich: Zondervan, 1986), 170–71.
[3] The same phrase is used in Exodus 19:17. Hess, *Joshua*, 300.
[4] These are called suzerain–vassal treaties. Such comparisons are also made with other covenant-making ceremonies in the Bible, not just Joshua 24.
[5] Howard, *Joshua*, 428 (emphasis original).

JOSHUA'S CALL TO SERVE THE LORD

move back to the promised line and so to Egypt. Within all this the focus is on God's actions: 'I took', 'I led', 'I multiplied' (his descendants), 'I gave' (three times). God is the actor here.

Abraham's inauspicious beginnings here root Israel's identity in the soil of grace. As the reformer John Calvin says:

> For why is it said that the fathers of the people served strange gods, and that Abraham was rescued from the country, but just to show how the free mercy of God was displayed in their very origin? Had Abraham been unlike the rest of his countrymen, his own piety would distinguish him. The opposite, however, is expressly mentioned to show that he had no peculiar excellence of his own which could diminish the grace bestowed upon him, and that therefore his posterity behoved to acknowledge that when he was lost, he was raised up from death unto life.[6]

The Exodus (24:5–7)

We move to the events of Exodus 2–15 where God sent Moses and Aaron to bring his people out of Egypt. The affliction mentioned refers to the plagues recounted in those chapters. The focus here is on God's deliverance from their enemies, emphasising the helplessness of the Israelites and the destruction of the Egyptians. This focus on God's defeat of Israel's enemies continues in the next sections.[7] There is a blurring of past and present generations through verses 5–6 (see the variation between 'you' and 'they'). This merging is common in such narrations because what God has done in the past is inherited and realised in the present.[8] It finishes with an emphatic emphasis on the present audience: 'You saw with your own eyes' what God did (verse 7).[9] The failed entry to the land is passed over but alluded to by referring to living in the wilderness a long time.

---

6 Calvin, *Joshua*, 4:272.
7 Hess, *Joshua*, 302.
8 See, for example, Deuteronomy 5:3 and Joshua 4:23.
9 Verse 7a also sees a brief moment of change in the speech from God speaking in the first person to Joshua speaking of him in the third person. It then returns to the first person for the remainder.

Possessing the eastern land (24:8–10)

We move to the events of Numbers 21–4 and the battles for the land east of the Jordan. God's actions for his people are emphasised: 'I gave them into your hands' and 'I destroyed them from before you' (verse 8). When one king, Balak, realised he could not defeat Israel in open warfare he summoned Balaam to curse them. But again, God acted: he made Balaam repeatedly bless the Israelites even when he intended otherwise. So God 'delivered' his people.

Entry into the Promised Land (24:11–13)

The rehearsal of history then moves into the book of Joshua itself with a reminder of the crossing of the Jordan, the battle of Jericho and the battles against the inhabitants of the land. Again, the emphasis is on God's action: 'I gave them into your hands' (verse 11). Verse 12 gives a vivid picture of God's action in sending 'the hornet' ahead of his people which drove out the inhabitants and two Amorite kings.[10] This image is used predictively in Exodus 23:28 and Deuteronomy 7:20. This 'hornet' is probably a reference to fear. There are other possible interpretations, but the point is very clear: God did it. As Marten Woudstra says, 'It means to stress once again the divine monergism displayed in the work of the Conquest.'[11] It is explicitly stated that Israel did not do this by their sword or bow. Hence the conclusion in verse 13 is that God 'gave' them the land and did so in a prepared state – tilled land, built cities and planted vineyards and olive groves.[12]

This survey of Israel's history is to impress at least two things on Joshua's audience. First, their history is only because of God's grace: they are not a deserving or worthy group and God does not owe them anything. Second, their history is only because of God's power:

---

[10] This could be a flashback to Og and Sihon but is more likely kings in the land itself; Adoni-Zedek and Jabin as the leaders of the south and northern coalitions are commonly suggested (Joshua 10:1; 11;1), e.g., Firth, *Joshua*, 392.
[11] Woudstra, *Joshua*, 349.
[12] See this predicted in Deuteronomy 6:10–11.

he is the one who has rescued, protected, won battles and provided for them. They only stand as they are – the nation of Israel – and only stand where they are – in the land of promise – because of God's grace and power.

2. The call to serve the Lord • Joshua 24:14–28

Joshua's call to faithfulness and the people's response (24:14–18)

The conclusion to this history overview is a call to 'fear' and 'serve' the Lord who has done all this for his people (verse 14).[13] Fearing God has been a minor theme so far in Joshua (see Joshua 4:24; 22:25) but is very appropriate here. It does not mean being frightened of God but rather having a reverence for him that leads to trust and loyalty. Here is it is allied with the idea of 'serving', which again has not been common in Joshua but was part of the call given in 22:5 and becomes the dominant theme of this passage from this point on (it is used fourteen times). Joshua uses 'serve' as an all-encompassing term for faithful living before God.[14] Such service is to be with 'all faithfulness' (verse 14, NIV), which combines two words: 'sincerity' and 'faithfulness'. It is to be service without hypocrisy or deviation.

Such serving of the Lord means they will throw away other gods such as those their ancestors served (verse 14, NIV 'worshipped'); either those of Abraham (referred to in verse 2) or those in Egypt.[15] Serving God is seen here as an orientation of loyalty to him in distinction to any other god; serving him means not serving others (see verses 16, 19–20, and 22–3). A challenge is then given in verse 15: serve the Lord or choose some other gods to serve, whether those of their ancestors or those of the inhabitants of the land

---

13 Fearing and serving God are often combined in calls from Moses to the nation in Deuteronomy (for example, Deuteronomy 6:13; 10:12, 20; 13:4).
14 Harstad, *Joshua*, 779.
15 The reference to Egypt could mean that earlier gods were still worshipped there, or that their ancestors adopted Egyptian gods, or it could even be a reference to the Egyptians who came up with Israel and became part of the nation (Exodus 12:38). See Leviticus 17:7; Deuteronomy 32:16–17; Ezekiel 23:1–8.

(here summarised as Amorites). We should note that Joshua is not actually asking them to choose whether they will serve God, as is commonly suggested. Rather, he is saying that if they are not to serve the true God, they may make their choice of false ones; this is a rhetorical device to show what an appalling idea that is.[16] Joshua, though, asserts that he and his household will serve the Lord. His 'house' includes family members and any others that Joshua leads as the head of the family.[17]

The people respond appropriately: it would be outrageous for them to 'forsake the LORD' and serve other gods (verse 16). They give a condensed version of the history they've just been told as the basis for this (verses 17–18). The logic is, given that this is what God has done for us, we too will serve him. Or, put differently, 'he is our God', the one who has acted as God for us.

Enforcement, warning, and covenant (24:19–28)

Joshua responds with a challenge: that they are not able to serve the Lord (verse 19). This surprising statement has been much debated. It is often taken to be forestalling a glib declaration of loyalty, or to make the Israelites pause to consider what they are promising. Such dynamics may be in play, but the logic of the verse ties this statement to God's holiness and jealousy.[18] Holiness is God's separateness and distinction from the rest of creation, and is linked with his moral purity. Jealousy is not 'envy' but rather God's burning desire for his people's loyalty.[19] Joshua is impressing on his hearers a right picture of God: realise who you are making this commitment to. The Lord is not some insecure deity who is glad of whatever attention his worshippers might care to give him; he's not like a feeble husband who sits around while his wife flirts with other men. He is holy and jealous and so rightly demanding of total loyalty.

If then they turn against this God, he will not forgive them; indeed, he will make an end of them. Once again, this does not

---

16 Harstad, *Joshua*, 783–5.
17 Although individuals could opt out of a family position; Goldingay, *Joshua*, 426.
18 There is a connecting 'for' which the NIV misses out: 'For he is a holy God . . .'
19 See similar uses in Exodus 20:5; 34:14.

mean God will not forgive sins at all; after all, the covenant includes stipulations for sacrifices to bring atonement. Rather, the point is that he will not forgive if they 'forsake the LORD and serve foreign gods'. As Calvin says, 'It does not refer to faults in general, or to special faults, but is confined to gross denial of God.'[20] As we have seen before, God is not demanding perfection but loyalty.

So when Joshua says they are not 'able' to serve God, he is highlighting the loyalty involved, such that 'two-timing' God will not be tolerated. This may compare with the pagan gods who are less demanding and so whom they could serve in such a half-hearted or syncretistic way.[21] Or the sense may be more that they cannot serve God in the way that they have been. If Joshua's command to 'throw away' other gods is taken at face value, he sees the Israelites as having been partial in their loyalty so far.[22] It may be that this is part of the handover of responsibility; in Joshua's absence they will stand before God directly, not under a single leader.[23] Joshua's statement therefore should not be read as a simple denial of their ability; otherwise, why does he accept their response. It may, however, operate at multiple levels and, as we discuss below, Joshua may foresee failure.[24]

The people respond with confidence: 'We will serve the LORD' (verse 21). Joshua calls them as witnesses to this statement, and so witnesses 'against' themselves, and they agree. So Joshua calls them to throw away foreign gods – paralleling verse 14 – and to 'yield' their hearts towards the LORD. We should note that the 'heart' is the centre of the person in their thinking, desiring and acting, not simply the place of feeling. The word rendered 'yield' means to turn or to bend, and so either pictures a heart inclined towards God (so ESV) or bending before him (so NIV). Whichever the right image

---

20 Calvin, *Joshua*, 4:278.
21 Trent C. Butler, *Joshua 13–24, Volume 7B* (Nashville: Zondervan, 2014), 324.
22 Fretheim, *Deuteronomic History*, 82–3.
23 Paul R. Williamson, *Sealed with an Oath: Covenant in God's Unfolding Purpose*, New Studies in Biblical Theology (Downers Grove: Apollos, 2007), 117.
24 Note that some commentators read this section as saying that God's demands are insurmountable and so Israel is promising the impossible. Joshua may indeed foresee failure but, if so, it is because of the fickleness of the people, not the unrealistic expectations of God.

is, the idea is that of wholehearted submission. The people respond with a third affirmation of their commitment to 'serve the LORD our God and obey him' (verse 24, compare verses 18 and 21). The effect of this back and forth between Joshua and the people is to make the people's stated commitment unequivocable.

That commitment is then represented by a covenant which Joshua makes for them. The status of this covenant is debated. The key issue is how this covenant relates to those made previously: is this a new covenant or a reaffirmation of an old one? The NIV interprets it as a 'renewal' of a previous covenant, as shown in the chapter heading and in the choice of the word 'reaffirmed' in verse 25 (the word could be translated 'put' or 'set'). We will discuss this further below.

The people's commitment is also recorded in the 'Book of the Law of God' (verse 26). Earlier references are to the 'Book of the Law' (Joshua 1:8) or the 'Book of the Law of Moses' (Joshua 8:30–35; 23:6). This may represent a growing literature that operates as a basis for the life of Israel that Joshua is now adding to.[25] It may also elevate Joshua and his ordinances as Scripture – and so as an equivalent to Moses (compare verse 29 where Joshua is described as 'the Servant of the LORD').[26]

Joshua also memorialises this event by setting up a stone. This is reminiscent of the stones set up after the crossing of the Jordan but also echoes other memorials through the book (see Joshua 4:19–24; 8:30–35; 22:34). It is set up under an oak tree which is clearly known ('the oak'). This is probably the oak at Shechem in Genesis 35 where Jacob buried the foreign gods his household had, so echoing an earlier moment of turning from idols and to the true God.[27] This is near the 'holy place of the LORD'. This is usually translated 'sanctuary' and commonly refers to the Tent of Meeting, but it is the first time this word has been used in Joshua. The stone will act as a 'witness' to what has been said. It has 'heard' everything the people said and so will hold them to account if they go against their commitment.

Joshua then dismisses the people to return to their inheritance,

---

25 Harstad, *Joshua*, 809.
26 Creangă, 'Joshua', 238.
27 See Genesis 35:1–5. It may also refer back to Abraham at this site in Genesis 12:6.

JOSHUA'S CALL TO SERVE THE LORD

thus summing up what has been achieved through the book: they are in the Promised Land and have each received their part of the promise. As Adolph Harstad writes, 'At the end of their trip home, they will find down-to-earth proof of the goodness of their covenant LORD.'[28]

KEY THEMES AND APPLICATION

Commitment to serving God
The main thrust of this section is Joshua's calling the people to serve God as opposed to other gods. In that way, it echoes the call of the previous speech, but there are differences in focus. The previous speech focused on the presence of other nations around Israel and so the temptation to mix with them and their gods. Hence, it sounded a note of warning for the future. The current speech focuses on their background and what God has done for them, and so calls for a decision of commitment in the present. They are twice told to 'throw away' other gods or foreign gods, they are challenged as to who they will chose to serve and they give a threefold affirmation: 'We will serve the LORD'. This is a moment of decision and of commitment. That is then represented in the covenant and the witness stone.

The equivalent in the New Testament would be passages like Mark 8:34–8, Luke 9:57–62 and Luke 14:25–35. In such passages, Jesus lays down the commitment needed to be his disciple and calls people to recognise the cost involved. We can also see the renunciation of false gods in a number of places, such as 1 Thessalonians 1:9–10, Acts 19:17–20 and the call to 'flee idolatry' in 1 Corinthians 10:14–22.

In teaching this passage today, we would want to show people the force of this call. There is its exclusive nature: God alone is to be served and so other gods are to be rejected. There is its wholehearted nature: this is not an external, superficial service but a heart aligned with God and bowed before him.

---

28 Harstad, *Joshua*, 812.

The need to remember God's work
While the focus of Joshua's call is wholehearted commitment to God, we must note the way he goes about this. Before the call of verses 14–15 comes the rehearsal of history in verses 2–13. Such an exclusive call finds its place and makes sense only in the light of God's actions to Israel. He saves them and provides for them before asking for such service from them. That is why the focus within the history is on its one-sided nature: God saved and protected while the people were helpless; God gave while the people only received. When the Israelites make their first affirmation in response, they too repeat a condensed version of this history: given what God has done for them, they will now serve him (verses 16–18). Salvation is always a gift of grace that leads to a life of discipleship (e.g., Romans 12:1–2; Ephesians 2:8–10).

This is a key dynamic in how God works: the description of what God has already done for us always precedes the commands of what he asks from us. Our commitment to him only follows from his previous commitment to us. This is seen in the logic of the New Testament letters which standardly detail God's saving actions before commanding a new way of life.[29] Salvation is only and ever by God's gracious action to us, but such salvation results in a new life of service to God.

This requires that we see the equivalent one-sided nature of God's work for us that is emphasised here and that we are underserving of it. Lutheran commentator Paul Kretzmann said:

> Thus Israel, without any merit on its part, through God's goodness and merciful kindness alone, had received a glorious land . . . We Christians are also obliged to confess, with regard to both the temporal and the spiritual blessings of the Lord, that we are not worthy of the least of all his benefits.[30]

---

29 This is most sharply seen in the book of Ephesians which has no commands in the first three chapters describing God's actions for us (apart from one command to 'remember'), but is then full of commands in the second three chapters.
30 Paul Kretzmann, 'Popular Commentary of the Bible: Old Testament', in Nichols, *ESV Church History Study Bible*, 337.

This is then significant in how we encourage God's people in wholehearted service to him. We do not simply enforce the need for such commitment. Rather, we start with God's gracious work through the Lord Jesus on our behalf; we need constant reminders and so appreciation of all God has done for us. This is at least part of the function of God's people gathering regularly together to rehearse our story, particularly in celebrating the Lord's Supper.

People's inability to serve God
We have seen the key focus on people's commitment to 'serve the LORD'. They say it three times, and we might even imagine their saying it louder each time. They are prepared to commit themselves formally to such a pledge of loyalty. The setting up of the stone seems to seal their ongoing faithfulness. However, later readers of Joshua would read those verses with a bitter taste and a mournful air. They would know that the people were 'untrue to their God' (verse 27) and so that stone did indeed come into play in bearing witness against them. They did 'forsake the Lord and serve foreign gods', and so God did 'turn' against them and 'bring disaster' on them (verse 20). This is seen in the very next book of Judges in partial ways, then through their history under the kings, and finally in exile.

This should temper any use of this passage to call people to grand statements of commitment in serving God. Such statements may be well meant but are naïve and overestimate our ability to keep them. Knowing the future of Israel brings a soberness to teaching this passage. Such calls for commitment can and should be made, but only in utter dependence on God, and with acute awareness of how we will fall short. That also leads into the next point about the new covenant.

Covenants and the new covenant
There are two issues to consider here over the covenant Joshua makes. The first, less significant issue is how this covenant relates to previous covenants made, specifically those with Abraham and with Moses. This is debated because the wording used for the 'making' of the covenant in verse 25 is the standard wording for the creation of

a new covenant.[31] Joshua's making of a covenant here is also unusual in that he is said to make it rather than God. For that reason, some have seen it as making a new covenant *to keep* the covenant – a form of binding promise.[32] Despite the unusual wording, however, it is usually still read as a reestablishing of the Mosaic covenant.[33] The 'decrees and laws' of verse 25 would most naturally be those already given through Moses.[34] In that sense, this looks back to chapter 8 and the reading of the Mosaic Law on Mount Ebal (Joshua 8:30–35). It is appropriate to have this reaffirmation at this stage as the people start their new life in the land.

The second, more significant issue is how this relates to the new covenant which believers today are under. As we mentioned in discussion of Joshua 8:30–35, the new covenant needs to be explained and applied, otherwise the teaching of this passage might lead people to live in the wrong period of salvation history. While there is continuity across the old and new covenants, there is also change. In particular, the new covenant involves God's Law being written on people's hearts so that they will obey it (see Jeremiah 31:31–4). It recognises that there was nothing wrong with the old covenant laws but there was something wrong with the people and so their obedience. Hence, as we noted above, we should see that, left to ourselves, we are unable to follow through on our commitment to God and will turn from him. What we need is for him to work in us and turn our hearts so that they will 'yield' to him. Indeed, he needs to give us new hearts. We may then make declarations of

---

[31] Covenants were referred to as being 'cut', and that is the wording in verse 25. That word is used for the initiation of the covenant with Abraham (Genesis 15:18) and through Moses (Exodus 34:10; Deuteronomy 5:2). By contrast, where a covenant is 'confirmed' or 'established', the wording is different, and this is usually by way of reassurance from God (for example, Genesis 9:9; 17:7; Exodus 6:4; Leviticus 26:9; Deuteronomy 8:18). The Israelites are only ever called to remember or to keep the covenant.

[32] Peter J. Gentry and Stephen J. Wellum, *Kingdom through Covenant: A Biblical-Theological Understanding of the Covenants* (Wheaton: Crossway, 2012), 390. They insist that 'cutting a covenant' always refers to a new covenant being made.

[33] Williamson, *Sealed with an Oath: Covenant in God's Unfolding Purpose*, 117.

[34] A counterpoint here is that they are in the singular, and so might refer to the 'decree/law' that Joshua was making. However, the singular can refer to the entire Law, such as in Ezra 7:10.

commitment but knowing they can only be fulfilled because of his past work changing us and will only be fulfilled by his ongoing work empowering us.

The choice of who to serve
Joshua's call to choose in verse 15 does not give the option of not serving any gods; rather, he asks them to choose which gods they will serve. In secular contexts today, that will seem strange because people will assume they can opt out of serving any god. But behind Joshua's words is a key biblical truth: we will always serve someone. The human heart is made to worship, and so sin is not only not worshipping God as we should but also choosing to worship something else instead (see Romans 1:21–3). This assumption and so the use of idolatry as a tool of cultural analysis is of great use.[35] In other, more religious, contexts, where pagan idols are physically present and form part of people's regular life, Joshua's call is more straightforward, if challenging. Will believers 'throw away' such idols that may be revered by their family and community? Will they choose to serve God exclusively?

---

35 See Brian Rosner, 'The Concept of Idolatry', *Themelios* 24, no. 3 (May 1999): 21–30; Timothy Keller, *Counterfeit Gods: When the Empty Promises of Love, Money and Power Let You Down:* (London: Hodder & Stoughton, 2010).

25

The End of An Era

Joshua 24:29–33

We come to the close of the book of Joshua. We have seen the land conquered in the first half and then divided as an inheritance in the second half. The last few chapters have sounded the note of covenant loyalty in ongoing life in the land as God's people. The book now concludes with the account of two significant deaths but three burials. The deaths are those of Joshua and Eleazar, which bring this period of salvation history to a close. The leadership of God's people will now change and be devolved to the tribes, with occasional judges raised up by God. However, sandwiched between them is the burial of Joseph's bones. This type of ending may not immediately seem worthy of much attention, but it is making significant points summarising the main lessons of the book.

Buried in the promised land

29 After these things, Joshua son of Nun, the servant of the LORD, died at the age of a hundred and ten. 30 And they buried him in the land of his inheritance, at Timnath Serah[c] in the hill country of Ephraim, north of Mount Gaash.

31 Israel served the LORD throughout the lifetime of Joshua and of the elders who outlived him and who had experienced everything the LORD had done for Israel.

32 And Joseph's bones, which the Israelites had brought up from Egypt, were buried at Shechem in the tract of land that Jacob bought for a hundred pieces of silver[d] from the sons of Hamor, the father of Shechem. This became the inheritance of Joseph's descendants.

33 And Eleazar son of Aaron died and was buried at Gibeah, which had been allotted to his son Phinehas in the hill country of Ephraim.

---

[c] 30 Also known as *Timnath Heres* (see Judges 2:9).

[d] 32 Hebrew *hundred kesitahs*; a kesitah was a unit of money of unknown weight and value.

JOSHUA

1. *The death of Joshua* • *Joshua 24:29–31*

Joshua's death is simply placed 'after these things' with no precise timing. He is 110 years old – there is no obvious significance in the number, but it is standard to record significant people's age. Joseph died at the same age (Genesis 50:26), and he will be mentioned next, subtly emphasising a link between them. Joshua is given his full title and is now, for the first time, called the 'servant of the LORD'. This is the title given to Moses throughout the book. This accords great status to Joshua, places him on a par with Moses and provides a link back to the opening of the book with 'the death of Moses the servant of the LORD' (Joshua 1:1).[1] He is buried in the land he inherited – see Joshua 19:49–50.

The key word from the preceding ceremony 'serve' is picked up in verse 31. We are told that Israel served the LORD during Joshua's lifetime and that of the elders who had also 'known' what the LORD has done for Israel (NIV 'experienced').[2] Hence, there is an extension to the people's commitment to God following Joshua's death under these elders (presumably those who heard his exhortation in chapter 23). This verse is double-edged in nature. It is wonderfully positive about the life of Israel during this time, pointing to their faithfulness in serving God loyally as they promised. It particularly heaps praise on Joshua. But it raises an ominous thought: what happens next? The reference to those who know what God has done suggests that as that generation dies out, so might loyalty to God. John Calvin said:

> Accordingly, attention is indirectly drawn to their inconstancy, when it is said that they served the Lord while Joshua survived, and till the more aged had died out. For there is a tacit antithesis, implying lapse and alienation, when they were suddenly seized with a forgetfulness of the Divine favors.[3]

---

[1] Woudstra, *Joshua*, 359.
[2] God's work here is in the singular so summing up all he had done from the Exodus to now. Woudstra, 360.
[3] Calvin, *Joshua*, 4:282.

For any later reader, that is exactly how it would have been read, because they would have known the subsequent history of turning away from the LORD. As Trent Butler comments, 'The same facts that have shown the faithfulness of Joshua can also function to introduce the unfaithfulness of a generation who forgot Joshua and his God.'[4]

2. The burial of Joseph • Joshua 24:32

The comment about Joseph has some background history to it. We read in Genesis 50 that Joseph made the Israelites swear that they would carry his bones up to the Promised Land. In doing so, he showed his confidence and faith in God's promises (Genesis 50:24–6). He is now buried at Shechem where the previous covenant ceremony was held, in land purchased by Jacob (see Genesis 33:18–20). It then became part of the inheritance of Manasseh, one of Joseph's sons (Joshua 17:2).

We should ask why we are told of Joseph's burial here. The answer is twofold. First, this signals the end of the Exodus journey. One of the patriarchs who went down into Egypt comes back up into the land and 'enters' their inheritance. Second, Joseph exemplifies the right attitude regarding the promise of the land. While in Egypt he said, 'God will surely come to your aid and take you up out of this land to the land he promised on oath to Abraham, Isaac and Jacob' (Genesis 50:24). He believed God's promise and so looked forward to its fulfilment; he also valued that promise and so desired to enter into it himself. He now symbolically claims his inheritance. As a result, mention of him here raises the question as to whether the Israelites will do the same.

3. The death of Eleazar • Joshua 24:33

Eleazar has been far less prominent than Joshua but came to the fore during the distribution of the land (Joshua 14:1; 17:4; 19:51; 21:1). He is also the father of Phinehas who is mentioned here and was

---

4 Butler, *Joshua 13–24*, 7B:343.

prominent in the events with the trans-Jordanian tribes in chapter 22 (Joshua 22:13, 31–2). We are told that Eleazar is buried in land allotted to Phinehas, and so he too is buried in his inheritance. His death marks the end of the process of distributing the inheritance to the tribes. Eleazar's close association with the allotment of the tribes' inheritance highlights that theme and connects back verse 28. As we will comment below, the question is subtly raised as to how successful Israel will be in taking the remaining land of inheritance that was allotted through his hands.

KEY THEMES AND APPLICATION

Fulfilment of God's promises

Each of these three men provides some link with Egypt: Joseph was the start of Abraham's family going down into Egypt, and Joshua and Eleazar were part of the generation who came up out of Egypt in the Exodus.[5] So between them they mark the beginning and the end of the Egyptian period. Joseph's deathbed statements, and now his burial here, show that this is finally the end of that time in slavery and the arrival in their true home.

God had said, 'I will give your descendants all this land I promised them, and it will be their inheritance for ever' (Exodus 32:13). Now each is said to be buried in the land of his inheritance (verses 30, 32) or the land given (NIV 'allotted') to them (verse 33). Their burials therefore mark the fulfilment of God's promise.

As we have mentioned before, the inheritance in the land is a picture for us of our inheritance in Christ. As Peter says:

> In his great mercy he has given us new birth into a living hope through the resurrection of Jesus Christ from the dead, and into an inheritance that can never perish, spoil or fade. This inheritance is kept in heaven for you, who through faith are shielded by God's power until the coming of the salvation that is ready to be revealed in the last time. (1 Peter 1:3–5)

---

5 Howard, *Joshua*, 442.

These three men being at rest in their inheritance should encourage us in looking forward to God's promises being fulfilled for us. David Oginde ends his commentary on Joshua with a question along these lines: 'Are you living in hope of this new promised land, and are you drawing others to Christ, the only gate to enter this new land?'[6]

The example of faith
Joseph is cited here as an exemplar of the attitude needed to inherit the land. He trusted and valued God's promises and so looked forward in faith to their being fulfilled. He died with his eyes on his inheritance: he knew his final grave was not in Egypt. Such an attitude would stand the Israelites in good stead, if they would follow in that pattern.

In the book of Hebrews, Joseph is cited as an example of the faith the author is seeking to encourage in his readers:

> By faith Joseph, when his end was near, spoke about the exodus of the Israelites from Egypt and gave instructions concerning the burial of his bones. (Hebrews 11:22)

We might reflect, as the book of Hebrews does, on our faith in God's promises. Are we living looking forwards, with our eyes on our inheritance? Or are we distracted and consumed with the here and now?

The question of the future and the need for a leader
The comment that Israel served God during Joshua's life and that of the elders is significant. We get the impression that such leaders lay behind the people's loyalty, but with them gone such loyalty would soon evaporate and they would fall into the very patterns which the last two chapters have warned against. In fact, the book of Judges repeats verses 29–31 but reorders them so that Joshua's death is recorded after the faithfulness of the people (Judges 2:7–9); then comes the ominous comment: 'After that whole generation had been gathered to their ancestors, another generation grew up who knew

---

6 Oginde, 'Joshua', 294.

neither the LORD nor what he had done for Israel' (Judges 2:10). What is explicit in Judges is already subtly conveyed here in Joshua.

This is an example of the problem of the 'next generation'. God does not repeat his acts of salvation for each successive generation, but rather calls them to look back and remember and live in the light of them. We have seen the significance of this principle in the calls to remember through the book (most notably Joshua 4:19–24). We have also seen it in the 'merging' of generations in Joshua's speech: the people are to live as if they were those who came out of Egypt and saw what God had done (Joshua 24:5–7). Now a question is raised of the next generation who do not know what God has done for Israel.

Hence the book ends on a challenging note: How will the people live? Will they trust God and so enter into their inheritance? The call of Joshua in chapters 23–24 looms large: will the people continue in faithfulness and so receive the fulfilment of God's promise themselves? Again, any later reader would know the answer to this question. They would see this as a high point in entering the land; it would go downhill from here. We have also seen tell-tale signs within Joshua itself. John Goldingay may overstate the point but surely captures the truth of it in saying:

> So the opening, the centre, the close and the individual stories in Joshua describe the people as wholly committed to Yhwh and to a life of obedience to Yhwh's directions, but also see them as continually falling down on such commitment.[7]

Marten Woudstra comments that 'an air of joyful optimism pervades the book of Joshua'.[8] We would have to disagree. There have been many optimistic moments, and much has been achieved, but by the end there is more an air of anxious concern. As Joshua dies, we worry for the future. The reader is left longing for a leader who will remain and who will lead the people into a constancy of obedience. As we have seen several times before in Joshua, we are then pointed to the new Joshua, Jesus, who does exactly that.

---

7 Goldingay, *Old Testament Theology*, 1:465.
8 Woudstra, *Joshua*, 32.

Appendix A: The Tribes of the Promised Land

The tribes that inhabited the land promised to the Israelites are described to us in a variety of lists. In Joshua, the first list comes in 3:10. This has seven groups which acts as a representative list of all the different tribes involved. This may be because of the resonances of completeness in the number seven. The apostle Paul picks up on this number in his summary of Israel's history, saying that God 'overthrew seven nations in Canaan, giving their land to his people as their inheritance' (Acts 13:19).

Other lists of these people groups can vary from one to twelve in number. When described as one group they are called the 'Canaanites' or the 'Amorites'. More commonly, five or six groups are listed. It is clear in certain passages that some terms are used as broader categories: for example, in Genesis 15 the one term 'Amorites' in verse 16 is expanded to ten tribes in verses 19–21. Similarly, in Exodus 13 there are five tribes listed in verse 5 which are then summarised by the single term 'Canaanites' in verse 11.

In Joshua, following the opening list of seven tribes in chapter 3, there are three lists of six tribes (each omitting the Girgashites) and then a final list of seven in 24:11. There are also other references which may or may not be intended to cover all the inhabitants. So in Joshua 5:1 there is reference to 'all the Amorite kings west of the Jordan and all the Canaanite kings along the coast'. This may well be a summary of all the tribes.

For further comment and a discussion of what we know of the different tribes listed, see the excursus by Harstad.[1]

---

[1] Harstad, *Joshua*, 175–9.

JOSHUA

	Reference	Canaanites	Perizzites	Amorites	Hittites	Hivites	Jebusites	Kenites	Kenizzites	Kadmonites	Girgashites	Rephaites	Other
Genesis	Genesis 12:6	Y											
	Genesis 13:7	Y	Y										
	Genesis 15:16			Y									
	Genesis 15:19–21	Y	Y	Y	Y		Y	Y	Y	Y	Y	Y	
	Genesis 34:30	Y	Y										
Exodus	Exodus 3:8	Y	Y	Y	Y	Y	Y						
	Exodus 3:17	Y	Y	Y	Y	Y	Y						
	Exodus 13:5	Y		Y	Y	Y	Y						
	Exodus 13:11	Y											
	Exodus 23:23	Y	Y	Y	Y	Y	Y						
	Exodus 23:28	Y			Y	Y							
	Exodus 33:2	Y	Y	Y	Y	Y	Y						
	Exodus 34:11	Y	Y	Y	Y	Y	Y						
Deuteronomy	Deuteronomy 7:1	Y	Y	Y	Y	Y	Y				Y		
	Deuteronomy 20:17	Y	Y	Y	Y	Y	Y						
Joshua	Joshua 3:10	Y	Y	Y	Y	Y	Y				Y		
	Joshua 9:1	Y	Y	Y	Y	Y	Y						
	Joshua 11:3	Y	Y	Y	Y	Y	Y						
	Joshua 12:8	Y	Y	Y	Y	Y	Y						
	Joshua 24:11	Y	Y	Y	Y	Y	Y				Y		
Judges	Judges 3:5	Y	Y	Y	Y	Y	Y						
Ezra	Ezra 9:1	Y	Y	Y	Y		Y						Ammonites Moabites Egyptians
Nehemiah	Nehemiah 9:8	Y	Y	Y	Y		Y				Y		

Appendix B: The Borders of the Promised Land

The borders of the Promised Land are a source of perplexity and some debate. We will not rehearse, let alone answer, all the issues here but simply provide some brief orientation.

The boundaries of the land were introduced in Joshua in chapter 1 as follows:

> Your territory will extend from the desert to Lebanon, and from the great river, the Euphrates – all the Hittite country – to the Mediterranean Sea in the west. (Joshua 1:4)

This echoes previous outlines of the land such as that given to Abraham:

> To your descendants I give this land, from the Wadi of Egypt to the great river, the Euphrates. (Genesis 15:18)

And to Moses:

> I will establish your borders from the Red Sea to the Mediterranean Sea, and from the desert to the Euphrates River. (Exodus 23:31)

These are also found in Deuteronomy 1:7 and 11:24.

These are the broadest definitions of the land given, especially to the east where it extends to the River Euphrates. However, this does not match the more detailed descriptions given in other passages. One of the most detailed is in Numbers 34:

JOSHUA

The LORD said to Moses, 'Command the Israelites and say to them: "When you enter Canaan, the land that will be allotted to you as an inheritance is to have these boundaries:

'"Your southern side will include some of the Desert of Zin along the border of Edom. Your southern boundary will start in the east from the southern end of the Dead Sea, cross south of Scorpion Pass, continue on to Zin and go south of Kadesh Barnea. Then it will go to Hazar Addar and over to Azmon, where it will turn, join the Wadi of Egypt and end at the Mediterranean Sea.

'"Your western boundary will be the coast of the Mediterranean Sea. This will be your boundary on the west.

'"For your northern boundary, run a line from the Mediterranean Sea to Mount Hor and from Mount Hor to Lebo Hamath. Then the boundary will go to Zedad, continue to Ziphron and end at Hazar Enan. This will be your boundary on the north.

'"For your eastern boundary, run a line from Hazar Enan to Shepham. The boundary will go down from Shepham to Riblah on the east side of Ain and continue along the slopes east of the Sea of Galilee. Then the boundary will go down along the Jordan and end at the Dead Sea.

'"This will be your land, with its boundaries on every side."' (Numbers 34:1–12)

This description has much more in common with the boundaries described in the book of Joshua in chapters 13–19. The southern boundary is virtually identical; the western boundary is the Mediterranean Sea in both cases; the northern and north-eastern boundaries are probably larger in the Numbers account, although exact placement is difficult to achieve.[1]

---

1 Wenham, *Numbers*, 231–3.

APPENDIX B: THE BORDERS OF THE PROMISED LAND

Nili Wazana has examined these two different types of description of the land. The first is expansive, using broad-ranging terminology (desert, river, mountains) and is based on extremities ('from . . . to'). The second is more limited and precisely described, giving a continuous boundary line. She argues that the former of these points to a type of 'world domination' as seen in later biblical texts that refer to ruling between seas and rivers.[2] Examples of these include Psalm 72:8; 89:25; Zechariah 9:10. This expansive view is particularly picked up in promises to the Davidic King, which sees him as God's instrument in ruling the world: 'The rule of the Davidic Dynasty as depicted in the Psalms is thus an image of God's reign as the Creator and guider of the world, who bestows on His earthly representative the authority to govern the whole earth.'[3]

Coming from a different angle, Paul Williamson argues that the imprecise nature of the land is deliberate, and he points to texts that suggest the expansion of the land in the future, such as Genesis 26:3-4, Exodus 34:24, Numbers 24:17-19 and Deuteronomy 19:8-9. He concludes, 'Canaan was simply the preliminary stage in the ultimate unfolding of God's programmatic agenda – an agenda which not only involves all peoples of the earth but also encompasses all regions of the earth.'[4]

We should therefore see the precise boundary descriptions in Joshua as delineating the actual territory to be lived in. But that limited territory must be held together with the expansive domain described in chapter 1, and which points to the biblical theological arc of God's reign over the whole earth.

---

[2] Nili Wazana, *All the Boundaries of the Land: The Promised Land in Biblical Thought in Light of the Ancient Near East* (Winona Lake: Eisenbrauns, 2013), 104–6, 118.
[3] Wazana, *All the Boundaries of the Land*, 121.
[4] Paul Williamson, 'Promise and Fulfilment: The Territorial Inheritance', in *The Land of Promise: Biblical, Theological and Contemporary Perspectives*, ed. Philip Johnston and Peter Walker (Leicester: InterVarsity Press, 2000), 22.